SIAM: PRINCIPLES AND PRACTICES FOR SERVICE

Other publications by Van Haren Publishing

Van Haren Publishing (VHP) specializes in titles on Best Practices, methods and standards within four domains:
- IT and IT Management
- Architecture (Enterprise and IT)
- Business Management and
- Project Management

Van Haren Publishing offers a wide collection of whitepapers, templates, free e-books, trainer materials etc. in the **Van Haren Publishing Knowledge Base**: www.vanharen.net for more details.

Van Haren Publishing is also publishing on behalf of leading organizations and companies: ASLBiSL Foundation, BRMI, CA, Centre Henri Tudor, Gaming Works, IACCM, IAOP, Innovation Value Institute, IPMA-NL, ITSqc, NAF, Ngi/NGN, PMI-NL, PON, The Open Group, The SOX Institute.

Topics are (per domain):

IT and IT Management	Architecture (Enterprise and IT)	Project, Program and Risk Management
ABC of ICT	ArchiMate®	A4-Projectmanagement
ASL®	GEA®	DSDM/Atern
CATS CM®	Novius Architectuur Methode	ICB / NCB
CMMI®	TOGAF®	ISO 21500
COBIT®		MINCE®
e-CF	**Business Management**	M_o_R®
ISO 20000	BABOK® Guide	MSP™
ISO 27001/27002	BiSL®	P3O®
ISPL	BRMBOK™	PMBOK® Guide
IT-CMF™	EFQM	PRINCE2®
IT Service CMM	eSCM	
ITIL®	IACCM	
MOF	ISA-95	
MSF	ISO 9000/9001	
SABSA	Novius B&IP	
	OPBOK	
	SAP	
	SixSigma	
	SOX	
	SqEME®	

For the latest information on VHP publications, visit our website: www.vanharen.net.

SIAM

Principles and practices for service integration and management

Dave Armes

Niklas Engelhart

Peter McKenzie

Peter Wiggers

Colophon

Title:	SIAM: Principles and Practices for Service Integration and Management
Series:	Best Practice
Authors:	Dave Armes, Niklas Engelhart, Peter McKenzie, Peter Wiggers
Reviewers:	Hans Boer (IBM Netherlands)
	Johann Botha (getITright)
	Daniel Breston (Qriosity)
	Brian Broadhurst (TeamUltra)
	Peter Brooks (itSMF South Africa)
	Dave van Herpen (Sogeti)
	Kevin Holland (NHS, UK)
	Charlotte Lee (IBM UK)
	Jeannine McConnell (ServiceNow)
	Markus Müller (ABB)
	Charlotte Newton (IBM UK)
	Tobias Nyberg (Galestro)
	David Nyman (Avega group)
	Harold Petersen (UXC Consulting)
	Léon-Paul de Rouw (Ministerie van BZK, Ministry of the Interior, Netherlands)
	Suresh GP (TaUB Consulting)
	René Visser (Pink Elephant)
Publisher:	Van Haren Publishing, Zaltbommel, www.vanharen.net
Text editor:	Steve Newton
Design & layout:	CO2 Premedia, Amersfoort
NUR code:	981 / 123
ISBN Hard copy:	978 94 018 0025 9
ISBN eBook (pdf):	978 94 018 0578 0
Edition:	First edition, first impression, November 2015
Copyright:	© Van Haren Publishing, 2015

Trademark notices
ITIL® is a registered trademark of AXELOS Limited.
IT4IT® is a registered trademark of The Open Group.
COBIT® is a registered trademark of ISACA.

Contents

3   People and Processes for Service Integration   69

4   Data and Tools   91

Foreword

Several years ago I was delivering an ITIL Foundation course in the UK. One delegate persistently asked how the ITIL ideas worked in a multi-vendor outsourced environment. My response was that this hadn't really been properly addressed yet. He countered with "there should be a book about it", I agreed and suggested he had effectively just offered to write it. He conceded. At that time, I happened to be charged with finding new titles for the itSMF International's publishing initiative, so was keen to hold that persistent delegate to his commitment.

That delegate was Dave Armes and at that point the book you now are now reading was conceived and started on its way. Then, as is the way with these things, nothing much happened for a while. But in the course of my work travels I met two more interested guys wrestling in their work environments with the implications of multi-vendor outsourcing on IT Service Management: Niklas Engelhart on a course in Sweden, and Peter McKenzie at a conference in Australia. Both were careless enough to agree they would be interested in contributing to a book on the topic. With three authors on board I felt confident enough to talk to publishers. The itSMF International route to market had gone by then but we were all delighted with the enthusiasm and support shown for the project by Van Haren Publishing.

So, that was my main role complete: bringing the talent together. Peter Wiggers in the Netherlands later joined the three. That international stretch across four countries has certainly added to the value, despite the time zone challenges it brought to planning and progress meetings. Incidentally most of the authors have still not physically met!

Since that first conversation with Dave, the concerns and focus on multi-supplier supply have increased. In fact it became so high profile it was allocated fashion status and a hyped-up acronym – SIAM. I was encouraged that – as with ITIL – our project was underway before the name was coined and stuck.

So, the popularity of the SIAM idea helped us lock down the title of the book, and we got the chance along the way to offer input to AXELOS' initial SIAM series of papers. Those papers were built around examples of one approach, while this book sets out to be generic – which all sounds to me like a good combination for those seeking a broad set of ideas to help with their own SIAM approach.

Like all best practice, this book is a documentation of what has seemed to work well for other people, and should form a sound starting point for those with similar issues in similar situations. Of course, as with all such 'best practice' guidance, there isn't a single answer, this book holds suggestions that you will need to adapt to your specific circumstances. The industry is seeing a stream of new SIAM ideas in blogs, webinars and conference presentations. That, I am sure, will increase in coming years and shows that this is an area of ITSM that needs – and will surely get - yet more attention.

This book sets out to provide a foundation for the future range of guidance. It is wide ranging and we hope you – yes you! – will feel inspired to document your experiences and share them with the community. The SIAM world will evolve, approaches will change and practitioners need to contribute to the development of the future best practice approaches.

The authors have the scars to show their real world experiences – and they have strived to help others learn from their work and avoid mistakes. I hope this book helps you reach the right path sooner than you might have without a steer from those who have travelled this way before and I also hope that when you are on that path you will mark the trail for those who follow you.

This kind of book can be started by the authors but the final polish comes from the collective wisdom of the enthusiastic reviewers who have given their time to add their thoughts and experience to the project. So we would like to recognize and thank the following for their support: Hans Boer, Johann Botha, Daniel Breston, Brian Broadhurst, Peter Brooks, Dave van Herpen, Kevin Holland, Charlotte Lee, Jeannine McConnell, Markus Müller, Charlotte Newton, Tobias Nyborg, David Nyman, Harold Petersen, Léon-Paul de Rouw, GP Suresh and René Visser.

Ivor MacFarlane

Preface

Why would we use a picture of formation skydiving on the cover of a textbook about Service Integration and Management? In fact there are quite a few analogous aspects. If we consider that the skydivers are 'Service Providers' providing a 'body flying service' and the load organizer is the Service Integrator (the SIAM service provider):

- The Service Integrator (load organizer) describes what the outcome must look like and the constraints for delivery – including the very important time limitations… Gravity works!
- The Service Integrator advises the Service Providers (skydivers) about the techniques that have proven to be successful, but ultimately the Service Providers must decide how they will do the job they are given. Failure makes the Post Implementation Review (video debrief) an uncomfortable experience and they will be held accountable for their performance.
- The common KPI (successful formation) is a success for all – or for none. A good individual performance of the Service Provider will avoid scrutiny and consequence for that Service Provider but is not the real goal.
- Every service provider must:
  - Know their slot;
  - Fly their slot well;
  - Not cause issues for the other Service Providers;
  - Take personal accountability for the outcome;
  - Not allow themselves to become a victim even if someone else is not doing their own job.

Once the task is underway the Service Providers must pursue the common goal – there is not a lot of opportunity for constant communication in free fall. It happens quickly (around 125 miles per hour) and – to quote the general rule of aviation – for every take off there WILL be a landing of some sort. The difference between a successful flight with a controlled and safe landing and a dangerous event depends on coordination of the fliers.

In this book we will show how mutual accountability which is a life-saver for skydivers is also vital for SIAM. It is the foundation for a 'maturity' of partnership that allows cooperating, yet competing, Service Providers to operate in line with the commander's intent. Each Service Provider must be relied upon to execute, and held accountable if they do not:

Know their slot, fly their slot…

Hold this skydiving metaphor in mind as you read this book as a reminder that any similarities to 'normal' ITSM are not the whole picture. There are both opportunities and potential pitfalls when deploying SIAM and we want our readers to benefit from our experience and increase the success of their own SIAM deployments.

September 2015,
The author's team

1   Introduction

The traditional IT organization that purchases hardware and software from suppliers, develops its own skilled resources and uses those components to deliver services to its business is no longer valid. All large IT organizations now need to consume services from an increasing array of Service Providers to remain competitive and keep up with the rate of change in the industry. They need to leverage lower cost resource pools and delivery models, including the ability to consume all things 'as a service'. This means that IT organizations are now required to integrate and orchestrate services provided by others, as much as deliver the services themselves. This requires organizations to change; change processes, change skills and change culture.

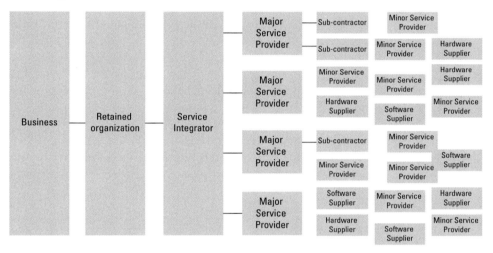

Figure 1.1   Service Integration

Many different names have been applied to the practices which integrate services and Service Providers, including; Service Integration (SI), Multi-Supplier Integration (MSI) and Service Integration and Management (SIAM). For the purposes of this book, the practice will be called Service Integration, and use the abbreviation of SIAM, so as to avoid any confusion with Systems Integration. The organizational unit primarily responsible for performing Service Integration activities will be referred to as the Service Integrator.

The authors of this book have collectively been working with organizations to help them manage complex IT for more than 20 years and for the last 10 have focused on the area of SIAM architecture and implementation. They work as consultants to, and leaders within, multi-sourced organizations and have delivered significant benefits through a number of different approaches to the challenges SIAM presents. The principles captured within these pages have evolved and have proven robust across a broad range and type of organizations, in most industries and across the US, Europe and Asia. The objective is to provide guidance to IT professionals and managers and shed an 'experiential light' on what matters in getting the best from a multi-sourced environment.

1.1   The growth of Service Integration

The concept of Multi-Supplier Service Integration is not new; it has been discussed in all parts of the IT industry for many years and in other industries as common practice for much longer. The traditional pressures of IT remain, with organizations having to do more with less, and in less time. But the industry is now developing and is at a point where suppliers and Service Providers have an increasingly broad set of offerings to help organizations. As a consequence, multi-sourcing has flourished with competition driving down cost, at the expense of a significant increase in complexity, as the number of organizations involved goes up. This complexity is increased even further when dealing with commodity 'as a Service' or cloud-based models where the costs are lower for the service received but the level of customization within the service is reduced, causing greater need for Service Integration.

The IT industry is now firmly within what Dan McNicholl, "Master of the Outsourcing Game, an Interview" (McNicholl, 2005), referred to as the fourth generation of outsourcing:
• Generation I – do it yourself;
• Generation II – large scale outsource to a single supplier;
• Generation III – multi-source across a number of specialist providers (loose federations);
• Generation IV – integrated Service Providers focused on common goals (tight governance).

As a result the definition of Service Integration is:

> Service Integration is the set of principles and practices, which facilitate that collaborative working relationship between Service Providers required to maximize the benefit of multi-sourcing. Service Integration facilitates the linkage of services, the technology of which they are comprised and the delivery organizations and processes used to operate them, into a single operating model.

To come back to the skydiving analogy, Service Integration ensures that all parties (including the customer):
1. Are fully aware of their required outcomes, expectations and accountabilities;
2. Are enabled to deliver those outcomes;
3. Are held clearly accountable for these outcomes.

1.2   What is different in a multi-sourced environment?

Why is implementing and managing a multi-sourced environment different? The additional complexity arises from the boundaries between the organizations involved and the rigidity of the contracts that bind them. The IT industry has learned to deal with the negotiation and collaboration required in a Generation II single-source model, but when complexity is significantly increased, the strain begins to show. Ensuring that there is a robust approach to the way that work must be done, and who is accountable for it is more complex when there are multiple parties involved, even more so when they represent different organizations and are bound by different organizations. Each piece of work needs to be:

- Specified;
- Documented;
- Contracted;
- Delivered;
- Integrated/orchestrated;
- Reported;
- Governed.

The growth of 'as a Service' and cloud-based offerings from Service Providers is driving the level of integration required between Service Providers ever higher by increasing the number of providers but decreasing the awareness those suppliers have of the customer's business. There is growing awareness of this widening gap. While Service Providers are able to ensure delivery of their own service levels, the integration required to support business services and business values remains the responsibility of the retained organization. When the gaps between the performance of these two services (those delivered from external IT Service Providers to the retained IT organization and those delivered from the retained IT organization to the business service/process) becomes too large, that is when customers need to consider SIAM. The objective of this publication is to provide a field guide to IT leaders and managers looking to successfully manage this transition and provide guidance, structure and lessons learnt to maximize the benefit of Service Integration and avoid the pitfalls.

It is widely understood that a trusting relationship is the most productive way for multiple parties to work towards a shared goal, yet still customers listen to a sourcing mantra in IT which is based on a foundation of mutual mistrust. This is evident in the tendency to call suppliers 'vendors', and to frame the governance as 'vendor management', i.e. with the commercial aspects foremost in mind. There is a growing set of data, which indicates that those organizations which embrace partners strategically in a broad range of areas will be the most successful.

The good news is that those commencing SIAM implementations do not have to start with a blank sheet of paper. Looking outside IT there are many engineering and manufacturing companies that manage a bewildering supply chain, which has to ensure components arrive at the right place at precisely the right time to build the final product. These components come from multiple different external companies – sometimes multiple companies for a single sub-assembly (parallel supply). More importantly, the contracts are aligned to the delivery and quality of the components as an outcome, they do not specify how. The automotive industry is a good example of this approach.

Examples from academia provide additional insights. Elinor Ostrom, (Ostrom, 2009) who was awarded 2009's Nobel Prize of Economics, looked at how real-world communities manage communal resources, such as fisheries, land irrigation systems and farmlands, identifying a number of factors conducive to successful resource management:

- One factor is the resource itself; resources with definable boundaries (e.g., land) can be preserved much more easily:
  - Clearly defined services
- A second factor is resource dependence; there must be a perceptible threat of resource depletion, and it must be difficult to find substitutes:
  - Pressure on IT budgets
- The third is the presence of a community; small and stable populations with a thick social network and social norms promoting conservation do better:
  - Our IT community, including Service Providers ('us', not 'us and them')
- A final condition is that there be appropriate community-based rules and procedures in place with built-in incentives for responsible use and punishments for overuse:
  - Our SIAM principles and practices

Service Integration provides community-based rules and procedures, which govern the ecosystem operation (skydiving in formation) and the benefits of effective Service Integration (completed formation with safe landings) – including the ultimate survival of our SIAM community, and depend on disciplined management of resources.

1.3   Why is Service Integration different?

Despite the changes in the industry, there is still no formalized SIAM competence that is recognized and industry standards have not yet caught up to provide the required guidance.

ITIL has provided guidance and structure to the management of IT since the late 1980s, but is based around IT services being delivered by a single set of processes, in the main, by a single organization. While ITIL is operating model agnostic, it is based on a more traditional single service provider archetype.

COBIT is an overarching reference framework for the governance of enterprise IT. This book refers to COBIT 5, which was published in 2012. It has evolved from an IT audit perspective to an IT strategy perspective covering every aspect of the way information technology should support the business objectives of the enterprise.

Important concepts and elements can be found as part of the enabling processes defined in COBIT, however, the concept of Service Integration is not yet fully addressed. The Plan process APO09 – Manage Service Agreements – covers Service Integration from a conceptual and high level point of view but in COBIT today the only hint of Service Integration is in process APO010.03 – Manage Supplier Relationships and Contracts – where activity number 8 states "Define and formalize roles and responsibilities for each service supplier.

Where several suppliers combine to provide a service, consider allocating a lead contractor role to one of the suppliers to take responsibility for an overall contract". The Build, Run and Monitor processes do not include specific references to the field of SIAM. Clearly there is a need for further elaboration of this area of expertise. APO09 and APO010 Manage Suppliers are the obvious places to look for more specific Service Integration content in future releases of the COBIT reference model, Figure 1.2.

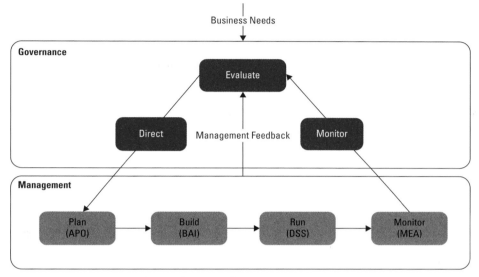

Figure 1.2   COBIT main structure (Source: (ISACA, 2012))

This publication stands on the shoulders of the people who created ITIL and COBIT and uses the structures they gave us to highlight only those things that need to be adapted to work more effectively in a multi-sourced environment.

1.4   Conceptual model for Service Integration

Whenever an organization procures services from more than one Service Provider, some level of integration will be required. Integration is a service in its own right and can be provided by either the customers own retained IT organization, or outsourced to an external party. (Different types of sourcing strategies are discussed in Chapter 2 **Basic Concepts and Terminology**.)

Whatever the model, the Service Integrator always has the end-to-end responsibility for the delivery of the aggregated IT services that are required to support the service customers and their business process outcomes. Whether the dependencies between Service Providers are functional, e.g. through integrated applications (front office, back office, middleware), or non-functional (server, storage, network) SIAM will always be required to provide coordinated management and governance.

A Single Point of Service (SPOS) is analogous to a SPOC (Single Point of Contact), where a service user or consumer has its interface for request, incidents, changes etc. A SPOS will be the customer's only interface to agree, design, release, operate, manage and govern services.

Some fundamental objectives of a Service Integrator are to:
- Reduce complexity to the customer by acting as a single point of service for all customers;
- Improve operative stability through standards and supplier coordination and collaboration;
- Reduce the time to market by effectively and efficiently integrating and orchestrating processes between Service Providers;
- Reduce the cost of IT service provisioning by:
  - Improved efficiency and effectiveness through removing gaps and overlaps between providers;
  - Ensuring the definition of the scope of each service is appropriate ('economy of scope');
  - Economy of scale through reuse of service management resources and capabilities;
  - Effectively orchestrating multiple providers' services to provide the required balance between service cost and service quality.

In fully mature and integrated environments the key responsibility of a Service Integrator is to act as a Single Point of Service (SPOS) with which the service customer objectives, requirements, desirable outcomes etc. are agreed upon and formally propagated further to every service and its provider.

1.4.1   SIAM integration model

From an overview perspective a SIAM model is a matrix where the integrator "covers" the participating providers and their services from the customer and its consumers. This can be done in an "open" fashion, where customer is fully aware of the underlying services, or closed, where customer is unaware of the underlying providers and services. The structure does not intend that all activities of the Service Providers be managed by the Service Integrator. It is just the interfaces to the encapsulated services, presented for integration, that are managed. The Service Providers are expected to manage the underlying aspects of their operations internally and according to their own processes. This is because of the responsibility being aligned to the accountability for the services.

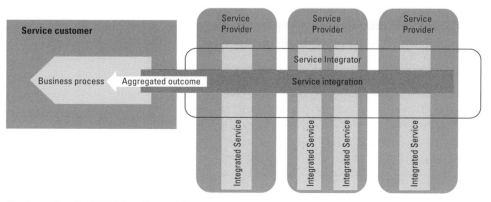

Figure 1.3   Overview SIAM integration model

SIAM is used for the governance and management of aggregated IT services and design and implementation of SIAM models are based upon IT Service Management principles. The Service Integrator needs to have the resources, capabilities and capacities to take end-to-end responsibility for the aggregated outcome and manage the integration of services. This includes both customer internal IT provider as well as third party providers. Characteristics of a Service Integrator include:

- A Service Integrator is accountable or enabling (depending on how one chooses to implement – see **An example model of Service Integration (SIAM)** later in this chapter) of the delivery of the aggregated services over multiple providers and their delivered services.
- The customer business processes and users consume every delivered service through the end-to-end aggregated service.
- The Service Integrator often sets up governance and management of integrated services within a SIAM function.
- The customer might or might not be aware of the underlying participating providers and their services.

It is not just the Service Integrator who needs to have SIAM capabilities; SIAM also depends on Services Providers having the ability to be integrated as well.

1.5   Benefits of effective Service Integration

In a multi-sourced environment, the benefits of outsourcing are typically well understood and can include:
- Access to a broader pool of resources and skills;
- Access to methods and pre-configured tools;
- Lower cost through optimized methods and broader resource pools;
- Flexibility.

When extending this model to the practice of 'Cloud Sourcing', additional benefits can be realized, including:
- Reduced implementation through pre-configured environments;
- Additional cost benefits through highly leveraged asset costs;
- Increased quality at lower cost through mass production.

However, very few services in corporate IT can be solely provided by a single external party. The retained organization typically contributes business-specific data, integration with other services and some unique insight into the business context of the IT solution. Thus, the externally sourced services must be selected, implemented, operated and integrated in a way that will be unique to each organization. This is the role of the Service Integrator, acting as an agent of the retained organization. In the Gartner paper 'Scoping the Office of the CIO' (Lee Weldon, Gartner, 2012) Weldon refers to this as "ensuring a consistent, transparent and efficient approach to the way the IT organization delivers value to the business" or "Do things right."

While the benefits of Outsourcing and Cloud Sourcing are clear at the individual service level, these benefits can be significantly® eroded if the required integration between services is weak. For example, if the integration of two services takes an additional set of resources within the retained organization, the costs will increase and the benefit will reduce. Likewise, if there are gaps between two services which limit the overall performance or availability of the business services they support, this will impact the experience of the end-user and thus the credibility of the SIAM function and the retained IT organization.

There are multiple benefits that the business can achieve through having a mature Service Integration function (or SIAM function as this book will call it). The list below provides the most important ones:
- Improved controls, supporting reduced risk and more consistent cross Service Provider service delivery;
- Increased clarity through coordinating cross supplier interactions, leading to reduced cost through duplication and improved service through better coordination of resources;
- Improved customer satisfaction through facilitating reduced cost and improved service;
- IT operating as a single team based on the Service Integration coordinating and managing the cross supplier interactions – there will be no finger pointing between Service Providers in case of serious service disruptions, due to single points of contact and accountability;
- Optimized resource usage in support of reduced cost of IT through standardized IT service delivery, which will free up resources to support business innovation;
- Ease of onboarding new services and Service Providers (e.g. SaaS) – new IT services and solutions that are initiated by the business can be integrated fast in a predefined structure using tested onboarding procedures;
- Fast switching of Service Providers by greatly simplifying transition – the overall Service Integration enables clearly defined service scope and standardized interfaces, which will facilitate a replacement of a Service Provider for a single service bundle when such a need arises without business disruption. This is because the standardization of process interactions means that changing one Service Provider has minimal impact on others.

1.6   An example model of Service Integration (SIAM)

One of the most widely publicized Service Integration models is that published by the UK Government as the UK Public Sector's SIAM Enterprise Model which is described in the whitepaper 'An example ITIL®-based model for effective Service Integration and Management' (Holland, Axelos.com, 2015).

This model describes the components of an accountable SIAM function where the Integrator takes accountability for end-to-end service delivery from the suppliers (see the diagram in Figure 1.4 from the whitepaper).

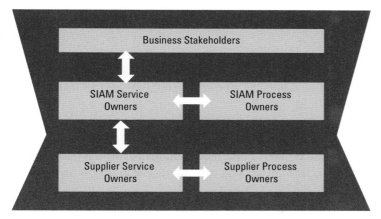

Figure 1.4   SIAM High-Level Conceptual Illustration

The model then goes on to describe the service components, which can be included in the SIAM function as part of a SIAM Enterprise Model, see Figure 1.5.

Business and Customer Organizations			
Business/Customer Relationship Management			
Service Catalog and Portfolio Management	SIAM Design	IT Information Security	Service Desk
Toolset Integration	Business and Service Continuity	Service Transition Planning and Support	Operations Bridge
Multi-Supplier Coordination		Service Validation and Testing	Operational Service Management
Supplier and Service Assurance		Knowledge Management	
Externally Provided Services		Internally Provided Services	

Figure 1.5   UK Public Sector SIAM Component Model

This model also introduces the concept of 'core SIAM' which includes
• Business/customer Relationship Management;
• SIAM Design;
• Service Catalog and Portfolio Management;
• Toolset Integration;
• Business and Service Continuity;
• Multi-supplier Coordination;
• Supplier and Service Assurance;
• IT Information Security;
• Service Desk;
• Service Transition Planning and Support;
• Operations Bridge;
• Knowledge Management;
• Service Validation and Testing;
• Operational Service Management.

As the paper 'An example ITIL-based model for effective Service Integration and Management' (Holland, Axelos.com, 2015) suggests, this is one way of structuring a relatively large scale and mature SIAM function. The model can be scaled through the correct organizational alignment, but in environments with existing Service Provider contracts and processes (where roles and accountabilities are already defined, and suppliers in place) a SIAM function can be a significant level of change to implement.

Experience indicates that models such as this can be used to provide an overall direction to the implementation of a SIAM function, although an 'enabling' approach may offer an easier way to get started.

An "enabling" SIAM function is responsible of ensuring that the standards, processes, reporting and other enabling functions are in place to allow e Service Provider services to be integrated into aggregate services, to meet the needs of the business. An illustration of the relationships in an enabling model is shown in Figure 1.6.

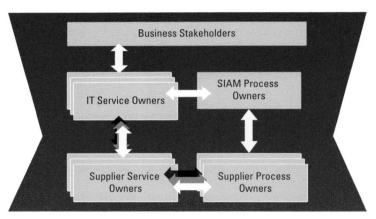

Figure 1.6   Enabling SIAM High-Level Conceptual Illustration

1.7   Managing the intersections

SIAM is founded on the same service management enablers as traditional (non-integrated) service management. There are different 'paradigms' or 'groupings' of enablers today, e.g. the '4P' of ITIL (People, Process, Products and Partners) or the 'seven enablers' of COBIT. Both of these are good practice for any service delivery situation. Since SIAM is more concerned with management and governance of Service Integration, and less with operational execution, this book has its center of gravity within COBIT but makes use of ITIL as well. In the end it is the generic area of ITSM and SIAM and not specific standards that are important to master in order to succeed. It is of course an option and even a possibility to change, extend, enhance or elaborate enablers according to any other paradigm. What's important is that SIAM implementations use a structured approach that covers every aspect of the management and governance of services.

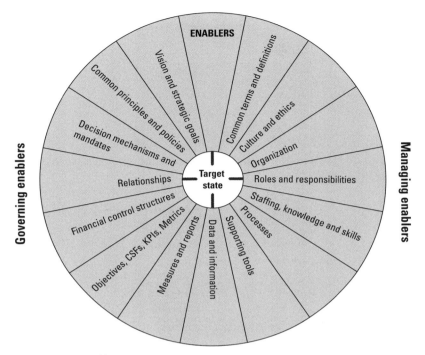

Figure 1.7 SIAM Enablers

The enablers described above can be established at three levels, each with its own characteristics and objectives:
- Strategic – visions and long term relationships. Support overall business.
- Tactical – midterm, budget level. Responsible to continuously support specific business process(es).
- Operational – daily operations, supports users and other operational stakeholders.

This allows the decisions to be made at the most appropriate level of governance and management.

The use of enablers and three levels of governance are, of course, not unique to SIAM, on the contrary they should be used in any well-formed service delivery. The differences or elaborations within SIAM are:
- It is a common set up and establishment of enablers (as far as possible), they are not bespoke or unique to each intersection between services;
- There might be flavors or variants in the implementation but the designed enablers have to be established in every intersection of an integrated delivery.

To manage the aggregated delivery of multiple IT services, enablers for management and governance should be applied to every intersection between the Service Integrator, the Service Providers and their services. These enablers are a vital part of the SIAM function and they should therefore be common to all services and every participating party should recognize and adapt to them. See Figure 1.8.

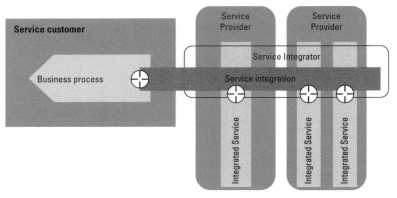

Figure 1.8   Enablers are applied to every intersection between integrating and integrated services

It is the Service Integrator's responsibility to design the way these enablers will interact from the requirements of the unique situation but they must be agreed and implemented by every participating Service Provider. It is also important to remember that different providers will have different prerequisites and competences to adapt and implement enablers. A Service Integrator must have the competences to deal with the situation where different providers behave, within certain limits, differently. It is important that the service customer should only experience the homogenous behavior of the Service Integrator.

This design will ensure that customer requirements and demands for service can be propagated through the Service Integrator to every participating service and the delivered, aggregated, service outcome will support the desired business values.

How to design and implement the different perspectives and dimension of the service enablers will be further discussed and elaborated in the following chapters of this book.

Practitioner tips:
- Different providers will have different prerequisites and competences. Don't try to force a rigid standard upon every party. A good Service Integrator parries and manages differences to provide a seamless appearance to the customer.
- It is not necessary to cover every corner from the beginning. Start with the most critical service and/or the most critical intersection and incrementally work forward – but make sure to cover every enabler, every time an increment is added.

1.8 Structure of this book

There are many dimensions to the Service Integration concept set out above. These are covered in the following chapters:

- Chapter 2 covers basic concepts and terminology as well as conceptual models for Service Integration;
- Chapter 3 describes the people and the processes that are needed;
- Chapter 4 discusses the implications for tools and data management;
- Chapter 5 covers sourcing as an important aspect of Service Integration;
- Chapter 6 covers governance;
- Chapter 7 focusses on continual service improvement;
- The book will conclude with final remarks in Chapter 8.

'Practitioner tips' are included throughout the chapters for key 'take-aways' to assist readers.

To provide context for the structure of this book, alignment to COBIT enablers has been provided for ease of understanding, as illustrated in Figure 1.9 and Table 1.1.

Table 1.1   COBIT enablers

Chapter	Covers...	...and is (partly) covering COBIT enabler...
2. Basic concepts and terminology	Definitions of the SIAM function and conceptual models for Service Integration	Principles, Policies and Frameworks
3. People and Process	People and processes to run a SIAM function	Process Culture, Ethics and Behavior People, Skills and Competences
4. Data and Tools	Tooling framework to record, gather and analyze data to share information	Information Service, Infrastructure and Applications
5. Sourcing multiple Service Providers	The sourcing process of a Service Integration ecosystem and contractual aspects	Organizational structures
6. Governance	Governance of Service Integration	Organizational structures Culture, Ethics and Behavior
7. Continual service improvement	Improvement over time	Process
8. Conclusions	Wrap-up and final considerations	Not applicable

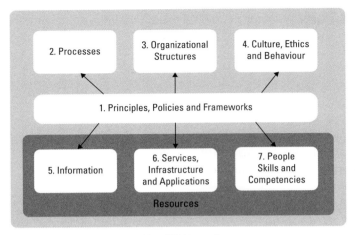

Figure 1.9   COBIT Enterprise enablers (ISACA, 2012)

1.9   Case studies

Throughout this book, reference will be made to three case studies that illustrate some of the approaches that have proven successful. Each demonstrates different perspectives on the challenge of establishing and managing a SIAM function with and without large scale contract change.

- A global automotive manufacturer implementing a large-scale 'accountable' SIAM function to drive cost efficiencies;
- A global energy production company implementing an 'enabling' SIAM function with little contract change, focusing cross-supplier collaboration to drive continual service improvement;
- A large European bank implementing an 'accountable' SIAM function to drive service improvement and cross-supplier collaboration.

1.9.1   Case study 1 – Global large automotive manufacturer

Situation/context:
The company was a global automotive manufacturer, operating in 42 countries. There had been a 10-year large scale, monolithic outsourcing deal worth multiple billions of dollars per annum. Over the 10 years some portions of the large deal had been taken to market and had created a situation of 'accidental multi-sourcing'. As they approached the end of the 10-year deal, a business case was made to consolidate the multiple service contracts, executed locally to a much smaller number of global service contracts. It was a significant step to commit to changing from the traditional model to a globally standardized service contracts.

Key features of the approach were:
- A vision of globally standardized service contracts to support a global level of optimization;

- The expiry of the previous global service contract created an effective 'greenfield' implementation. They committed to globally coordinated change across all IT outsourcing contracts simultaneously;
- The company was a very mature consumer of outsourcing services;
- Multi-billion dollar IT spend per annum.

Solution aspects and constraints

There was clearly a transition risk since it was a very new approach, with the intention of a single big bang transition date, and a major transition. To mitigate this risk, about a year of planning and another year to take the contract bundles to market was planned.

Cost efficiency was a driver for the market approach but the ongoing maintainability of the resulting commercial regime was a significant consideration. It was unlikely that the company could justify such a large-scale transition again, so the solution had to permit future changes on a Service Provider by Service Provider basis without significant impact (and therefore transition cost) to other Service Providers.

One of the Key Performance Indicators for the IT organization was ratio of maintenance expenditure to new project expenditure – i.e. how much of the total IT expenditure was 'keeping the lights on' compared to how much was adding new capability to the business lines. The goal was to decrease the maintenance cost as a proportion of the overall IT expenditure allowing more budget for the enhancement of services.

The contract bundles were aligned to:
- Infrastructure types (e.g. mid-range hosting, network etc.);
- Business unit aligned application contracts with responsibility for application and integration for each business unit (e.g. manufacturing applications);
- An end-to-end application Service Integrator responsible for overall application and information integration;
- A technical infrastructure Service Integrator that included the SIAM function, later changed:
  - This bundle was split into two components during the bidding phase. It was recognized that the infrastructure system integration scope was substantially different to the Service Integrator role;
  - The Service Integrator role needed to operate across all IT services whereas the infrastructure Service Integrator was limited to the infrastructure bundles;
  - This was a recognition that the scope of the Service Integrator had to be aligned to the outcomes required of it.

During the planning phase the companies who would be invited to bid on the future contract bundles were given the opportunity to engage in mapping the end-to-end processes. This was an innovative way to ensure that the future suppliers could influence the way the processes were built in order to be compatible with the way the solutions would be proposed.

This avoids asking suppliers to perform 'unnatural acts' meaning delivering to the contract specification in a way that unnecessarily drives up cost.

Standardization was a key feature of the solution, to support:
- A desire for standardized contracting to minimize transition/implementation costs and maximize efficiency – most importantly to reduce the cost of any future transitions;
- Reduced impact of change in one supplier to the other suppliers or the customer, allowing innovation within suppliers without unnecessary external dependencies;
- Addressing the concern from the customer about management of conflict of interest;
- Candidates who wanted to bid for the integration management were required to demonstrate that the conflict of interest created between the Service Integration role and any Service Provider roles could be managed;
- Globalized contracts to reduce over 1,000 local arrangements of outsourcing contracts to less than 100;
- A key principle of alignment of authority and accountability was implemented to ensure that the service encapsulation allowed optimal outcomes for both the company and the Service Providers.

Implementation plan
- The transition plan involved all contract services transitioning to the new roles and responsibilities, billing and service measurements on a single night at midnight;
- The new terms and conditions transitioned immediately even though many suppliers used incumbent staff adopting a traditional shadow/reverse shadow approach. What was a key (and innovative) aspect was that the new Service Providers engaged the previous incumbent as *they* required but the new suppliers were accountable for the outputs and SLAs. The customer was not required to manage those engagements;
- Service Desk was a separate Service Provider contract – it was treated as a Service Provider bundle and not part of the Service Integrator;
- A single, standardized cross functional scope of work was used across all contracts – all suppliers had standard methods for engaging the Service Integrator and other suppliers. This allowed a high degree of integration and automation of processes and cross Service Providers orchestration;
- It recognized the Service Integrator as an agent of the customer and had authority to instruct Service Providers (within defined boundaries);
- The Service Integrator provided an ITSM tool as a single source of truth that acted as a communications hub to all other Service Providers in a highly automated and standardized way. All interactions between the Service Providers' tools and the Service Integration tools were via a web service interface. Smaller service providers had the option of using email gateways to send/receive spreadsheets in a predefined XML format that was processed in the same way as the web service. The retained organization used the Service Integration tools;
- All SIAM reporting was performed based on the ITSM tools and data. Service Providers had access to the consolidated data but their reporting of SLAs was their responsibility and they were therefore required to ensure they captured the necessary data.

Results and lessons learned

The implementation was considered successful and the SIAM contract was renewed at the end of the first five-year term.

- The transition was successful, with almost no impact to business operations resulting from the big bang approach due to the very high levels of risk and contingency planning;
- Approximately 15% saving were achieved due to new outsourcing deals and contract models;
- Another similar saving was achieved after transition from aligning the system integration planning to the Service Integration model – whilst increasing the amount of project work completed each year. This was a significant improvement in the KPI related to the ratio of maintenance to new function expenditure;
- The transition used service delivery staff to augment implementation – this allowed good engagement, transition to service and reduced training costs because the BAU people were involved up front. The down side is that it was difficult to perform a transformation activity with service delivery priorities for the staff;
- Even though the retained IT organization was considered 'thin' at less than 10% of total headcount estimates, it was large enough to require communication and education related to the new model. The retained organization was generally a 'change ready' team and viewed the changes as an opportunity;
- In the early stages of implementation, the SIAM function learned that a standard process, when implemented manually in different geographies, could be used very differently. This caused a significant re-work of the change process automation.

Since the implementation was a very early one with very high risk due to the size and relative novelty of the solution, a significant amount of planning and risk mitigation had to be performed. Much of the planning and design had to be considered from a first principles perspective. This is why it took two years to plan, including the contract negotiations.

1.9.2   Case study 2 – Global energy company

Situation/context

The IT department of a global energy company, operating in 26 countries and supporting all corporate functions, had been through a major program of outsourcing over a three year period. During that time, they had selected major Service Providers split across five major service areas:

- Infrastructure and end-user services, including service desk and desk-side services;
- Application maintenance services split across two Service Providers, one for subsurface applications and another for surface and enterprise applications;
- Application development services had been procured through a framework agreement with two providers who were shortlist bidders for new development projects;
- Security services including security tools and identity and access management;
- Service integration services.

In addition to these major contracts, there were smaller, local delivery teams, both retained resources and local service providers embedded in the operating assets across the world. The retained organization was focused on governance and management of these major Service Providers and local delivery teams.

The objectives of the outsourcing program had been to:
- Reduce cost – operational and project;
- Improve service;
- Reduce the time taken to develop and deploy new services;
- Access new skills and expertise.

Post transition of the outsourcing agreements, based on budgets and customer and consumer satisfaction feedback, it was generally agreed that something had to change – the objectives were not being achieved.

The major problems to be resolved included:
- The retained organization had become too focused on the outputs of the Service Providers and lost sight of the service being delivered to the end user:
  - Reporting and metrics were based on an amalgamation of each Service Providers information and would take four to six weeks to go through all the reviews before they could be published;
  - Retained staff had become either:
    - Reactive to the Service Providers – providing approvals upon request, rather than providing the structure for delivery; or
    - Prescriptive to the Service Providers – directing individual resources within the Service Providers at the task level, therefore accepting delivery risk back to the retained organization;
- The SIAM function was focused on delivering a three year transformation of staged process implementation which was struggling to gain acceptance from the Service Providers;
- The mandate for all Service Providers to use the same IT Service Management tooling, coupled with a poorly defined and executed implementation, meant that the integrated tools suite was hampering rather than enabling the delivery of services;
- The retained organization's focus on service provider boundaries had led to barriers to effective communication which was impacting decision making and planning.

Solution aspects and constraints
- The customer did not want to go into wholesale contract change in the middle of the contract terms. The planned renewals in 2017 would offer the opportunity to contract in new ways but in the interim, they needed to achieve some of the benefits expected from the first round of outsourcing.
- They were constrained by the need to get people focused on a single set of data that was meaningful in terms of the end-user experience without triggering all the contractual exclusion clauses that would allow Service Providers to abdicate from their accountabilities.

Findings from data analysis needed to be released from the long-winded discussions about exemptions and scope-boundaries and focus on how to achieve outcomes. The ecosystem as a whole needed to be able to react to real-time metrics and near real-time data.
- They needed to measure the experience the end-users were receiving from IT and focus on service providers' results in that context. They wanted to use that data to drive investment and transformation initiatives rather than the two year-old long-term plans that were established at contract signature with each Service Provider in isolation.
- They needed to find a way for all partners to collaborate on the things that would either:
  - Bring direct benefit to them in terms of service improvement or cost reduction; or
  - That they could invest in, in the short term, trusting that benefit would be coming for them in the next iteration.
- They needed to enable the organization to react quickly to new findings in data and new priorities from a business perspective, without getting caught up in contractual discussions to adjust targets and priorities.
- There was a necessity to provide communications and updates about the successes and future plans to all stakeholders, using language that they would recognize as a meaningful achievement or goal.

Implementation plan
A set of objectives were defined to address the situation:
1. Change the focus of the retained organization from supplier-focused to customer-focused:
   a. Retained resources needed to be able to understand any issues with the service being provided to the end-users and prioritize based on that end-user impact;
   b. Implement measurement of end-to-end business services and aggregated business service lines to measure service as received by the user;
2. Establish a culture of collaboration and improvement within all of the teams:
   a. Internal collaboration between teams;
   b. External collaboration between retained IT and Service Providers;
   c. External collaboration with the business to understand priorities;
3. Establish a set of baseline measures and invest in reporting to give a single foundation data set to support collaboration and act as a basis for all future improvement planning;
4. Integrate the required functions within the organization to facilitate more rapid decision making and closer collaboration;
5. Update the SIAM contract to enable a mix of objectives based on short-term and long term service outcomes;
6. Establish ongoing communication of both the vision and the progress that has been made in terms that mean something to the stakeholders.

Results and lessons learned
For this company, the experience has been a positive one in many ways. Closer collaboration between the different parts of IT and Service Providers has led to more positive and creative working relationships. An internal IT re-organization has re-emphasized the importance of the business service line model by aligning the teams into business domains which bring together strategy, projects and operations for each domain into a single team.

The specific results achieved by this transformation include:
- Significant savings were realized through contract re-negotiation based on reducing the number of contractual SLAs to those that really matter and increased confidence and efficiency;
- Greatly improved IT metrics:
  - 65% reduction in incident and service request backlog;
  - P1 incidents down by 30%;
  - P2 incidents down by 45%;
  - Reduction in overall incidents resolution time by 30%;
  - Improved customer satisfaction to 90%;
  - 40% reduction in planned down-time;
  - Failed change <1%;
  - Expedited change <7%;
- Implementation of new IT capabilities:
  - Deployed online user self-service with 150 cross-supplier service request types;
  - Reduced time to report from four weeks to real-time;
  - Implemented cross-supplier incident resolution SLAs (92% compliance);
  - Implemented service request targets at both the request and task level and improved achievement to 90%;
- Related achievements:
  - All Service Providers worked on, or integrated to a single toolset driving real-time reporting and dashboards. Tools are integrated to achieve effective real-time data and analytics;
  - A CMDB linked to end-user experience monitoring and measuring the top 40 application services. All Service Provider services required to deliver the business service are measured and monitored in real-time with integration into the ITSM tool to record incidents.

The principle lesson learned through this transformation has been that a successful SIAM implementation is not something that can be done *to* an organization. Even with the best outsourced partners the retained organization must be willing to adapt to the new approach as well. In this case study the following changes were made affecting the retained organization:
- Moved from supplier-focused to customer-centric;
- Established a culture of collaboration and improvement across the ecosystem;
- Established a set of baseline measures and invested in reporting;
- Adapted the organization to enable rapid decision making and closer collaboration;
- When sourcing SIAM services, recognized that the contract must be implemented in the right way;
- Continually communicated both the vision and the progress made towards it.

By establishing the right culture, even without significant contractual change, significant value can be achieved.

1.9.3   Case study 3 – European bank

Situation/context

The IT organization of a European bank (supporting all corporate functions) had implemented and managed their first generation of outsourcing contracts over a five-year period. During that time, they had established and managed major Service Providers split across major service areas:

- Application maintenance services split across three external Service Providers and a large number of small internal application management groups;
- Data center and end-user infrastructure services, including service desk and desk-side services from a infrastructure service provider; this Service Provider was also contracted to ensure end-to-end control as the service guardian;
- Network services from a network provider;
- Telephony services from a telecom provider.

The retained organization was focused on the governance and management of these major Service Providers.

When renewals of the contracts were approaching, the opportunity was used to re-evaluate the current environment and a number of deficiencies were identified. The major deficiencies were:

- End user satisfaction was too low, although service level performance by the external Service Providers met the required service levels;
- Uncontrolled growth of infrastructure resources;
- There had been many scope discussions amongst the service guardian provider and the other Service Providers. Service guardian was forced to work beyond their scope as they were end-to-end responsible;
- Service Integration function was only half implemented; several Service Providers operated directly with the bank, bypassing Service Integrator. This made the Service Integrator ineffective;
- Service level performance of the internal resolver groups was lacking;
- Sub-optimal problem management existed as a result of inconsistency of problem management service level definitions amongst the contracts.

Resulting from the analysis, the following objectives for the outsourcing program were set:
- Reduce operational cost;
- Improve service;
- Improve end-to-end control by the Service Integrator and collaboration across Service Providers.

Solution aspects and constraints

As part of the solution, a distinction was made between major Service Providers and other Service Providers including internal departments. This new solution was required to improve control over these major Service Providers.

The new contracts with the major Service Providers contained several additional elements, which were equal for all major Service Providers:
• Acknowledgement of, and adherence to, the Integrator role of the service guardian;
• Acknowledgement by the retained departments that they were internal Service Providers;
• Transparency of data amongst the Service Providers (with the exception of commercial data);
• A multi-supplier common KPI model, in which every major Service Provider is accountable for contribution to end-to-end results;
• Multi-supplier governance structures.

Implementation plan

A program was set up to renew all outsourcing contracts at the same time, using the same set of consistent terms, conditions and service levels – in effect a standardized cross functional scope of work.

The outsourcing engagement program was run by in collaboration between infrastructure, networking and telephony procurement departments of the bank, supporting consistency across the contracts. This was the first, very important, cross-departmental collaboration required.

In the negotiations phase, the approach was to establish agreed roles and responsibilities with the service guardian first. As a result these roles and responsibilities became a constraint for the other major Service Providers with limited room to make changes. The same roles and responsibilities were shared with the internal Service Providers.

The transformation plan included several improvement projects:
• Definition of a multi-supplier RASCI table (Responsible, Accountable, Supporting, Consulted, Informed) for all ITIL processes in scope using round table workshops with all major service suppliers led by the service guardian provider;
• Inclusion of the defined RASCI table into the OLAs amongst all Service Providers, including internal;
• Development and implementation of an onboarding procedure to ensure positioning of new Service Providers in the service support structure;
• Implementation of the common KPI model and multi-supplier governance.

Results and lessons learned
• The expected cost savings were achieved as a result of the contract renewals;
• End-to-end availability of the critical business services went up from 95% at the start of the service guardian role to over 99% as a result of the changed emphasis on the aggregated services;
• A communication plan targeting all levels of stakeholders is needed to support the changed expectations and required behaviors;

- Open communication and discussion is needed to gain mutual trust and respect. False consensus – where people appear to agree in order to avoid conflict but do not follow through – is not helpful;
- These types of changes do not happen overnight – there is a cultural change aspect required as well;
- For the common KPI model: first year was to learn and start cooperating, second year to stabilize measurement and reporting, and improve practices, real improvement on the KPI outcomes occurred in the third year.

1.9.4 Summary

These case studies were implemented independently from each other, without the knowledge from the UK government example (Holland, Axelos.com, 2015). That they were developed independently and have some different approaches is not a surprise given that the community of practice for Service Integration was not established. What is interesting is the factors that are similar and seem to be correlated with 'successful' implementation. It will be these similarities that are recommended throughout the rest of this book, noting that there is not (at least not yet) a 'one size fits all' answer. The book will highlight as 'practitioner tips' those patterns highly correlated with success, and cautions against 'anti-patterns' that are highly correlated with problems.

The one, astoundingly clear, observation is that Service Integration is not just a technology problem. Changing the way the people think about Service Providers as partners in an ecosystem (symbiotic relationships) and ensuring clarity of roles are critically important factors. Changes to processes can support this ecosystem thinking and role clarity. The contractual agreements can (should) support the process models. The technology makes the processes an order of magnitude more efficient and has enormous value in analytics. However, experience shows that without a change to the way in which people work, the other elements will not deliver the expected value.

There are still differences of opinion on many topics within the Service Integration community. For the reader to make their own decision, the reasons for these differences of opinion must be analysed. The authors of this book have spent many hours, collectively and independently, on such analysis and the recommendations contained are the result of this. However the authors encourage the readers, as famously quoted by Thomas J. Watson (of IBM fame), to THINK!

2 Basic Concepts and Terminology

The objective of this chapter is to set the scene and introduce the basic concepts of Service Integration. It provides the reader with a common reference model for the language and terminology that will be used in the remainder of the book. After establishing some common ground with regard to sourcing definition, this chapter will discuss the need for Service Integration. It will also answer the question of what SIAM capability to outsource (and what to retain) and why this should be done, both in general and in more detail. The chapter will then discuss the various ways in which Service Integration is implemented and provide a set of guiding principles.

2.1 What is sourcing?

2.1.1 Separation of duties

The term sourcing refers to the acquisition of resources or services to deliver a particular part of the IT value chain. The very origin of economic science starts with separation of duties. This has been so since the moment John and Jack, two prehistoric people agreed that John would go and hunt for both of them, while Jack would stay in the cave and make weapons. The labor was divided, and each activity had its own source.

This created challenges as well! Firstly, there was an instant mutual dependency: Jack became dependent on John for food, while John needed good weapons to hunt. Secondly, coordination became important: John and Jack needed to agree what kind of weapons were needed, and whether meat and/or vegetables were required for a balanced diet.

Separation of duties has proven to be a very successful strategy for humankind. Humans have evolved from dividing labor between individuals to dividing labor between organizations. Sourcing strategy has become an important part of every company's IT strategy. And the two challenges mentioned above have not gone away:

- Mutual dependency: sourcing can be characterized by the level of mutual dependency that a sourcing agreement creates. In the prehistoric example above, everyone would label Jack and John as partners. But would an organization call every service provider they work with a partner? This cannot be done, and therefore a differentiation of Service Providers must be used. The Henderson portfolio as discussed in Section 2.2.1 provides a continuum for this.
- Coordination: most of the concepts discussed in this book would also apply for organizations that do not outsource at all. However, the coordination of activities, processes and data interactions is a key element in managing and controlling external Service Providers in the multi-service provider ecosystem and is at the heart of Service Integration.

2.1.2   Sourcing types

This section will introduce briefly some of the most common forms of sourcing, focusing on services, leaving third-party supply of hardware and software products out of scope for now.

- **Insourcing** relates to the situation where the work in scope is being done by a person, group or department internally within the enterprise. All of these are the enterprise's own employees. Insourcing is often used as a term when organization takes back work that was previously outsourced in some way. However, it can also refer to work that has never been sourced to an external party as well.

NOTE: do not confuse insourced with 'retained' (as defined in Section 2.1.3); insourced services are services that are delivered by internal Service Providers, which should be treated by the Service Integrator as Service Providers.

- **Staff augmentation** refers to individuals who perform a temporary role in the organization. There are situations where leading IT roles in organizations are being fulfilled by sub-contractors. They are contracted based on an hourly rate. They simply fulfill a gap in resources that the organization could not meet from its own employees. This can be used as one way of dealing with staff attrition or skills shortages.
- **Out-tasking** is a form of labor division where a set of tasks is being performed by an external party. The customer organization decides specifically what needs to be done and how, and retains complete control and responsibility over the results. Again, contracts are based on hourly rates and typically do not include service levels. Examples of out-tasking are designing a website or conducting an end user satisfaction survey.
- **Outsourcing** is the most common and central type of sourcing and the object of Service Integration. Typically an outsourcing contract exists with service scope, service level agreements and more pricing arrangements. Although customization to the specific requirements of the customer are common in this model, the outsourcing service provider adds value by leveraging economies of scale because he can share resources. Throughout this book this is the type of contract that is referred to. A special and growing type of outsourcing is the 'as a Service (aaS)' service option around cloud where the Service Provider, the service scope and the assets used to deliver it are far more inter-woven and the levels to which it can be personalized and/or customized are much less.
- **Sub-contracting** typically refers to a situation where the capabilities of a Service Provider are supplemented by those of another organization. Specific elements of the service scope can be sub-contracted to a third party in a way which is transparent to the end customer.
- **Divestiture** is the most extreme business model change where a former business unit providing IT services to the business is sold to an external partner. Consequently, the sourcing strategy will have to be redefined. The newly created enterprise will most likely continue to provide IT services to the business, but in a competitive Service Provider landscape. On the other hand, it will be able to become active in the IT services market in order to develop new customer relationships.

2.1.3   The retained organization

Most enterprises will use a combination of the sourcing types above. Traditionally, management and control of external Service Providers has been the area of responsibility of a supplier management department, in which contract managers were responsible for a portfolio of third party contracts. Having multiple, large service contracts with different companies in parallel, however asks for a new kind of discipline: Service Integration.

While the practice of Service Integration needs to be performed by and with the retained organization, in defining which function within the organization executes that practice, a model for defining the different elements of that organization must firstly be established. For the purposes of this book, five elements of an IT organization will be used to describe the different capabilities, as shown in Figure 2.1.

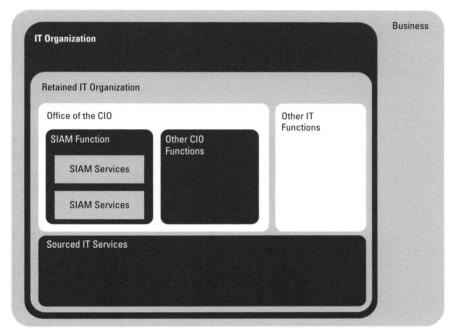

Figure 2.1   Aspects of an IT Organization

- IT Organization represents the entirety of the organizational unit that is accountable for the delivery of IT services within the organization.
- The Retained IT Organization is those aspects of the IT organization that are not sourced from a third party. This can include staff augmentation, but these people are operating on behalf of the IT organization.
- Office of the CIO (OCIO), as defined by Gartner (Lee Weldon, Gartner, 2012), is the part of the organization that focuses on the two key aspects of "ensuring a consistent and strategic approach to the use of information technology across the enterprise" and "ensuring a consistent, transparent and efficient approach to the way the IT organization delivers value to the business".
- The SIAM Function typically focuses on some or all of the aspects of the second objective of the OCIO and is accountable for ensuring that things are 'done right' i.e. in the way that

most effectively balances the performance of the individual services with the performance of the business service that they support.

• SIAM Services are component services that can be sourced from one or more third party organizations to deliver aspects of Service Integration. They perform one part of the integrating role, for example a Service Desk or a reporting and management information service.

Due to the fact that much of the current literature about SIAM has been written by Service Providers, there is considerable confusion between the capabilities of the SIAM services that are available from the market as opposed to those required to deliver an effective SIAM function.

Multiple customers have developed their own way of dealing with this important management challenge in different ways. When deciding the scope of the SIAM function, the key determinant is what that function will be accountable for; will it be *accountable* for the delivery of services, or will it simply be an *enabling* function? The choice made will have a significant impact on the size and capabilities of the SIAM function required.

A good example of the difference between an accountable vs. enabling SI function can be found in the whitepaper "An Introduction to Service Integration and ITIL" (Holland, Axelos.com, 2015). In this paper, Kevin Holland describes the aim of the SIAM function as "to provide a single point of visibility and control for the service management and delivery of all services provided by internal and external suppliers". Within this definition, the addition of "and delivery" changes this from an enabling function to an accountable one.

The implementation of a fully accountable SIAM function represents significant change to most IT organizations, requiring contractual, cultural and organizational change at all levels. An enabling SIAM function can represent a smaller scale change that can be implemented without significant impact to existing contractual frameworks while still delivering significant benefits. For a detailed explanation of one such story, please review the global energy company case study in Section 1.9.2.

While some fundamental benefits may be realized from an enabling SIAM function, there is distinct additional value to be had from an accountable SIAM function which, in addition to clarifying points of accountability, also provides ways to mitigate the potential risks of different sourcing models (see Section 2.4.)

2.1.4   Service Integration and SIAM versus service orchestration

The concept of service orchestration is referred to in multiple publications on service-oriented architecture. Sometimes the definitions and examples used come very close to the meaning of Service Integration in this book. On other occasions, however, service orchestration is associated primarily with automated aggregation of individual services. Overall, there does not seem to be a consensus on what service orchestration is.

In general one could say that orchestration refers to the execution of an already existing composition, without changing the components, whereas integration is about creating something out of individual components, which was not there before.

Despite some elasticity of meaning, the term service orchestration could be used as an alternative or even as a synonym for the term Service Integration. However the authors have decided to take a pragmatic approach and adopt the generally accepted term Service Integration and Management (SIAM) throughout this book.

2.1.5   Service Integration and SIAM versus cloud service brokerage

As the cloud services market has become mature, cloud service brokerage (CSB) has evolved as a new discipline. Gartner defines CSB as "an IT role and business model in which a company or other entity adds value to one or more (public or private) cloud services on behalf of one or more consumers of that service via three primary roles including aggregation, integration and customization brokerage." (Gartner, 2015.)

As the cloud service landscape is complex it makes sense to establish the cloud service brokerage role as part of the SIAM function. The goals and objectives of CSB are no different from those of SIAM, although the focus and the practices may differ to some extent, depending on the type of cloud service. For example, a public cloud service is designed to be a standardized commodity, which does not enable the kind of customization and partnership that a bespoke service from a major service provider can bring.

2.2   Business relationships in outsourcing

One of the first questions that any organization looking to outsource should ask is "what kind of partner are you?" As the number of Service Providers increases along with the need to integrate them, an alternative question should be asked, "What kind of _integrator_ are you?" As the dependency between services that can be consumed and the Service Providers that deliver them becomes ever more tightly-coupled, the answers to these two questions become the foundation of an effective multi-sourcing strategy. Working with clients across the world and in different industries has highlighted one lesson more than any other, Service Integration is not something that can be done to an organization, the retained organization needs to understand the cultural shift necessary to truly integrate their Service Providers and embody that shift within its own principles and practices.

The answers to these questions will clearly influence the selection of Service Providers as there must be some common shared values and principles upon which to base the relationship. There is growing evidence that they can also drive improvements in the organization's ability to identify new trends, respond to them and increase revenue and profit. To explore this question further, consider the ways in which organizations look to develop, maintain and benefit from business relationships and the specific relationships that they build. The 'how' and the 'what' of the business relationship.

2.2.1   Relationship types

The differing types of relationship that can be created between an IT sourcing customer and provider are almost endless in their complexity and variety, but as early as 1990, John C. Henderson of MIT was demonstrating the importance of "effective coordination across the information systems community" and "building partnerships as a management strategy." His paper 'Plugging into strategic partnerships: The critical IS connection' (Henderson, 1990) explores this concept and introduces 'determinates of partnership' which are divided into two categories:

1. Relationship in Context (RiC) is the "degree to which the partners believe that the partnership will be sustained over time":
   a. Mutual benefits;
   b. Predisposition;
   c. Commitment.
2. Relationship in Action (RiA) relates to the partners' "ability to influence policies and decisions that affect the operational performance of the partnership":
   a. Shared knowledge;
   b. Mutual dependency on distinctive competences and resources;
   c. Organizational linkages.

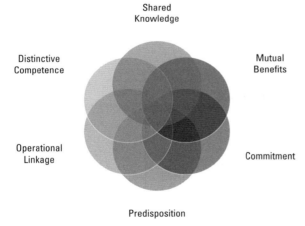

Figure 2.2   Henderson determinants of relationship

These relationship determinants indicate the type of relationship between two organizations or teams. In a subsequent study, Henderson similarly developed a 'Portfolio of Relationships' which classified the different relationship types as: Transactional, Value-Added, Special and Unique, see Figure 2.3.

When forging partnerships and sourcing services, it makes sense therefore to understand the type of relationship and outcome that is required, and to procure, integrate and manage accordingly.

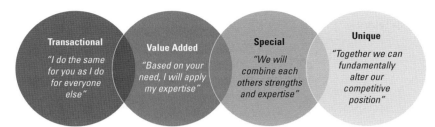

Figure 2.3   Henderson Portfolio of Relationships

Sadly, this is all too often not the case. Clear definition of the scope of the service provides a level of certainty for the known future, building and maintaining the right relationship helps deal with the unknown. Moreover, it is difficult to change the relationship midway through the term of the contract if there is no CCN (Contract Change Notice) for that.

A similar model of relationships is discussed in the paper 'Maturity model for IT outsourcing relationships' (Solli-Saether, 2006) where three relationship types are discussed and linked together in terms of a maturity model:
• Cost Stage: IT outsourcing is driven by cost concerns;
• Resource Stage: outsourcing is driven by the need to access resources (people, skills, innovation) of another organization;
• Partnership Stage: emphasis is on intangibles such as trust, understanding, flexibility etc.

These stages and the critical issues of each are visually represented in Figure 2.4.

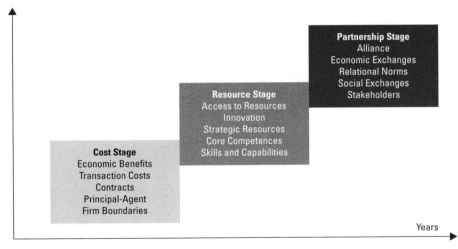

Figure 2.4   Critical Issues in each stage of outsourcing maturity

Within this model, progress to the next stage of relationship comes from solving all the problems at the previous stage. In the case of the Cost Stage, this implies that the customer achieves intended cost savings, transaction costs are acceptable, the contract prevents opportunistic behavior and there is a satisfactory separation of duties. The paper also highlights some of the inhibitors to successful relationships in the early stages of outsourcing. In a significant time of change retained IT staff may transfer to a service provider or even be made redundant; this reality can lead to mistrust between the people involved from the start.

Combining these models leads to the conclusion that successful integration of Service Providers requires a clear understanding of the type of relationship being sought and the level of maturity in their integration capability to 'mature' the relationship to a sufficient stage to support the relationship required.

> **Practitioner tip:**
> Successful integration of Service Providers requires a clear understanding of the type of relationship being sought and the level of maturity in their integration capability to 'mature' the relationship to a sufficient stage to support the relationship required.

2.2.2   Benefits of relationship planning

To attempt to quantify the impact of sourcing strategies, the IBM Center for Applied Insights studied the views of 1,351 sourcing decision makers from around the world in the 2013 study entitled 'Why partnering strategies matter' (Patrick M. Kerin, 2013).

Within the analysis, four partnering strategies emerged, see Figure 2.5.

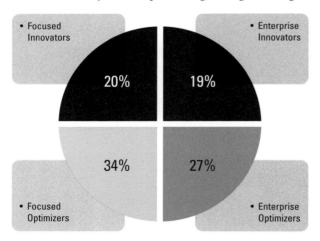

Figure 2.5   Partnering Strategies in the IBM study "Why Strategies Matter" study

1. Enterprise Innovators are sourcing more areas of their business and are sourcing services to drive innovation – changing how they operate, their role in the value chain, how they monetize value or even the way their entire industry works.
2. Enterprise Optimizers source a similarly broad set of business and IT functions, but their focus is on driving greater levels of effectiveness and efficiency.

3. Focused Innovators are sourcing a narrower set of services and are engaging partners to help innovate in specific areas
4. Focused Optimizers have a more traditional view to services and are targeting optimization in specific areas through partnerships.

Within the respondents of the IBM study 'Why partnering strategies matter':
- 40% were C-level executives;
- Approximately one third were IT leaders and two thirds were business leaders;
- 65% had 1,000-9,999 employees, 35% had greater than 10,000 employees;
- 18 different industries were represented;
- 12 different countries (30% growth markets and 70% mature markets).

The financial performance of the organization involved was based on an analysis of publically available financial information and firmographic factors that could also affect the financial performance were controlled through multivariate analysis.

Among the significant findings was the simple bottom line that:
- "Outsourcing motivations have changed, so should sourcing strategies. Why? Those who have made the shift are also outperforming – racking up twice the revenue growth and five times the gross profit growth of their peers".
- A change in the sourcing models requires a corresponding change in the way that these partners are integrated together and managed on an ongoing basis.
- Revenue growth and Gross Profit growth were the first parameters to show a strong correlation.

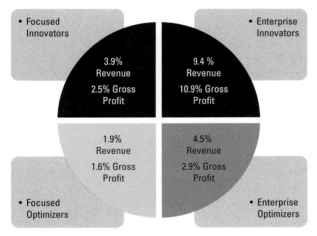

Figure 2.6   Partnering Link to Financial Performance (3 YEAR CAGR%, FY 2011)

This was then further explored through in-depth analysis with other factors such as geography, company size and industry, and found to be a common correlation across many measures of financial performance.

Whether Service Provider relationships are a driver of business performance or business performance drives service provider relationships, there is clear and empirical evidence that successful organizations have a clear view of the type of relationships that they want and need with their Service Providers and manage them accordingly.

2.2.3　Impact on Service Integration

Relationship models take on an additional level of complexity when utilized to help plan our approach to sourcing IT services:

- The type of relationship with Service Providers needs to be able to support the type of services being delivered to the retained IT organization:
- They also need to be aligned with the resulting service being delivered to the business;
- AND, they need to support the type of relationship between the business and IT.

For example, if an IT organization (including all of its component parts) and the business have a unique relationship, the service to the business requires a significant amount of flexibility and is likely to change in a very dynamic way. Sourcing one component of that may be viable through a transactional approach, but sourcing the entire service is more likely to require a special or unique relationship.

Due to the fact that there are a finite number of Service Providers, particularly on a global scale, one customer may have multiple contracts with a single service provider. The relationship model for each contract sets an expectation of behaviors that contribute to, and have an impact upon, the overall relationship with the service provider. It is possible to have a 'unique' relationship with an organization and procure transactional services within that relationship. However, the organization's overall relationship between the two should be able to support the most mature level of service relationship between them.

When relationship expectations are not met, this can lead to ruptures in the relationship that can have broader implications. For example, if an organization procures multiple services from a single service provider:

- If the service provider fails to deliver in accordance with their contract in one service, the result will be a negative impact on the overall relationship;
- If the customer fails to meet their obligations under the terms of one contract, the result will be negative for the whole relationship;
- If there is a mismatch in the expectations, e.g. the customer is expecting the flexibility and customization of a special relationship from within a commodity service, this will also impact the overall relationship.

Any negative factors for the overall relationship will ultimately have a similar impact on the services being delivered e.g. reduced trust, poor communication, and protectionism. It becomes clear, therefore, that the practice of Service Integration, and one of the roles of any SIAM function, is to ensure that the retained organization has the skills, capabilities and awareness to identify and maintain these working relationships at both a contract and organizational level.

The findings of both the studies referenced above, support the hypothesis that the more collaborative the business relationship, the greater the value that can be achieved from the overall ecosystem. There is also a significant impact on the size, and cost of the retained organization. The nature of the intended relationship and accountabilities need to be understood and reflected in Service Provider agreements. They also need to be communicated effectively to avoid duplication of cost and systemic confusion that will arise if people discover by chance that they have overlapping responsibilities and accountabilities. When it comes to integrating the services, the role of (and therefore the design of) the Integration layer needs to support the relationships required, and recognize the different relationship types in the ecosystem:

- Will the retained organization be resourced and structured to measure all of the services, or review the output of Service Provider measurement systems?
- Will the retained organization be focused on managing the Service Providers or collaborating with them to achieve greater levels of mutual value?

Given these considerations, the answer to the question "what type of integrator are you?" should be addressed early in the journey of design and execution of the final IT operating model. There is evidence (as detailed above) that indicates there are business benefits for those who are able to leverage the power of unique relationships with selected partners. However, if the organization is looking to procure specific commodity services, then a small set of transactional or special relationships may be a better answer. Either way, the decision needs to be made, and made early to ensure that the required levels of governance, tooling, process and resource can be applied to make the overall business successful.

The long-term nature of outsourcing relationships means that the same people will need to build and maintain effective working relationships over an extended period of time and to progress through the stages of maturity (Solli-Saether, 2006). There are important and significant cultural challenges to be overcome and a level of maturity required, as detailed in the case studies in Section 1.9, and the difference between the success and failure of overall ecosystem relies on the leadership of the retained organization and the Service Integrator.

2.3 Sourcing the Service Integrator function

When outsourcing IT services in general the first question that comes to mind is: Why? Although the answers may seem obvious, they need to be mentioned here before the same question can be answered specifically for the subject of Service Integration.

The most common decision arguments for outsourcing include:
1. Cost. Many outsourcing decisions are taken for economic reasons. It is cheaper to outsource IT services because IT Service Providers are able to deliver with less costs, due to economies of scale and competitive pressure.
2. Core competence. Organizations that want to focus on their core competences decide to outsource IT services because these are considered as commodities, and as non-business

critical. IT infrastructure services in particular are considered as a commodity. Note that this does not imply that business-critical IT services will never be outsourced, but it is far less likely.

3. Skills. For certain activities or services, where specific skills are needed, organizations are willing to outsource. SFIA (the Skills Framework for the Information Age) provides a structured overview of IT skills and can help to identify where skills are lacking. 'IT Performance Management' (Wiggers, Kok, & de Boer - de Wit, 2004) links this to the technology lifecycle. Especially at the start and at the end of the technology lifecycle skills are scarce in the market and outsourcing can be a welcome solution. Consider for example mobile apps (in 2015 considered to be at the start of the technology lifecycle) and legacy applications (to be considered at the end of the technology lifecycle).

The 'Why?' question is important, not only because this increases awareness of the reason for an outsourcing decision, it also establishes the foundation for the kind of relationship the organization wants to have with the party that it will work with, as well as the selection and performance criteria.

2.3.1   Why outsource Service Integration?

The 'What to outsource?' question is an important one regarding Service Integration. The outsourcing of a Service Integration role is not that obvious and indeed many organizations have retained the Integrator role. And there are good reasons to retain the Service Integration role:

- The retained IT organization has end-to-end accountability over the IT services that are provided to the business units. They are the single point of accountability towards the business units, as it has been their decision to outsource part of IT service delivery to external Service Providers. In order to keep that control it makes perfect sense to organize the Service Integration role as a retained function.
- Outsourcing the Service Integration role introduces complexity in the Service Provider ecosystem as one needs to think about which IT service bundles can be outsourced to the same Service Provider and which can't.

Let's take a closer look at the general arguments for outsourcing Service Integration, see Table 2.1.

Service Integration does not directly contribute to the cost reduction of IT services. It does help prevent a significant increase of IT costs as a result of moving to a multi-service provider model. Indirectly, though, good Service Integration can reduce cost through reduced duplication, reducing commercial risk to the Service Provider (by clear processes, measures and data etc.), and can lead to a significant reduction in cost when it gets to the point of switching partners more easily. Service Integration mitigates the risks of inefficiencies due to lack of collaboration and communication.

Table 2.1   Pros and cons of outsourcing service integration

Outsource Service Integration because of...	Pros	Cons
Cost	Enabling indirect cost reduction through multi-sourcing of best-of-breed Service Providers	No direct cost reduction
Core Competence	Operationally managing IT Service Providers is not a core competence	IT strategy and business alignment is a core competence
Skills	Able to focus on business process skills	Need to retain IT Service Integration skills to enable switching of Service Providers

The 'core competence' argument has been used quite often in the area of Service Integration and it is closely linked to the 'skill' argument. As an example, consider crisis management, resolving major incidents. This is definitely a task that is part of an Integrator role in a multi-service provider environment. However, resolving complicated, deep technical IT infrastructure issues in the middle of the night with a group of highly technical people is not regarded as a core competence by many organizations. But ensuring that the business impact is identified, communicating to the stakeholders in the business units or even to the public (when an important public web site is down) should be regarded as a core competence. Based on this kind of reasoning, a split between the tasks to be retained and those tasks that can be outsourced becomes possible. A systematic approach using a Service Integration reference model as a checklist will enable an organization to define the scope of the to-be outsourced Service Integrator.

One way to label this distinction is to make a difference between a strategic integrator, a tactical integrator and an operational integrator role:
1. The strategic integrator role will focus on defining the principles and standards that will govern the environment, control IT service supply and report on its performance towards the business;
2. The tactical integrator role will focus on organizing the service support structure by developing and managing SLAs and OLAs and enforcing cooperation between the Service Providers;
3. The operational integrator role will facilitate the day-to-day execution of the service delivery.

The strategic integrator will always need to be retained, but the tactical and operational integrator could be outsourced.

Typical examples of retained roles and functions as part of the strategic integrator:
• Sourcing strategy;
• Regulatory compliance;
• IT security policy setting and guidelines.

Table 2.2   COBIT processes and Integrator roles

COBIT process (ISACA, 2012)	Strategic Service Integrator	Tactical / Operational Service Integrator	Service Provider
EDM01 Ensure Governance Framework Setting and Maintenance	X		
EDM02 Ensure Benefits Delivery	X		
EDM03 Ensure Risk Optimization	X		
EDM04 Ensure Resource Optimization	X		
EDM05 Ensure Stakeholder Transparency	X		
APO01 Manage the IT Management Framework	X		
APO02 Manage Strategy	X		
APO03 Manage Enterprise Architecture	X		
APO04 Manage Innovation	X		
APO05 Manage Portfolio	X		
APO06 Manage Budget and Costs	X		
APO07 Manage Human Resources		X	
APO08 Manage Relationships		X	
APO09 Manage Service Agreements		X	
APO010 Manage Suppliers		X	
APO011 Manage Quality		X	
APO012 Manage Risk		X	
APO013 Manage Security		X	
BAI01 Manage Programs and Projects			X
BAI02 Manage Requirements Definition			X
BAI03 Manage Solutions Identification and Build			X
BAI04 Manage Availability and Capacity			X
BAI05 Manage Organizational Change Enablement	X		
BAI06 Manage Changes			X
BAI07 Manage Change Acceptance and Transitioning		X	
BAI08 Manage Knowledge		X	
BAI09 Manage Assets			X
BAI010 Manage Configuration			X
DSS01 Manage Operations			X
DSS02 Manage Service Requests and Incidents			X
DSS03 Manage Problems			X
DSS04 Manage Continuity			X
DSS05 Manage Security Services			X
DSS06 Manage Business Process Controls	X		
MEA01 Monitor, Evaluate and Assess Performance and Conformance	X		
MEA02 Monitor, Evaluate and Assess the System of Internal Control	X		
MEA03 Monitor, Evaluate and Assess Compliance With External Requirements	X		

More elements of the tactical integrator role include:
- Service framework definition;
- Performance management and control;
- End-to-end process ownership.

Whereas the operation integrator roles could be:
- Crisis management;
- Multi-service provider problem management;
- Multi-service provider service improvement;
- Consolidated service level measurement and reporting;
- End-to-end process management.

With regards to COBIT, Table 2.1: COBIT processes and Integrator roles below provides a high-level indication of the positioning of each process, see Table 2.2:
1. The strategic enterprise IT, covering CIO and strategic roles as well as the strategic SIAM function;
2. The tactical and operational Service Integration processes, which may be either retained or outsourced;
3. The Service Provider processes, where Service Providers can be both internal and external.

Note that for the service provider processes the operational Service Integrator will need to provide process orchestration (e.g. end-to-end incident management ownership).

2.4   Service Sourcing archetypes

When speaking of Service sourcing, four different archetypes can be identified that have evolved over time. In reality, especially for larger organizations, there will be a mix of different archetypes due to legacy, specific requirements and organizational maturity.

This section will introduce the SIAM perspective to the different archetypes.

2.4.1   Sourcing Archetype A - Internal

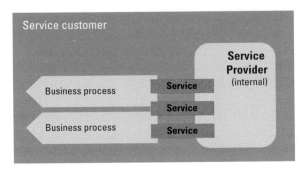

Figure 2.7   Service Sourcing Archetype - Internal

Each part of IT is run and delivered within the service customer organization, usually as a shared service unit. A single internal provider that delivers every IT service to a single customer might seem like a simple, non-complex, situation where implementation of SIAM is unnecessary since:

- The Service Provider has good specific business knowledge and usually good knowledge of IT components legacy, dependencies and the development history;
- Every resource and component (assets) is owned by the service customer giving it full control over how to govern and manage them;
- There are no dependencies to the principles, technologies or calendars of other services and their providers;
- Every decision body is within the service customer line organization which facilitates the governing of IT services and their providing units;
- Controlling the IT service delivery can be managed by governing the line-organization's internal units that deliver them. Hence the need for service orientation might be neglected or reduced (which, of course, in fact is an undesirable consequence).

However, a shared service unit can be large and complex, consisting of multiple organizational units and functions, delivering everything from infrastructure operations to application development and maintenance. The benefits of implementing SIAM are often significant in this archetype, since there are a number of services or units that need to interact to deliver a desired outcome to one or more business processes.

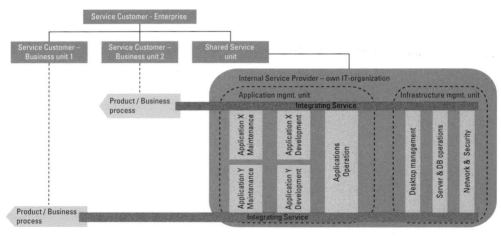

Figure 2.8   High-level example of integration of services within archetype A

Formal SIAM implementation is often neglected in archetype A since IT service delivery is a totally internal affair. But the complex situation often forces a shared service unit to establish SIAM structures and capabilities in an informal, or even unconscious, fashion. This situation can be called 'accidental SIAM'.

The prerequisites to implement a formal SIAM in this archetype are as follows:
- Establishment of SIAM can be done in an incremental fashion by replacing informal structures with formal SIAM enablers (processes, supporting tools, consolidated supporting functions etc.) giving priority to where it is mostly needed, or delivers the highest ROI;
- Every decision body is retained within the same organization. This supports efficient and effective SIAM over multiple, internal, delivery units;
- Exclusive possession and access to ITSM tooling suites, no integration of management tools with external parties necessary;
- Legacy and dependencies between IT-components are well known. Every dependency is manageable within the same organization.

Challenges of implementing SIAM in archetype A include:
- Investment in tools support, competences, organizational development etc. will not pay off unless economies of scale can be realized;
- SIAM relies upon the fact that it is IT services that are integrated, and not IT components or units/providers. Depending on the maturity of the shared service unit, the cultural and organizational change of moving to a true service-oriented IT-provisioning can be more cumbersome and profound to the organization than expected. This can be exacerbated in environments with prevalent 'shadow IT' that are dependent upon specific technical components or data sources within the centralized IT function.

2.4.2   Sourcing Archetype B - External

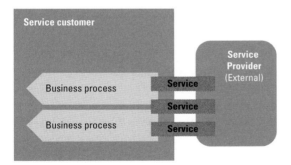

Figure 2.9   Service Sourcing Archetype - External

Here no IT services are provided by the service customer organization, either from within the business units or by a consolidated internal shared service unit or IT organization. In this archetype every IT service is delivered by one single external IT Service Provider. It shares the complex structures often found in archetype A; a large and complex organization, consisting of multiple organizational units and functions, delivering everything from infrastructure operations to application development and maintenance. On a smaller case, this archetype can also be considered to be in-place in the event of a completely separated business process, as a delivery model where there is very little dependency on other processes and IT-components

From a SIAM perspective this archetype adds the following challenges and complexity compared to archetype A:

- **The Service Provider lacks business knowledge on both non-functional and functional integration requirements**. The service customer cannot rely on formal, informal or tacit knowledge of the IT Service Provider to 'fill in the gaps' when integrating IT services. E.g.
  - Implicit understanding of business vital dates and deadlines when DB storage or server performance limits should not be exceeded. There are a number of different techniques to deal with this situation. One is to retain business-, enterprise- and system architect functions within the retained IT organization and make them part of the SIAM function. Another is to elaborate and focus on business outcomes of services, and not the technology used to deliver them (or in other words – mature in-service orientation);
  - The service customer does not have exclusive access and ownership of the resources and IT components (service assets) used to produce and deliver IT services. In an archetype B every asset used to deliver services is owned and managed by the external service providing party. Every attempt from the service customer to change the behavior, or in any other way influence this, must be done through the interfaces of managed services;
  - The service customer and its consuming business processes and users have external dependencies to the Service Provider concerning calendars, technologies, processes etc. This will force both parties to plan, integrate and map accordingly. If the provider delivers its service to only one customer or exclusively isolates every asset from taking part in IT services delivered to other customers, this won't be a problem. However, an external Service Provider often delivers services to more than one customer and wants to make effective and efficient use of its assets.
- **The Service Provider line organization and its decision bodies are separate from that of the service customer**. This might impose slower decision processes when changing, or in any other way influencing the behavior of a service or its assets compared to the archetype A situation. A service customer must change its behavior accordingly to deal with this situation.
- **In archetype B, governance can only operate on, or through, managed IT services**. In archetype A it is possible to govern the delivery of IT services 'indirectly' through the line organization units delivering them or the components used to deliver them. This is not possible in archetype B and might cause a change, or elaboration, to the service customer principles and standards of governance. It requires that the service customer has the capabilities to define and govern their IT-provisioning requirements by outcome and contribution to the business processes, or product, and not by 'organizational unit' as might be the case in archetype A.

The resemblance to archetype A is obvious; a number of services delivered by a single organization need to interact to achieve the desired, aggregated, outcome. A major difference and the first questions to answer in archetype B (as well as archetypes C and D that will be introduced shortly) are:

1. "Who should be accountable for delivering the integration service and the aggregated outcome?"
2. "What common functions should be retained within the service customer organization?"

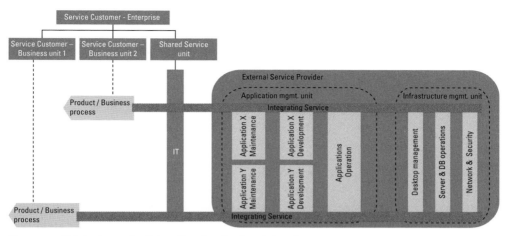

Figure 2.10   High-level example of integration of services in archetype B

The answers to these questions lead to two possible sourcing models within this archetype:
• Model 1: Retained Service Integration (customer is the Service Integrator);
• Model 2: Outsourced Service Integration (single service provider is the Service Integrator).

Model 1: Retained Service Integrator in archetype B

This model refers to the situation where the retained customer organization performs the Service Integration activities themselves. One may rely on individual subcontractors to augment skills and capabilities, but the accountability for Service Integration remains with the customer.

In this model there is a large risk of duplication of responsibilities and roles. The retained organization could very well struggle to provide added value to the business on top of the single Service Provider.

Model 2: Outsourced Service Integrator in archetype B

The primary Service Provider model is a traditional outsourcing model, where the customer has an outsourcing relationship with a single Service Provider. This Service Provider is in control of the end-to-end scope of the contracted services. Any service provided by a third party is contracted by the primary Service Provider – as a subcontractor.

The primary Service Provider manages its subcontractors directly. Any requirements from the customer related to the scope of the subcontractor are contracted using 'back-to-back' agreements, meaning the requirements are mirrored from one contract to the next. De facto the primary Service Provider is the Service Integrator.

The big advantage of this model is the clarity of responsibilities. There is one party responsible and that is it. Whenever the major Service Provider uses other Service Providers for part of the services, they will be directly managed; requirements will be propagated to the subcontracting Service Provider, which will be controlled completely by the major Service Provider.

The main disadvantage of this model is the dependency on a single Service Provider. There is no guarantee that the major Service Provider will be able to excel in every single service provided. The risk of Service Provider lock-in is medium to high in this model, as the major Service Provider will have a monopoly on the knowledge of the customer organization's IT services.

How this is implemented is dependent to the specific situation and requirements – integration of application services for 'off-the-shelf' products and highly standardized infrastructure services such as cloud services will lean towards an outsourced accountability. Integrating services that support vital business functions and IT services of high strategic value to the service customer will almost certainly lean towards retained accountability.

From a SIAM perspective archetypes A and B share many of the prerequisites and challenges of an implementation. The core prerequisite "A single provider delivers every service and owns every asset used" is shared between the two. The major difference is that there are two different legal parties involved and that the Service Provider might deliver IT services to more than one service customer.

Critical success factors to meet the above challenges and succeed with SIAM in archetype B (and the archetypes still to be discussed) can be summarized as:
• Be true to the concept of service orientation – IT services should be procured, delivered and governed by service and not by the delivering organization/unit or the components used to produce the service;
• IT services should be defined, designed and delivered to support a business outcome.

Both of the above statements are true for any IT service delivery situation but are particularly critical with SIAM, where a number of different services, involving two or more legal parties, must interact to deliver an aggregated outcome to the service customer and its consumers.

2.4.3   Sourcing Archetype C - Multiple
In this archetype, services are provided by multiple providers, to achieve a 'best of breed' delivery. Service Providers can be both external and internal to the service customer organization. This archetype introduces the Service Integrator to facilitate aggregation of multiple services from multiple providers. It is of course possible, and maybe even preferable, to implement a formal Service Integrator in any of the previous archetypes as well.

But if SIAM was optional or beneficial in the previous archetypes, it is mandatory, or crucial, moving to archetype C. If SIAM is not focused formally, the service customer and providers will be forced into a situation referred to as 'accidental multi-sourcing' or 'informal SIAM'. The result is characterized by bilateral and isolated agreements between the Service Providers and the service customer. But since services still require integration to deliver

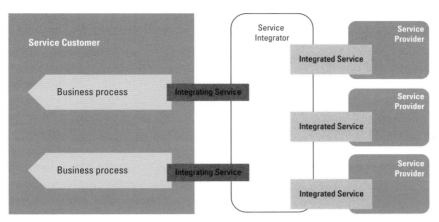

Figure 2.11   Service Sourcing Archetype - Multiple

the desired aggregated outcome, someone is 'accidentally' forced to take on the role of the Service Integrator. In almost every case this responsibility will fall upon the service customer and usually then by its shared service unit/IT-organization.

The role of the Service Integrator in archetype C can be sourced in a number of different fashions. The most relevant sourcing models will be described here; in practice, combinations of these sourcing models can exist as well:
- Model 1. Retained Service Integration (customer is the Service Integrator);
- Model 2. Independent Service Integrator;
- Model 3. Service Guardian;
- Model 4. Operational Service Integrator.

Model 1: Retained Service Integrator

This model (as shown in Figure 2.12) refers to the situation where the retained customer organization performs the Service Integration activities themselves. This is similar to the retained sourcing model as described under archetype B (single Service Provider), but now managing multiple Service Providers.

A large number of customers find themselves in this model by accident as, over time, a number of Service Providers are contracted to deliver different services and the retained organization becomes the Service Integrator by default. This is still quite common for many organizations. The IT procurement department manages the contracts on an individual basis and no formal integration role has been established. In less complex organizations, this situation may be sustainable, but for larger organizations this has typically resulted in reduced service quality and increased cost.

Model 2: Independent Service Integrator

The second, more-mature version of Model 1 is where an organization has consciously designed and implemented a Service Provider eco-system and designed a SIAM function to manage it. Here, the knowledge and skills of the organization have matured and, as a

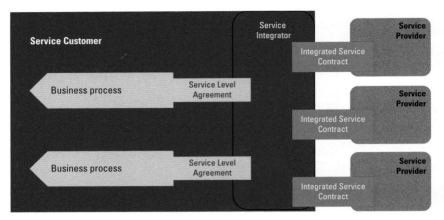

Figure 2.12   Retained service integrator sourcing model

result, it has been decided to consciously insource the Integrator role and activities in order to become independent of the IT Service Providers.

Being independent of third parties can be an advantage if the IT function is able to handle the responsibility themselves. Retaining the SIAM function is a significant responsibility and, as such, retained resources will typically be more senior and require a broader range of skills. Keeping skills current and up-to-date can also be a challenge and will usually need to be supported by a skills development roadmap. The lack of knowledge infusion from outside can therefore be a disadvantage of this model, something which can be mitigated by soliciting third party advice.

Model 3: Service Guardian

The Service Guardian model (see Figure 2.13) consists of one single major Service Provider who, in addition to its responsibilities as a Service Provider of one or more specific service bundles, takes the responsibility for end-to-end IT services as well. It is the sole responsibility of the Guardian to manage the other Service Providers on behalf of the customer organization and to provide guidance on the resolution of multi-service provider incidents and problems. It does make sense that such a Guardian Service Provider manages the service desk as well, but this is not mandatory; as long as end-to-end incident management is owned by the Guardian role, the service desk can be managed by a different Service Provider.

In order to execute its role, it is important for the Guardian to establish Operational Level Agreements (OLAs) with the other major Service Providers. These OLAs should document that both organizations will work together to provide services to the customer organization. Please note that this (our) definition of OLA is broader than the ITIL definition, which limits OLAs as agreed documents between departments of the same organization.

The disadvantage of this model is that the Guardian Role Service Provider is not independent; often when an issue needs to be resolved, the Guardian Role Service Provider is one of the parties. This requires disciplined operation and internal separation of duty that is respected

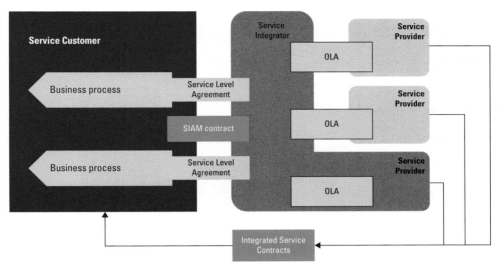

Figure 2.13   Service Guardian sourcing model

by all stakeholders in the enterprise. The big advantage is this model, however, is that the Service Integrator is committed to the service delivery themselves. Communication lines will be short and service level penalties can be at stake. This will motivate the Guardian Role agents more than when they manage a contract on behalf of the customer as an Operational Service Integrator.

Model 4: Operational Service Integrator

The Operational Service Integrator model (see Figure 2.14) is similar to the Guardian Role model, with the exception that the Service Provider undertaking the Integrator role does not actually provide any service delivery themselves. They are completely independent of the other Service Providers. This ensures a simpler implementation of the separation of duty. The fact that it is a different enterprise, both independent and neutral, also brings natural authority in resolving conflicts between Service Providers; for a Guardian Role Service Provider this authority must be based on trust and internal separations of duty.

This model has the advantage of external knowledge infusion and separation of duties. A large disadvantage of this model, however, is the lack of direct commitment for the Service Integrator to the service delivery. To explain the difference, consider a ham and eggs breakfast: the chicken was involved, but the pig was committed! Similarly, an independent Service Integrator will be involved in a major incident, but the data center provider will be committed. It needs SIAM service levels, with penalties to implement real commitment for an independent Service Integrator.

A different kind of disadvantage is that the appetite of Service Providers for an Integrator role can be less if the scope is limited to that role. Parties may tend to focus their sales force on a service bundle, where much larger revenues are at stake.

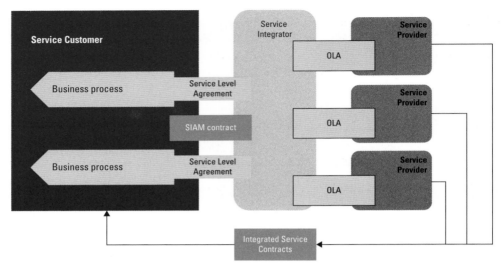

Figure 2.14   Independent service integrator sourcing model

From a SIAM perspective archetype C adds challenges and complexity compared to archetypes A and B:

- Multiple truths on how to manage IT service provisioning and what resources, capabilities, components etc. are to be used in IT service management. SIAM is then not only a question of how to integrate the outcome of multiple services, it is also a question of how to integrate the management of service provisioning. This will force the customer and the providers even further to define and deliver services by supporting their business outcomes and not by the product or function used;
- **The accountability for the aggregated outcome of multiple, integrated, services must be assigned to a single provider** to avoid accidental multi-sourcing and integration. This can be assigned to any participating party, including the service customer, depending on the situation;
- Integrated services will propagate activities and behaviors between them, e.g. a change of one service will cause a change to another service. This phenomenon is present within both of the previous archetypes as well, but in this archetype it will propagate between different legal parties and therefore must be formally agreed and managed;
- **Multiple providers will have multiple ways of establishing and executing ITSM processes**. Mapping and aligning process behaviors between the different Service Providers, and the service customer, must be done. Rules and principles for how operational process orchestration is managed must be agreed between participating providers and the service customer;
- Different providers will use different terms, definition and concepts for IT service management and delivery. Mapping and aligning these must be conducted and agreed upon;
- **Different providers will use different tools to support IT service management and delivery.** How, and if, the mapping and integration of these tools will be established must be conducted, agreed upon and implemented.

- **Different providers will have different calendars** e.g. for maintenance windows and releases. Calendars should, if possible, be aligned. If this is not possible, at least continuous communication of different calendars must be performed.

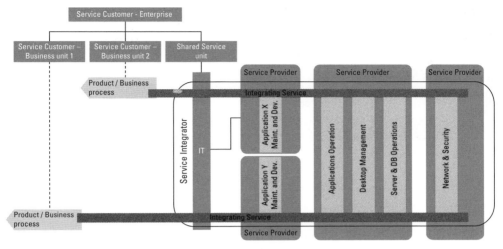

Figure 2.15   High-level example of integration of services in archetype C

Practitioner tips:
To meet the above challenges and succeed with SIAM in archetype C:
- SIAM is about integrating services, not providers or components. Be true to the concept of service orientation – IT services should be procured, delivered and governed by service and not by the delivering organization/unit or the components used to produce the service;
- IT services should be defined, designed and delivered to support a business outcome;
- Formally appoint and implement a Service Integrator. Every participating provider and the service customer should acknowledge the Service Integrator responsibilities, scope and behaviors.

2.4.4   Sourcing Archetype D - Matrix

The following statement can be used as a guiding pattern of archetype D - "Service Integration is about enabling Service Providers to be both successful and accountable for the delivery of their services in supporting the needs of the business".

Service Integration archetype D evolves further from archetype C from the perspective that Service Providers will consolidate and standardize the services delivered to multiple customers, or rather make reuse of the assets used to produce, deliver and manage services. They will replace isolated, customized services and duplicated assets. This will increase a provider's effectiveness and efficiency. The additional complexity here, as exemplified in the case of public cloud services, is that there is a need to understand the balance of the benefits

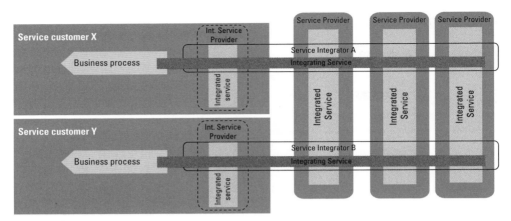

Figure 2.16 Service Sourcing Archetype - Matrix

between commoditizing the Service Provider's services and their ability to be integrated within each customer.

For archetype D the same sourcing model can be applied as discussed under archetype C:
• Retained Service Integrator (Figure 2.12)
• Service Guardian (Figure 2.13)
• Independent/Operational Service Integrator (Figure 2.14)

An important addition is that archetype D not only focuses the Service Integrator's abilities to integrate services, it also focuses the Service Provider's capabilities to enable their services to be integrated. There is a many-to-many relationship between service customers and Service Integrators.

From a SIAM perspective archetype D adds challenges and complexity compared to archetypes A, B and C:
• **Integrator needs to apply different SIAM behavior to meet the behaviors of different providers.** Every Service Provider will have its own implementation and flavor of SIAM and capabilities to integrate their services. A Service Integrator must have the capabilities and maturity to apply different SIAM strategies to meet these different implementations and behaviors;
• **Provider needs to apply different SIAM behaviors to meet the behaviors and requirements of different Service Integrators.** Vice versa every Service Integrator will have its own implementation and flavor of SIAM and capabilities to integrate the services from different Service Providers. A Service Provider must have the capabilities and maturity to apply different SIAM strategies to meet different Service Integrator behaviors.

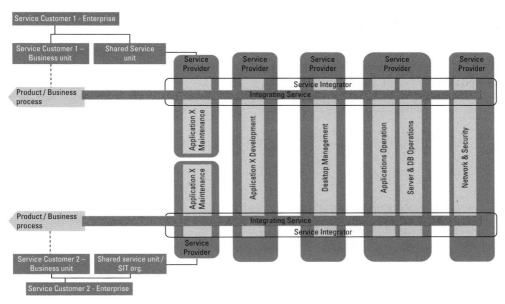

Figure 2.17   High-level example of integration of services in archetype D

Practitioner tips:

- The above challenges are easy to express but will in most cases, as far as Service Integrators or providers are concerned, require a great deal of investment in service management assets (tools, processes, capabilities, organizational structures etc.) and time to change behaviors and organizational cultures;
- Make sure to design and establish formal techniques and structures for collaboration and coordination between every participating party;
- Every participating service KPIs and metrics must be traceable back to one or more of the service customer's business goals and objectives.

2.5   SIAM guiding principles

Implementing SIAM is undertaken according to the specific situation, desired outcome, organizational maturity and types of relationship between customer and providers. Accordingly, the resulting SIAM implementations will be different and unique. However there are some guidelines and principles that are universal to any situation.

These are not hard and fast rules but it is recommended that you understand these guidelines and principles and assess how they should be implemented in a specific situation and environment, or manage the risks of not following them.

2.5.1 Integrate the intersections

SIAM takes place at the intersection between the Service Integration service (horizontal), the integrated services (vertical), and the organizations delivering them.

A key concern when implementing SIAM is to manage those intersections of services (see Section 1.7 Managing the intersections).

The horizontal perspective, or integration across providers, is about managing every participating service and its provider in order to meet the specific outcome required from that particular service. See Figure 2.18.

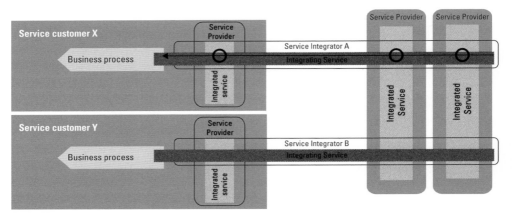

Figure 2.18   The horizontal perspective of managing intersections

A Service Provider might provide its services in multiple integration environments and hence will be under the governance of multiple integration services and their Service Integrators. This is the vertical service perspective. The vertical service perspective is sometimes called the asset perspective, the same assets (resources and components) are used to deliver multiple services, while the service delivered to each customer is unique. See Figure 2.19.

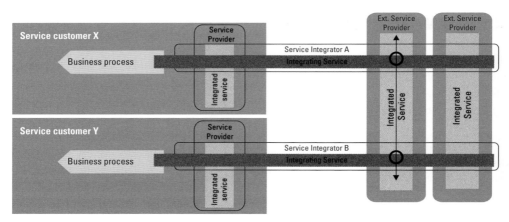

Figure 2.19   The vertical perspective of managing intersections

These two perspectives form the integration intersections between the Service Integrator
and the integrated services and have to be managed according to SIAM. See Figure 2.20.

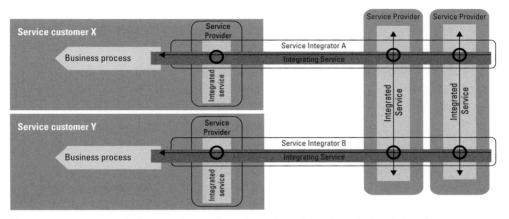

Figure 2.20   SIAM manages both perspectives of intersections between integrating and integrated services

2.5.2   Service Providers are not enterprises

The ITIL definition of a Service Provider is: "An organization supplying Services to one or
more Internal Customers or External Customers."

From a SIAM perspective the TOGAF (Open Group, 2015) distinction between an
Enterprise (a legal body) and *Organization* is also relevant. An enterprise might consist of
multiple organizations. An organization might be a unit, department or team, each one
acting as its own decision body when it comes to service provisioning.

To support SIAM a Service Provider is the organization that holds the power of decision-
making to manage and provide a specific service, it is not the legal body. This definition
allows SIAM principles to be implemented within a single enterprise with multiple service
delivering units. This is important because different Service Providers have different
requirements on how to manage and deliver their services despite the fact that they are parts
of the same enterprise. The examples from archetype A and B above illustrate this situation
– the management principles for managing applications services can differ significantly from
those used to manage infrastructure services.

The enterprise and the provider might coincide and when it comes to concluding legal
agreements and contracts, the parties will of course be the legal bodies.

This definition of a Service Provider provides better conditions for implementing efficient
and effective SIAM in every dimension (strategic, tactical and operational) than a definition
where the Service Provider is the same as an enterprise.

> **Practitioner tip:**
> Where possible, make use of existing organizational units and structures within an enterprise when defining Service Providers within a retained organization.

2.5.3   Every Service Provider encapsulates its services

Every Service Provider is a unique decision-making body with the powers of managing and delivering its services, using the resources and capabilities it sees fit. This is in fact a contradiction to the idea of integration, where different parties should behave uniformly to achieve a common goal. But since different types of services require different management resources and capabilities, providers will exhibit different behaviors. This will, in turn, require the Service Integrator to align multiple behaviors to be able to deliver aggregated services to the customer in a uniform fashion. Accidental multi-sourcing is often the situation arising from 'accidental multi-sourcing' discussed in archetype C above. Accidental multi-sourcing is a manageable situation if the Service Providers are few and mature and the services are stable and/or standard. If however, the providers and services are many and varied a more structured approach is necessary.

Furthermore, a provider might also deliver its services to multiple customers, facilitated by different Service Integrators. This will call for the Service Provider to adopt to multiple behaviors as well, to satisfy the requirements from multiple Service Integrators and their customers.

> **Practitioner tip:**
> Using a principle of service management encapsulation for IT services offers a flexible alternative to forcing every provider to establish multiple ITSM behaviors, or to use global ITSM and SIAM standards.

Service management encapsulation is a technique where a part (in this case a Service Provider or a Service Integrator) 'hides' its service management behaviors from other parties. The only way for another party to interact with, change or influence the behaviors of a service is through formal, open, interfaces. This gives a provider or Service Integrator the power to retain its unique service management behaviors, independent of the number and type of external parties it is integrating with. The formal and open interfaces will be negotiated and designed to meet every unique point of integration, or intersection, between an integrating service and an integrated service.

Interfaces are designed and established by the SIAM enablers, discussed in chapter 1, and will cover areas such as process integration, classification standards, role responsibilities, KPIs and metrics. Two examples of encapsulation and interfaces are:
- The provider (or Service Integrator) change manager role description has two perspectives, or parts:
  - A single internal clause, that describes the responsibilities, scope and content of the change manager when managing the provider's services; and

- A set of external addendums, one for each integrating service (or integrated service if it is the integrator change manager), that describes the change manager role specific to each intersection.
- A provider (or Service Integrator) uses the same ITSM tool suite in the management of all services delivered. Different Service Integrators will demand different reports, or may use different reporting engines:
  - The encapsulation capability of the provider is then to create and manage different sets of reports, or data exports, for different Service Integrators;
  - The Service Integrator encapsulation capability is the opposite of this: ie to receive data with different formats and/or content and compile them in a single, homogenous report for the customer (perhaps through the use of its own ITSM tool suite).

There are two types of encapsulation and a Service Integrator might use both types in the same integrating service:
- Open encapsulation ('white box') is the most common to functional services (e.g. application management) - when the service customer is aware of the participating services and its providers. The customer typically dictates to the Service Integrator what services and providers to use. In open encapsulation customers have the opportunity to demand certain ITSM behaviors as part of the delivery (e.g. classification standards, metrics and reporting).
- Closed encapsulation ('black box') is commonly used within non-functional service delivery (e.g. storage and network services) – when the customer isn't aware of which services and providers are used. Closed encapsulation is also applicable to cloud services and XaaS (Everything-as-a-Service). In closed encapsulation customers do not have the opportunity to demand certain ITSM behaviors in the delivery, they may even not be aware of the fact that a service delivered is in fact an aggregated service consisting of multiple integrated services.

The Service framework of overall capabilities, resources, structures and interdependencies, used to manage the production and delivery of its services, is often referred to as its Service Management Architecture (SMA). It covers functions, processes, products, process, people, organization etc.

To meet the requirements of service management encapsulation a Service Provider or Service Integrator's SMA must be enhanced or elaborated to cover the following two dimensions:
- The internal, or hidden, dimension – focuses on the core behavior that is used to manage any delivered service in any relationship;
- The external, or open, dimension – manages the interfaces between every participating service and its Service Provider. It is in this dimension Service integration enablers are established.

Optimizing the balance between these two dimensions remains one of the most significant challenges for any large Integrator or Service Provider with multiple customers. A thin external dimension will hide much of a providers internal behaviours, giving the provider good opportunities to standardize its ITSM behaviours in a cost efficient way. This will on the other hand leave the provider with poor capabilities of acting flexible and agile when dealing with multiple integrating services and customers. It is vice versa if applying a too vast and comprehensive external dimension.

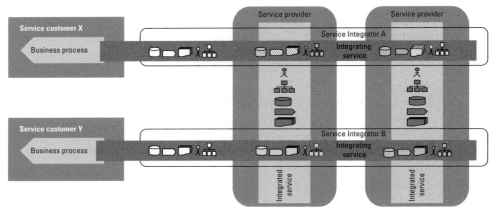

Figure 2.21   Encapsulation of service management architectures

Integrators and providers should both have capabilities to establish multiform, external interfaces to their uniform, internal SMA.

The Service Integrator must manage multiple interfaces from multiple Service Providers and the Service Provider must meet the integration interfaces of multiple Service Integrators, and their end customers and consumers.

> **Practitioner tip:**
> Define your core ITSM behaviors and how open interfaces to them can be designed and managed.

2.5.4   The integration of services is a service

There are many reasons for a service customer to establish formal Service Integration, including;

- Reduced complexity in IT service provision;
- Reduced number of Service Providers to govern;
- Mitigation and transfer of risk, or being able to better utilize best of breed services.
- The essence of Service Integration is to provide a service customer with the same experience as if a single party delivers a single service that fulfills the outcome.

In the case of an 'accountable' integration, the Integrator will appear as a Single Point of Service (SPOS) to the customer and the integrating service will be perceived as one, single service delivering the outcome. Every other, integrated, service will be invisible to the service customer.

If it is a 'enabling' integration, every participating service provider and its services are visible to the customer. Here it is even more obvious that Service Integration is a service of its own because the customer actively seeks to procure a service to manage the delivery of multiple services, having them delivered as an aggregated or composite service.

From a service customer and consumer perspective it follows that:
- A Service Integration service will be procured, governed and managed by the same ITSM standards as any other IT service;
- A Service Integrator is perceived as any other service provider.

Practitioner tip:
There should not be a difference to the customer and consumer whether the delivered service is an integration service or not, the way that it is governed treated should be the same.

2.5.5   Services are assets

Service assets are defined as "the resources and capabilities that a Service Provider uses to deliver and manage services". To a Service Integrator the main asset type used to produce and deliver aggregated services are other services.

A Service Integrator should be able to govern, manage and utilize an integrated service by the same ITSM standards as any other service asset. This statement is also a requirement on service encapsulation above.

Practitioner tip:
There should not be a difference between managing a participating service from managing any other service asset.

2.5.6   Propagation of responsibilities

The Service Integrator has responsibility for delivering the agreed, aggregated, outcome to support a business and its processes. This responsibility must be propagated outwards from the Service Integrator to every participating provider. Furthermore, this propagation should be limited to the specific responsibilities that each participating Service Provider is accountable for. The integrator must have the capability to identify, specify, contract, monitor and report every consistent part of an aggregated outcome. It must also have the capability to identify which integrated service contributes to which goals and its related metrics.

This will establish a foundation from which the propagation and management of responsibilities can be made, without losing connection to the originating, consuming, business goals. Propagation of responsibilities should be clearly specified in contracts and agreements. See Figure 2.22.

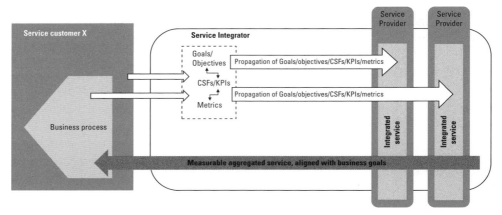

Figure 2.22   Propagation of business goals and requirements to service outcomes

Practitioner tips:
- Make sure that the business goals and desired outcomes are identified and agreed upon.
- Use a goal breakdown structure to support the propagation of responsibilities.

2.5.7   ITSM operates on services (and not on the provider or its assets)

Processes operate on services, roles are established by service, ITSM tools and consolidated functions support services etc. This is the standard ITSM message and correctly so, much is to be gained by acknowledge this approach. Nevertheless ITSM is not always implemented in this way due to different circumstances.

If the provider is internal, or a single outsourcing partner (see archetypes A and B above), ITSM sometimes tends to be implemented by the provider. E.g. a provider might establish a single CAB instance and a single change manager to cover all of the delivered services.

Whilst this may be a reasonable approach in single provider environments, when in SIAM environment a Service Provider must make an effort to establish involve services in the ITSM by the service. In an integrated environment there will be multiple providers involved and hence multiple decision-making bodies. In order to have SIAM and aggregated, end-to-end, services that are able to respond in an agile, efficient, effective and measurable way, the ITSM capabilities of all the participating parties should be established by services. This will also add flexibility to the integration landscape by giving providers and Service Integrators the opportunity to apply different behaviors to different services, delivered to different service customers. Of course the most important thing is that the customer doesn't need to adapt to different behaviors dependent on different providers.

There should be sound arguments for NOT doing it

Practitioner tip:
Stay true to the concept of service when establishing SIAM.

2.5.8 Agreements are defined and established by service and not provider

The same approach holds for agreements as for processes and roles - take care to establish them by the service and not by the provider or component. Apart from offering a more agile and efficient integration environment, it is also an important prerequisite for the propagation of responsibilities amongst services (see 'Propagation of responsibilities'). Of course commercially and legally binding contracts are signed between the legal bodies of the providers. SLAs and other service-specific agreements might be attached as annex agreements.

Practitioner tip:
Stay true to the concept of service when establishing agreements.

2.6 Process integration

How to integrate processes is a core area and capability within SIAM.

Remember the guiding principles from above:
- Every Service Provider (should) encapsulates its services;
- ITSM is established, and operates, on and within a service (and not its provider);
- The integration of services is a service.

Then processes are /should be the only interaction interfaces between services. Service integration can only achieve the desired customer outcome by integrating the processes of the participating services.

But since the establishment and execution of ITSM-processes will be unique to every provider, and also encapsulated within the services, processes must have interfacing capabilities to deal with different process behavior between different services and providers.

When a number of different providers and their services are integrated to achieve a desired customer outcome, managing those services must be done in a controlled and coordinated fashion. This is often referred to as 'process integration' or 'process orchestration'.

Process integration is:
- The management of coordinated and concurrent execution of multiple instances of processes;
- That are operating multiple services;
- Delivered by multiple providers;
- Achieving a uniform, specific, expected and measurable outcome;
- With the Service Integrator as the conductor.

When it comes to SIAM a [*item*] (incident, change etc.) to the customer will, in most cases, require that multiple providers contribute by operating their services to achieve the solution to the [item]. The Service Integrator then has the responsibility to trigger processes at every participating Service Provider necessary. The triggering of processes will create [items] within those Service Providers services, but the only way to control a specific [*item*] is through the process that created it. Within the object oriented paradigm of system development this is often referred to as 'Instantiation'.

Instantiation not only creates an instance of an [*item*] – it also establishes the references between the triggering process (the parent) and the instance process (the child). The parent needs to retain knowledge of those childs in which providers are participating to solve the [*item*]. From the other perspective the Service Provider child instance must have knowledge of which parent instance it is contributing to. See Figure 2.23.

An example:
1. The Service Integrator receives a change request from the service customer. Initially this will trigger and instantiate the Service Integrator's own change process to start execution of the specific change.
2. Upon assessment of the change request the Service Integrator realizes that two of the integrated services on which the aggregated outcome is dependent must be changed, in order to meet the request.
3. The Service Integrator then triggers the change processes within each of the two integrated Service Providers to create a change of their respective service accordingly and creates a unique reference for each process.
4. Hereby the Service Integrator's change process has created two child instances from its parent instance, retaining knowledge on which instances participates in the solution to the originating request. The child instances will have knowledge on which originating request they are contributing to.

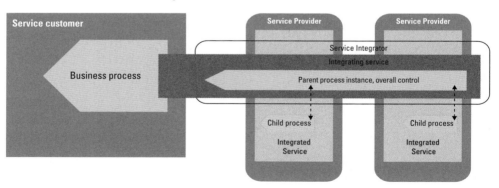

Figure 2.23   Parent-child process instances

When setting up process integration interfaces between two or more services and its providers the following, but not limited to, list of perspectives can be used as a guideline to map every specific process:

- **Events and triggers between the processes** – how to start a child process/interaction trigger between processes during execution/how to finish a child process or 'definition of done'?
- **What inputs** and **outputs** are expected from each participating instance of process?
- [*item*] **reference and identification** – how instances of processes will be referenced. How to identify which children a parent process has, or what parent a child process belongs to?
- **Naming and sequence of states** – which process-states are used by each participating provider and how do they map to the integrating service process?
- **Priority levels/matrix** – which process-priorities are used by each participating provider and how do they map to the integrating service process?
- **Risk levels/matrix** – which risk levels are used by each participating provider, how do they affect process execution and how do they map to the integrating service process?
- **Roles and responsibilitie**s – naming and responsibilities of roles within each provider and how do they map to the integrating service process?
- **Decision mechanisms and mandates** – which decision-points are used by each provider, which decision mechanisms are needed and how do they map between each other?
- **Mechanisms for escalation** – due to which prerequisites will process decisions or execution escalate vertically. How should this be dealt with in an integration environment and how do they map to the Service Integrator?
- **Channels of communication and forums** – what standards for process communication between Service Integrator and provider processes are there? How should this be dealt with in an integration environment and how do they map between every participating party?
- **Requirements and standards of documentation** – what standards are there for the documentation of [items] (e.g. changes and releases) between Service Integrator and provider processes? How should this be dealt with in an integration environment and how do they map between every participating party?
- **Metrics and measures** – how are processes measured? How are [items] measured? What objectives, KPIs, metrics etc. does the service customer have? How should these be propagated to every provider?
- **Reporting** – how are processes reported? How are [items] reported? What requirements does the service customer have? How should these be propagated to every provider?
- **Management tools** – what tools are used to support process execution and management, by which participating party? How can these be mapped or integrated?

Note concerning supporting tools: Processes are often supported by ITSM tools and it might be tempting to build Service Integration on the idea that every participating provider should use the same tool, or even the same instance of that tool. However, whilst this may seem a nice idea in theory, in reality participating providers will often not be able to migrate to the tool preferred by a specific Service Integrator. This is because a provider might deliver services to multiple customers and/or Service Integrators and won't have the capability to host multiple tool suites.

Instead parties are often dependent on system integrations and/or manual mapping between different tools. In the worst case, to be avoided if possible, 'swivel chair integration' is the only alternative (copy-paste between two different tools).

See Chapter 4 **Data and Tools** for a further discussion on tools integration in a SIAM environment.

Practitioner tips:
- Don't try to map every aspect of the above perspectives, aiming at a full translation of processes. Instead, focus what is relevant to build a well-functioning integration interface to meet the specific situation and desired outcomes.
- Start with the core or most critical process(es).

2.6.1   Direct and indirect management of integrated processes

To design and implement the process integration described above, interfaces are a prerequisite to succeed in this process integration. Fundamental to process integration is how the process execution is triggered, where instances of processes are created and how control over multiple instances of processes is continuously retained during execution by the Service Integrator.

In the example in Figure 2.24 the two child processes are totally unaware of each other and the parent process controls and coordinates the operation of the child processes. This is an example of indirect management of interdependencies between processes. Here the Service Integrator takes on an operative role of managing different instances of processes and retains a tight control over the execution of multiple instances of processes. This is the preferred management principle when the Service Integrator is accountable or when providers are not mature in participating in integrated deliveries.

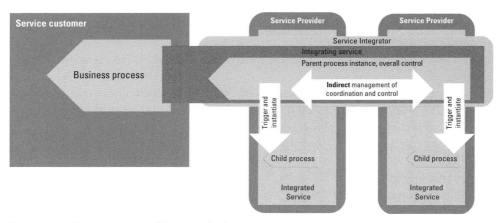

Figure 2.24   Indirect management of interdependencies between processes

If the Service Integrator is enabling and the Service Providers are mature in participating in integration environments there will be an opportunity to further develop effectiveness and efficiency by using direct management of interdependencies. In direct management each child instance, and its provider, has the capability to interconnect with another child instance. This will give the power to locally manage process orchestration within the child instances. This leaves the Service Integrator and the parent process instance to superintend and govern the different child instances. Giving the Service Provider, its services and processes the ability to manage directly will grant a more efficient execution of every participating process instance. See Figure 2.25.

Relations and behaviors are further discussed in Section 3.2 **Enabling a culture of collaboration**

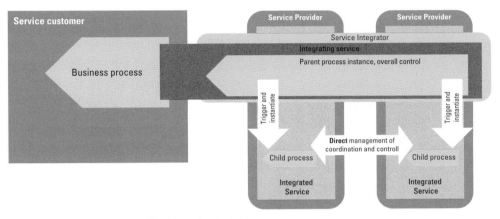

Figure 2.25   Direct management of interdependencies between processes

2.7   The Integrator and the Integrated

It takes two to tango and if someone is the Service Integrator, integrating services, there has to be one or more parties playing the part of the Integrated. To be fully successful, SIAM must cover both perspectives.

In an integrated environment the **Integrator** operates in the dimension of 'service packaging' or 'bundling services', integrating services provided by a number of external and /or internal providers. The Integrator has the responsibility to deliver an 'aggregated outcome' to support a service customer and service consumers. The focus of SIAM is then on the capabilities and capacities required **to Integrate** multiple providers and their services in order to meet a common objective.

The **Integrated** perspective is also important to achieve efficient and effective SIAM. At a first glance it might seem that delivering services through a Service Integrator is the same as delivering these directly to an end customer and its users (the Service Integrator 'acting' as the end customer). But there are a few differences with SIAM that need to be addressed. This will be covered in the following sections.

2.7.1   Contracts and agreements – backward propagation of requirements

In traditional service provisioning a Service Provider will sign underpinning contracts with supporting providers to deliver an aggregated service to its customer in a 'black box fashion'.

In SIAM however there is a possibility (widely used) to have an enabling Service Integrator (as opposed to an accountable Service Integrator) where commercial contracts are signed directly between the Integrated Service Provider and the end service customer, whilst the service delivery and its agreements (SLA and OLAs) will be implemented between the Integrator and the Integrated.

This will then force the integrated party to fulfill the requirements of the legal contract through the Integrator, a third party. The design and scope of the SLA and OLAs must then be elaborated to meet not only the requirements of the Integrator; but also the requirements of the end customer. This is known as 'backward propagation', when an integrated party sets the demands for the Integrator. See Figure 2.26.

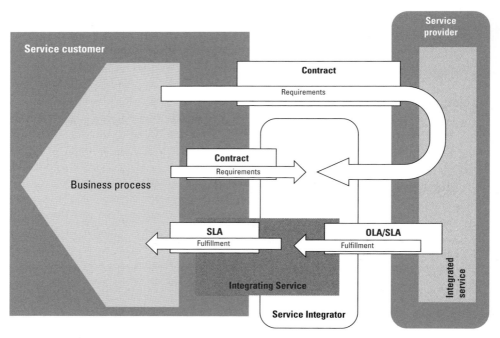

Figure 2.26   Backward propagation of requirements

'Forward propagation' is the more straightforward when a contract is signed with the Service Integrator, who in turns signs contracts with Integrated Service Providers. And fulfillment of contracts trails back the same way. See Figure 2.27.

Practitioner tip:
There is no need (or sometimes even no possibility) to avoid backward propagation, just make sure it is aligned!

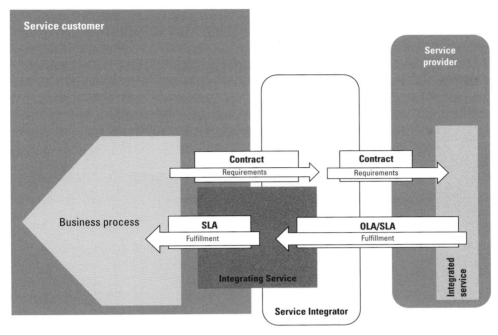

Figure 2.27   Forward propagation of requirements

2.7.2   Assets are communicating vessels

A Service Provider might take part, as Integrated, in more than one integrated environment.
Hence serving more than one Integrator. If a provider delivers its services to only one
customer, every asset used can be designed to meet the requirements of that single customer,
or its Integrator proxy.

But as soon as a provider has two or more Integrators, or customers, to deliver services
through/to, the provider must enhance its assets to cope with this situation. If a provider
strives towards effectiveness and efficiency in its service provisioning, it will try to consolidate
and make reuse of its assets, e.g. by creating a shared service center or a shared infrastructure.
This will then cause assets to function as potential 'communicating vessels' between services
and their integrators.

Using orchestration of a change as an example; if the analysis of a change request shows
that any of the assets used by an integrated service needs to be changed, and that same
asset is used by yet another aggregate service, the initial change request will cause a change
request to that other aggregate service. Then the assets become a communicating vessel
between aggregate services and customers. Figure 2.28 depicts a simple example but in
reality a change might propagate out to a very complex network of changes. To cope with
this situation an integrated party must be very well equipped when it comes to configuration
management and interdependencies between assets and services.

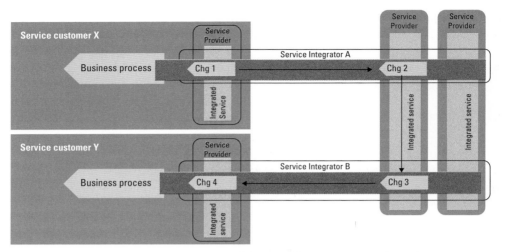

Figure 2.28   Shared assets creates communicating vessels between different integrating services and customers

At first sight this situation might seem to be normal to a commercial, third party, provider that delivers services to multiple customers. But the major difference in SIAM relates to the Integrator role because e.g. a request for change can be proposed and initiated not only directly from the customer but also from other parties, indirectly via the integrated providers. This is much like the situation with backward propagation of requirements discussed above. Service Providers probably deal with this situation to some extent even without participating in Service Integration, while delivering services to multiple customers. Requirements from one customer might impact the services delivered to other customers. The differences between Service Integration and integrated providers are that SIAM is formalizing the integration responsibilities and their specific contribution to the aggregated outcome. Hence moving the integrated from the characteristics of informal 'accidental multi-sourcing'.

Both the Integrated and the Integrator must establish capabilities and resources to support this SIAM requirement. How these capabilities are/should be designed is dependent on the situation:

Accountability – Service Integrators will have to manage the risks and impact of being affected by communicating vessels. Assessing and influencing the participating providers into acknowledging a provisioning, and use, of assets so that these risks can be managed, mitigated or/and avoided. The counterforce is of course the providers' requirements and objectives to be efficient and effective in the delivery of services to multiple customers and Service Integrators.

A Service Integrator that is accountable will need to be more formal, strict and distinct when establishing the relations between parties than an enabling Service Integrator. Accountable Service Providers should also be careful to gain, and retain, the powers of choosing and changing which providers and services to use. If the Service Integrator is enabling, it is the customer who owns the risks of being affected by [items] from other customers and this must be obvious and agreed between the customer and the Service Integrator.

Relationship types – depending on the type of service, Integrated Service Providers will need to adapt to different behaviors.

Transactional Service Providers should develop strong capabilities and resources to avoid, or minimize, the impact of communicating vessels (e.g. good in configuration management, fast throughput, parallel execution, good encapsulation and modularity of components etc.). This way a provider and its services can be taken out of the 'equation of communicating vessels', making it more attractive to be used as a partner in integrated environments. Adopting the same strategies also applies to Service Providers of value-adding, special or unique services, but they can be harder to achieve or at least more costly to the provider. This type of provider and service is harder to substitute and the Service Integrator is more often the enabling type to these. A Service Integrator should assess the provider's capabilities to communicate and coordinate with multiple customers/integrators, negotiating and agreeing on future plans and schedules. In doing so, the impact of communicating vessels can be identified and managed proactively.

2.7.3 SIAM is recursive

SIAM is recursive and can be applied to any number of levels. Let's consider a customer that implements a SIAM function for the end-to-end management of the customer IT environment. One of the suppliers will typically be a network service provider who in turn has multiple subcontractors. That supplier could (and this book postulates it should) establish a SIAM function to aggregate the subcontractor services.

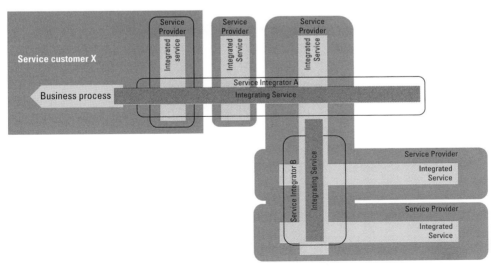

Figure 2.29   SIAM is recursive, to any number of levels

The SIAM function ensures that the aggregation of services at each level is not visible to its customer, irrespective of whether a Service Provider is a single organization or another Service Integrator.

SIAM treats a Service Provider (internal or external) as a 'black box' and therefore expects this aggregation to be achieved in the same way it delivers aggregation upwards.

In a recent example, a business has identified an opportunity to lift the SIAM concept up above IT to apply to all shared services as an aggregated whole. This has not yet been implemented but shows – at least in theory – how powerful this concept of recursion can be.

3 People and Processes for Service Integration

This chapter discusses the people and process related aspects of a SIAM function. Organization features and the way that the processes interact are quite different in a Service Integration framework. The Service Integrator has to stand back from the actual execution of the processes and focus on the outcomes of the processes and how they support the end goals of the business and /or its retained IT organization. The people and processes support the management and governance principles and rely on the tool and data support to perform the functions required.

The goal of the Service Integrator is to create an environment where the suppliers of the actual IT services are:
• Made aware of their responsibilities;
• Enabled to perform their responsibilities;
• Held to account for their performance.

Therefore it becomes clear that the organization of people around the Service Integration functionality, that will define the processes, is an important first step.

3.1 The people perspective

Given a 'new' SIAM function with its separation of duties from those of Service Providers, there is an immediate and obvious implication for organizational reporting and these implied constraints are valid regardless of whether the SIAM function is retained or outsourced. There needs to be a clear functional distinction between those in the SIAM function and those performing delivery roles. Chapter 6, Strategies for Governance and Management, will further discuss 'separation of duties'.

The reporting line of the SIAM organizational unit must be set up so that it will not impede the capability (or perceived capability) of the SIAM function to perform the role of arbitration of cross supplier disagreement. This applies to all the components of SIAM, whether outsourced or not. In short there cannot be a perceived conflict of interest between the SIAM function and any Service Provider. There will inevitably be occasions where there will be a dispute about the relative contribution to an incident or outage. In a multi-sourcing environment this is likely to impact SLA and KPI achievement, which in turn will impact service credit calculations. Organizations cannot be in a situation where the independence of the umpire (the Service Integrator) is questioned on the basis of conflict of interest. If this happens, the matter will escalate needlessly to an executive level debate.

Let's examine some of the possible combinations of sourcing:
- Retained Service Integrator with only outsourced delivery organizations;
- Retained Service Integrator with some insourced delivery organizations;
- Outsourced Service Integrator with some delivery also being performed by the same organization as the Service Integrator;
- Outsourced Service Integrator with a mixture of insourced and outsourced delivery organizations.

This is not an exhaustive list but even with this list it is apparent that the potential for claims of conflict of interest exists in most of the scenarios. It is easy to see why a SIAM function with outsourced components could be perceived to be a conflict of interest where they compete for business in the Service Provider space. What is sometimes a surprise is that a fully retained SIAM function can also be perceived as a conflict of interest when some Service Providers are also retained. Regardless of any current combination of sourcing, a robust implementation of SIAM must be able to cope with changes, so the recommendation is to model the SIAM implementation in a modular way such that the conflict of interest can be managed through any future changes.

It is relatively simple to manage this conflict of interest *provided* it is considered at the outset. It is usually harder to deal with after the battle scars start to develop because the trust is damaged at that stage and more work has to be done to rebuild trust than to avoid the loss in the first place. During the planning for the global large automotive manufacturer implementation (see Section 1.9.1), consideration was given to excluding any supplier for the Integrator role from other delivery contracts unless separation of duties and conflict of interest management plans could be demonstrated.

How do organizations manage the perception of conflict of interest? The best way is to establish the separation of duties at the organizational level.

For a fully retained SIAM capability, particularly where there is retained delivery, creating a reporting chain that is distinct from the delivery reporting chain is adequate. This implies that the Service Integration function reports to a strategic level of management. Clearly reporting at a CIO level would be sufficient but in a large organization this may not be possible. The 'correct' level will vary by organization but the hallmark of the reporting line is that it reports at a level that demonstrably is driven by the bigger picture and longer-term outcomes – above the tactical fray as it were.

For an outsourced service or mixed sourcing SIAM capability, there is likely to be a little less direct control of the supplier reporting lines. In most cases, the engagement or tender process would ask the supplier how they intend to implement a conflict of interest (CoI) management plan. An experienced SIAM supplier would be expecting this question. As with any tender process it is best to establish the requirement for a CoI up front rather than try to retrofit the plan. It is always easier to negotiate before contracts are signed.

What would be expected in a CoI management plan? Some of the features of a comprehensive plan would include:

- Separation of duties between any Service Integrator and delivery teams;
- Similar to the retained organization, a reporting chain for the Service Integrator that reports at a strategic level rather than to a manager of a delivery team – for example reports to the account director;
- Published policies and escalation procedures for Service Integrator staff;
- CoI training plans for the Service Integrator staff to ensure they are aware of their responsibility and the methods to escalate resolution of requests for inappropriate action.

It is important, regardless of sourcing, that the Service Integration function is seen as an agent of the customer - that means that there should be no behavior from the supplier personnel that differs from that of the customer. They must be seen as an independent mediator when it comes to the resolution of disputes.

Having established the need for an identifiably separate SIAM function and agreed the reporting line, it must now be considered what the staffing and structure of the SIAM function will be. Scoping considerations discussed in the following section will drive the definition of staffing levels within the SIAM function.

Practitioner tip:
Consider separation of duties and conflict of interest during design.

3.1.1 Competences required

The competences required for staff managing and operating a Service Integrator overlap with several other areas of competence, but the blend is typically different to the directly managed IT service management. Competence is used here to mean the combination of practical and theoretical knowledge, cognitive skills, behavior and attitude used to improve performance:

- **Knowledge** – awareness or understanding of someone or something, such as facts, information or descriptions which are acquired through experience or education
- **Skills** – ability to carry out a task with pre-determined results
- **Behaviors** – the range of actions and mannerisms made by systems, individuals and organizations in conjunction with their environment of other systems, individuals or organizations
- **Attitude** – evaluation (ranging from negative to positive) of systems, individuals and organizations

For teams that are used to directly managing delivery staff (regardless of sourcing) there is a change of mindset when it comes to the delivery of Service Integration. This is probably best characterized as a change from 'managing the people who deliver services' to 'managing the organizations delivering services'. It is the difference between managing the methods versus managing the outputs.

Where the SIAM function will be outsourced, this can be quite a cultural change. Given that the outsourcing industry is quite competitive, the role of the Service Integrator is to make sure that potential competitors are successful – giving rise to a 'coopetition' scenario. 'Coopetition' is a term that was coined by eliding the words 'competition' and 'cooperation'. It is the scenario where organizations both cooperate and compete for business simultaneously but in different transactions. For instance two suppliers may cooperate in the delivery of their respective current scope but are competing for other (new) business. There is a need for the Service Integrator to celebrate the success of the delivery parties – even if in other areas of the industry they compete. Some of these cultural issues will be addressed shortly.

Clearly organizations need their SIAM staff to be experienced practitioners of ITSM in general. An understanding of the practical implementation of frameworks like ITIL and COBIT is a baseline competence requirement. There have been examples of contracts scenarios where *all* staff working for any delivery team were required to be ITIL foundation certified as a base requirement.

However this will not be sufficient for the Service Integrator staff – and most certainly not for the leaders of the SIAM function. Other competences include (but are not limited to):
• Business relationship management;
• Communication skills;
• Commercial acumen;
• Negotiation and conflict resolution skills;
• Influencing skills;
• Ability to manage interpersonal relationships;
• Contract management.

These 'softer competences' are necessary because the success of the SIAM function will be dependent on their ability to engage with suppliers where, by definition, they have neither a direct contractual relationship nor direct management control. They exercise contractual relationships on behalf of (and as agent of) the customer. Given that these competences are required to build trust in a collaborative environment, the behaviors of one 'weak link' can be quite destructive.

Frameworks to assess competences include:
• 'The Skills Framework for the Information Age – SFIA' can be used. SFIA has some useful skills categorization but the primary focus is on technical skills;
• The European e-Competence Framework (e-CF – currently version 3) has more focus on soft competences, primarily in the 'Enable' and 'Manage' sections.

Many organizations – particularly large and public sector, have adopted one of these skills frameworks. They can be used to support the competence assessment for their organization but the competence mix will be dispersed across the framework and some of the softer skills are not obvious, although can be found in the detail.

Whilst developed primarily for project management, The International Project Management Association has developed the IPMA Competence Baseline (ICB - actual version has 10 'People' competences along with 14 'Practice' and 5 'Perspective' competences). Whilst the last two categories are heavily focused on project management, the people competences listed are very useful for SIAM people. It is recommended that these are reviewed even by organizations using the SFIA or e-CF frameworks to assess if they can be used to augment them.

> **Practitioner tip:**
> Plan for supporting staff development – particularly soft skills.

3.2   Enabling a culture of collaboration

As part of the transition towards a multi-supplier ecosystem with a SIAM function, a specific focus on organizational and cultural change is needed, as implementing Service Integration can represent a significant shift for the employees of the retained IT organization. To refer to the "Five Dysfunctions of a Team" (Lencioni, 2002), trust is a key platform for building functional teams.

To promote a cooperative spirit across Service Providers the following elements have proven to be useful:
1. Relationship charter. The relationship charter is intended to illustrate some of the behaviors the retained IT organization expects its Service Providers to exemplify in order to meet its expectations – collaborative behaviors being one of them.
2. Trust and colocation / regular in-person or video joint workshops, communication program to develop mutual understanding and shared knowledge.
3. Joint governance. Formal multi-supplier governance, where representatives of the major Service Providers meet, chaired by the Service Integrator (whether the role is established within the retained IT organization or with an external party) to discuss common interests and concerns.
4. Shared KPIs. Better collaboration between suppliers can be achieved by implementing cross-supplier aspirational KPIs aligned to the objectives of the retained IT organization.

3.2.1   Relationships charter
Whilst the service credits defined in Service Provider contracts are an essential tool in procurement or supplier management they are not enough to secure productive outcomes in a multi-supplier environment. Indeed contracts can drive down collaboration amongst Service Providers.

The joint development of a relationship charter is a way to strengthen relationships at the start of a contract period. Figure 3.1 shows an example that can be used as a template. The relationship charter is a tool to underpin productive and collaborative behaviors to which parties agree. The customer expects its Service Integrator to exemplify these behaviors in order to meet its expectations. With an Enabling Service Integrator, the customer will address its expectations to the participating providers as well. They will typically fall into a number of categories such as customer focus, mutual trust and transparency, end-to-end engagement and cost effectiveness.

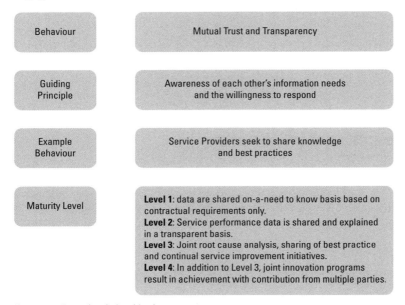

Figure 3.1   Example relationship charter

Within each category there are typically three dimensions of behavior definition:
• Guiding principles – high-level statements of expectations of the Service Integrator and Service Providers;
• Exemplifying behaviors – the behavior and attitude expected from the Service Integrator (and all Service Providers') team members, as individuals or as teams, to exhibit as they perform their roles;
• Maturity level – this should show both current state and next target state maturity levels, to enable the setting of medium term goals. For each exemplifying behavior this template uses four levels (L1 – L4) which describe, on an incremental scale, how that behavior and capabilities contribute to performance and a more valued relationship. L4 represents a mature partnership which delivers consistent added value.

More important than the exact wording in such a relationship charter is the process of jointly defining one. Having a joint workshop on this subject will enable a better understanding of the various counterparts amongst the Service Providers. Do not forget to invite internal Service Providers into these sessions as this is about the role of providing services and not about client versus supplier.

The maturity matrix can be used to measure the relationship between the organization and their major Service Providers on a regular basis.

3.2.2 Multi-supplier relationships

The Service Integrator should have an active role in achieving a collaborative culture by promoting the mutual knowledge and understanding of each other's people and capabilities. There are multiple ways to do this:

- Co-location – selected employees from different Service Providers working face-to-face with the retained IT organization should be co-located.
- For global delivery units from different companies that are in the same region a communication program can be developed. Meeting face-to-face with counterparts in other Service Providers can have significant benefits. A Service Integrator took the initiative together with retained IT organization, the infrastructure service provider and two Indian-based application Service Providers, to set up a collaboration program of the three global delivery centers of the three companies, which were all based in the same time zone in India. The program consisted of regular joint workshops to discuss cross-supplier process improvements and service performance as well as regular video-conferences. As a result employees from all three Service Providers got a better understanding of the supplier ecosystem and their own and the other companies' roles in it. In this way the companies who are competitors in many ways, are actively collaborating to serve this customer.
- Plan, design and implement the use of any 'virtual office tools' needed to support the specific situation.

3.2.3 Joint governance

The Service Integrator should organize formal multi-supplier governance forums, where representatives of the Service Providers meet to discuss common interests and concerns. If the Service Integrator is accountable such a forum will be chaired by the Service Integrator and the customer will probably not even attend. If it is an Enabling Service Integrator the forum might be chaired by the customer. When shared KPIs are to be implemented, this will be an anchor point to these regular 'round table' meetings. Joint, multi-supplier governance supports a collaborative culture in multiple ways. It enables communication and transparency, stimulates mutual understanding and builds trust. Building personal relationships amongst counterparts will be fruitful when problems and issues need to be resolved. For more details please refer to Chapter 6.

3.2.4 Shared KPIs

In a multi-sourcing environment the end-to-end service level achievement depends on how the Service Providers proactively collaborate in reaching the end result, for instance in diagnosing and restoring the service in case of availability problems perceived by the user. Although 'fix first, settle later' is a common phenomenon in the IT service delivery industry, the natural behavior of Service Providers is to focus on their responsibilities and/or accountabilities in line with the scope and service levels defined in the contract. Therefore, contractual requirements setting and expectation of collaboration can prove to be of value. Sharing KPIs amongst Service Providers can be a way to achieve this. More details, including a real-life example, can be found in Chapter 5.

> **Practitioner tip:**
> The goal state is a teaming culture with common goals and partnership behaviors.

3.3   Defining the scope of an SIAM function

Early SIAM implementations were limited to defining IT Service Management process. Typically the Service Integrator scope was defined by a framework such as ITIL and (often) limited to a specific subset of lifecycle phases, such as; service operations, service transition and continual service improvement. Since specific functions span multiple processes, this often leads to duplication of effort across Service Providers. Scoping a SIAM function purely on processes is an inadequate scope and also leads to inefficiencies between Service Providers, the SIAM function and other parts of the retained organization. The standards defined in the strategy organization, the solutions developed and deployed in the projects organization and the operational services delivered from the service delivery organization are all interconnected, whereas historically SIAM functions have been operations focused.

More recent implementations tend to define the functional roles of the SIAM functions – definition and management of processes is just one of these functions.

3.3.1   Service desk

The role of the service desk capability is often actively debated. Is it a function of SIAM or is it a service provider function? There are arguments to both sides of this debate. It should be noted that the modeling of the service desk as part (or not part) of the Service Integrator is an independent question from the sourcing of the service desk or the service desk design (single desk, multiple desks, federated or 'follow the sun') There have been occasions where the modeling discussion was used as a proxy for the sourcing or design discussion and this causes confusion.

The strongest argument for the case that the service desk should be a service provider is based on the separation of duties principle and management of conflict of interest. The service desk is an execution role and when it comes to root cause analysis, process review or continual service improvement, it must be held to account in the same way as any other service provider. It is likely to have SLAs and service credit regimes in the same way as any other service provider.

The argument for the case that the service desk is part of the SIAM function is based on the end-to-end role it has and the need to interact with all the service providers. It will participate in many of the processes alongside the other suppliers and assist in assigning, reassigning and following up things like incident tickets. Kevin Holland's UK government case study (Holland, Axelos.com, 2015) shows the service desk within the SIAM function.

There is also a commercial argument that is related to 'wallet share' or having a level of commercial footprint to make the deal attractive to a major outsourcing company. The logic is that it may not be commercially attractive to bid 'just' for the Service Integration component without a guarantee of a larger account. If anything is to be commercially bundled with the Service Integrator contract then the most obvious candidate is the service desk. Provided there is a clear separation of duties between the SIAM roles and other roles, including service desk roles, then there is no impediment to the bundling of these contracts in a commercial sense.

Figure 3.2 is a representation abstracted from a particular organization that was wrestling with this issue. It shows that there are aspects of being both a supplier and a cross-functional support organization associated with the service desk.

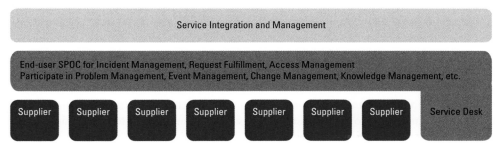

Figure 3.2   Example of the Service Desk relationships

It is fair to say that there is no one-size-fits-all answer to the way the service desk is modeled and commercially bundled. What does seem to be a consistent message across current implementations is that the service desk is a special case of a delivery organization. It has aspects of service delivery but has to be recognized in the process definition *and* contractual arrangements as a special case to support the additional process interactions that will be discussed later in this chapter. For example, other Service Providers must recognize that the service desk will have a requirement for interaction that is, in many ways, more aligned to the Service Integrator than other delivery teams.

> **Practitioner tip:**
> Consider the role and design of the service desk carefully. Separation of duties is important.

3.3.2 Key capabilities of the Service Integrator

Capabilities that support many different processes are another way of integrating services and providers and support/delivering standardization. The COBIT enablers are all candidate functions for federation by the Service Integrator. In Table 2.1 in Section 2.3 a suggested list of SIAM processes is listed based on COBIT. Typical competences included in a successful SIAM function are:

- **Audit and Performance Management.** This concentrates upon management of the performance of the services and auditing compliance to policies and interaction processes. Whilst there is a focus on IT outcomes, there will be some policy constraints that will need to be measured to support organizational goals and requirements. Security policy is usually top of the list but it is likely there will be other policies related to insurance, protecting workers' rights, ethical behavior and other areas common in outsourcing contracts.
- **Reporting and data dissemination**. While each Service Provider (internal or external) will have a requirement to report the status and performance of their own services, the aggregation and publishing of the reporting is a key SIAM function. The Service Integrator is also required to create an end-to-end view of services that are a superset of the component service reporting from Service Providers. Many implementations have also found it advantageous to provide a data warehouse function for Service Management data. This is necessary for Service Integration that builds aggregated services – services that consume sub-services from other providers, because it is more efficient to collate the data from other providers than to try to duplicate it. Collection, collation and dissemination of ITSM data becomes a core function of the Service Integrator.
- **Tools.** Where centralized and shared tools are implemented, the coordination of change to the toolset and the governance of their configuration will need to be centralized also. This does not mean that the operational application management needs to be centralized, but the governance and control must be.
- **Process Management.** Definition and maintenance of the end-to-end processes that allow cross provider collaboration. As discussed previously, in some early implementations this was considered the primary – or even the only – function of the Service Integrator.
- **Provider/Supplier Management.** In any multi-sourced environment where the existence and execution of an SIAM function needs to be a core element of contract creation and execution, aligning this role to the SIAM function provides potential benefits. While not appropriate for a wholly sourced SI, where SIAM is retained, this is a logical inclusion.
- **End-to-End Continual Service Improvement.** CSI is embedded at every level of the framework but it will be the Service Integrator that is accountable for the overall management and prioritization of CSI functions.

Obviously when the SIAM function is wholly outsourced, these functions would come from the same supplier. That supplier will be utilizing their own teams or selected subcontractors as a way of reducing their commercial risk. If however the SIAM function is led by the retained organization, with some staff augmentation services from other providers, it is NOT required that all sourced SIAM functions come from the same supplier. Having a SIAM team that is in itself multi-sourced gives a strong message about the collaborative nature of SIAM and embeds advocates of the model into all included Service Providers. It is recommended that there is a focus on the conflict of interest management plan for each supplier and that the culture of 'agent of the customer' is well established. Both of these recommendations require commercial maturity in both customers and suppliers to implement – this means that all parties understand the long term relationship and are, therefore, not motivated by short-term gains.

In case study 2 (see Section 1.9.2) the retained organization has brought together service desk, reporting, process design and coordination, supplier management and shared tools into a single SIAM function, which includes resources from all of its major providers. In addition, cross-IT continual service improvement initiatives were then executed and governed by a working group that included representation from all parts of retained IT and all Service Providers. Each member of the team then became the champion of the SIAM function and the focus on improved outcomes within their own teams, along with any barriers to collaboration, could be addressed quickly and directly.

3.3.3 Accountable and enabling Service integrator

Another way of defining the scope of an SIAM function is through its accountability of the Service Integrator. Different emerging models have defined this accountability in different ways.

- Accountable: An 'accountable' Service Integrator is one which is accountable for the delivery of the ongoing operational services that it integrates. This type of model is typically used when the SIAM function is sourced from a third party that takes some level of commercial responsibility for the other parties delivering into the environment. In its most refined state, this is a 'black-box' or 'closed' type of Service Integration. The customer is not aware of what services or which providers are participating to deliver the aggregated outcomes.
- Enabling: An 'enabling' Service Integrator is one that is responsible for the integration and management of the services in the environment, but not accountable for the service deliveries and outcomes themselves. In this type of environment the customer has full knowledge of which services and providers are participating. It is also often the case that the customer dictates what services and providers to use. In this situation the SIAM function is focused on identifying and eradicating:
  – Gaps and overlaps between services and suppliers;
  – Gaps and overlaps in reporting and metrics between services and suppliers;
  – Inefficiencies caused by the boundaries between two services or supplier.

The accountability of the Service Integrator will have a direct impact on the approach, competences, resources and relationships with the other suppliers the SIAM function establishes. Accountable SIAM, especially those that rely on third-parties to take some level of commercial accountability, will be far more prescriptive in their approach to Service Providers. While this may work well when the desired relationships are transactional (see Relationship Types in Section 2.2.1), it can cause inefficiencies and reduce the value that Service Providers can bring for the more mature relationship types. An accountable Service Integrator will require the SIAM function itself to be more actively directive with Service Providers due to this accountability, hence the potential for inefficiency.

An enabling Service Integrator will establish SIAM functions that are typically more suited to the more mature outsourcing environment. In this context the customer has overcome the initial reflexive distrust of external suppliers and the suppliers have understood that in long-term outsourcing relationships contracts will be 'win-win' or 'lose-lose'. Any tactical thinking is counterproductive to the supplier. This means that the overall relationship can be more trusting because the parties are more trustworthy. Typically, each Service Provider may have more than one contract and therefore has a broader relationship than any one single service. In this environment, the Integrator role becomes about enabling Service Providers to deliver at their best through optimizing the environment, interactions are more collaborative and goals are more shared.

In large and/or complex Service Integration environments the Service Integrator might act as accountable to one portion of integrated services and enabling to another set of services.

3.3.4   Process control and execution

In a multi-sourced environment, as discussed in more detail in Chapter 4 **Data and Tools**, a key question which needs to be answered is *"Which processes and data need to be mandated as consistent across all suppliers and which can be left to individual (or groups of) suppliers to manage and maintain?"*. This question is critical to the balance between the effectiveness and efficiency of the individual Service Providers and their services and that of the overall customer services delivered from IT.

Depicted in Figure 3.3, there is the concept of data partitioning which shows that for any process there are three possible partitions of data:
1. Data which the Service Integrator mandates to be both maintained and supplied by the provider to the Service Integrator;
2. Data which the Service Integrator mandates to be maintained by the provider;
3. Data which is maintained at the discretion of (and to support the internal processes of) the provider.

An example of this would be for configuration data. The Service Integrator might define a subset of configuration items (CIs) which are to be provided or, alternatively, that all CIs are sent but with minimalist data. Both strategies have been observed for CI data. For one early customer implementation, the customer wanted all CIs to be provided by suppliers to a federated CMDB. They did not want all CI attributes; rather they wanted 'thin' data associated with each CI. They expected that the providers would maintain significantly more detail. In a more recent implementation the Service Integrator has defined that they only want the CI information to the 'service' level to facilitate aggregated services. Whilst these examples used different partitioning of the data, in both cases Figure 3.3 is helpful in defining the expectation.

When dealing with professional IT Service Providers and procuring their services through contracts within which service performance is defined and committed to, it has to be assumed that all of the essential processes of IT management are included within that service to a level that allows them to meet their obligations. More importantly, these providers have been selected on the basis of the value proposition that each brings based on their own internal

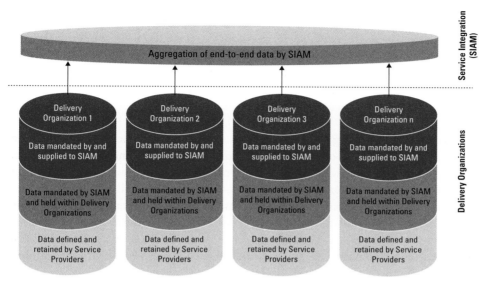

Figure 3.3   Data Classification for Service Integration

delivery capabilities. The goal is to facilitate collaboration by only enforcing standards that enable collaboration between providers.

From this assumption, follow-up questions are:
• "What level of processes and data need to be mandated as consistent across all suppliers…" in order to deliver the optimal balance of effectiveness and efficiency?
• Across which scope will each provider apply these processes?

The conclusion will be that there is a two-layer view of each process. At the top level, the end-to-end view defined by the Service Integrator will define the actors in each process and when and how transfer of control of the process will occur between parties. The execution of the process within each party is the responsibility of that party. The Service Integrator provides the framework to define how the Service Providers collaborate in the execution of the process.

This is typically implemented by overlaying the process onto swim lanes. Where the process flow crosses a swim lane, it represents a transfer of process responsibility. It is the role of the Service Integrator to ensure these transfers are clearly defined in terms of both when and how they occur.

Practitioner tip:
The data required in the single system of record should be considered carefully. More data is not the same as more information.

The service strategy and service interaction models will have an impact on just how granular this process diagram needs to be. Some traditional outsourcing will be quite interactive because the way the services are defined does not encapsulate the service well. For instance if 'infrastructure hosting' is with one supplier but the asset and license ownership is a retained responsibility, then the deployment process will be very interactive between parties. Where the services are better encapsulated, then this is less of an issue.

For example, when procuring a cloud-based email service, since the service is relatively autonomous, many of the processes used to design, develop, transit and operate the service can be delegated to the Service Provider. The results of those processes are enshrined in the contract through the usual commitments for warranty and utility. Those processes which must be common across all services such as configuration management and change management, can be simplified in terms of their scope by considering as much of the email service as possible as a single CI. For example:

- The email service becomes a single (or reduced) set of configuration items in the customer federated CMDB with no software license management as part of asset management since this is included in the service;
- Changes are only raised in the central change management system if they are anticipated to affect any functional or non-functional characteristic of the service, such as availability, performance, service continuity, security or external integrations.

This use of service level configuration items is very useful when integrating cloud services. Typically the cloud suppliers do not (and often will not) supply the detail of the underlying configuration. Attempting to map or reverse engineer the underlying solution is most certainly not a good use of customer resources and may be actively harmful because it encourages designers to rely on a level of implementation detail that may change without warning.

Using this approach to defining process scope is a way to realize the balance between provider and service effectiveness and efficiency while maximizing the accountability of the provider. It also enables the provider to deliver maximum value through internally optimized processes, procedures and tools.

3.3.5 Planning process scope for SI

In planning the process scope of the SIAM function it has proved valuable to break process control down into three levels. By separating each process into direction, control and execution, it provides an additional level of granularity that can be used to delegate processes appropriately:

- Process direction:
  - Owns the overall process design and standards which govern its use and mandatory requirements for outputs and controls. One example would be a process owner role.
- Process control:

- Operational management aspects of the process and process performance evaluation by service and provider. One example would be a change manager in the change management process.
- Process execution:
  - Performs specific activities within the process. This can be split between many different services, providers and support teams, based on a variety of scope boundaries. To avoid gaps in the process execution, the process control must provide a coherent integration for the parties to engage. There is also typically a 'service owner' role – the party responsible for any service from end-to-end service, that assists with assurance at the execution level.

As shown in Figure 3.4, this construct can be used to design appropriate levels of process control and execution in a multi-sourced environment.

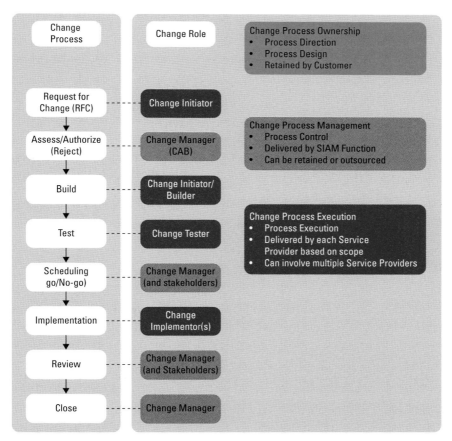

Figure 3.4   Process Control in a Multi-sourced Environment (Source: ITIL News, n.d.)

3.3.6   Using service models for the service strategy phase

System integration and Service Integration are related and work well together but they are not the same thing. In particular, in an organization that is built along the design/build/run structure (as proposed by both COBIT and IT4IT) there will be system integration and

Service Integration done by different parts of the organization. It is highly recommended that the two are kept aligned by the use of service models. If service design, build of services and then operation of the services are aligned, there will not be the sorts of discontinuities that occur when organizations design technology, build projects and then try to operate as services.

A service could be as simple as an infrastructure hosting service or as complex as an ERP system service.

> **Practitioner tip:**
> When possible, align system integration and Service Integration.

In several organizations, engaging with the system integration and project areas to align the service mapping view has been helpful. Based on these experiences, some simple 'business rules' have been created that are related to the IT services, to design and build – and therefore operate:
1. What needs to be designed and built is defined as services;
2. Every service has an operational owner, the service owner – the person who is responsible for running that service;
3. Services can contain other services from other Service Providers – these are called 'aggregated' services. Note that 1+1 = 3 in Service Integration. An aggregated service is more than the sum of the participating services. It is a service of its own, with its own warranties and utilities;
4. The service owner is accountable for ensuring that the service meets its SLAs and that all the ITSM processes are executed with respect to that service.

These rules allow us to implement the principle of model driven design of our services. There are some powerful implications of these rules. The accountability of the service owner (rule 4) coupled with the nature of aggregated services (rule 3) derives a cascading delegation model for accountability to sub service owners. If a service owner has *effectively* delegated to a sub service, then the sub service owner can be held accountable where they cause a service impact. If, however, the impact is caused by a service gap or a component that has not been delegated then it is the higher-level service owner who is held accountable. Obviously this is a recursive structure – effectively creating a cascading delegation model.

In the example shown in Figure 3.5, a notional aggregated service from supplier A is given. There are eight subservices in the service deconstruction model. Supplier A retains three subservices but there are also three from Supplier B and two from Supplier C. Supplier A must ensure that they have obtained appropriate services (from both a functional and non-functional requirements basis) and that they have effectively delegated the subservice accountability. Anything in the aggregated service that is not effectively delegated becomes the responsibility of Supplier A. It is the Service Integrator that sets the rules for what constitutes effective delegation and provides frameworks to facilitate the engagement.

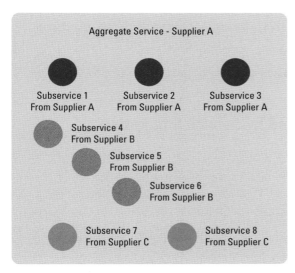

Figure 3.5 An example of an aggregated service

There are implications for ITSM processes such as:

- Configuration management – ideally, implement a CI taxonomy that uses service CIs and a rule that states that the only relationship that can cross a Service Provider boundary is a service CI to service CI relationship. This is a very helpful rule for clarifying cross provider dependencies.
- Service catalog – there can now be clear aggregated service definitions implemented as classes in the service catalog, ready for instantiation for consumers. This also highlights the importance of release and lifecycle management of service catalog items.
- Event and incident management – all impact analysis reported from Service Providers is required to be reported against the service and not against the technical component underneath that service. This allows the owner of an aggregated service to consume service information from the sub-Service Providers rather than duplicating this monitoring.

These rules also support more rigorous service encapsulation that allows a maturing of service management over time because people are encouraged to think of the aggregated services as a whole.

> **Practitioner tip:**
> The use of this kind of approach to service mapping elevates the importance of the feder-ated service catalog and fundamentally changes the approach to configuration manage-ment in the SIAM model. The service catalog becomes the descriptor for the components that are available for reuse by other suppliers to build higher-level services.

From a configuration management perspective, it becomes clear how the Service Integrator will be focused on the service CIs almost exclusively as they become the 'unit of currency' between Service Providers. This leaves the mapping of components to services and the role of the Service Provider. This focus on the aggregated service instead of the technical components that build the service is far better aligned to an 'as-a-service' paradigm than the more traditional technical level mapping that is often found in the CMDB.

3.4   Other processes impacted by Service Integration

As discussed, all processes will have the multi-layer orchestration view. The top layer is the end-to-end ownership and direction. The next level is orchestration and defining transfer of control across various Service Providers. Finally the instantiation and execution of the processes is a concern to every participating and impacted service (remember from Chapter 2 – processes operate on services). For example, the resolution of one incident from the customer perspective will in fact cause multiple incident, problem, change etc. processes to be started within multiple services.

Typically, swim lane diagrams would be used to show these transfer of control points. The process ownership and direction will typically be a governance-related activity so it is usually not shown on the actual process execution swim lanes. Whilst each Service Provider may execute the sub-processes differently internally, the principle of standardization allows the common method for transfer of control. Where there is not standardization of engagement then transfer of control will unavoidably be more complex because the transfer method will differ depending on the end points.

Some processes are more impacted by the introduction of a SIAM than others, how much and which is always dependent on the situation and types of relationships and service delivered. In a 'non-functional and operations service environment' the event and incident process might be complex to integrate. In application lifecycle management service environment the change and release processes will be the ones to address.

Other processes do require significantly more thought at the design phase. Some examples are included below.

3.4.1   Knowledge management

The service desk will be critically dependent in terms of the way that knowledge management processes and end user self-help are designed. If there is a single service desk/user self-service portal for level one support then the delivery and maintenance of knowledge articles will require some thought. It is likely that a different Service Provider to those consuming them will maintain the knowledge articles. This implies that the quality review, style and templates will need to be standardized.

> **Practitioner tip:**
> Don't underestimate the importance of knowledge management processes for cross-
> supplier collaboration and enablement.

Given that the efficiency and effectiveness of end user support is defined by the way that users can be helped at the first point of contact, one Service Provider needs to be encouraged to enable a different Service Provider to perform better. There is clearly a win-win scenario here as both the service desk and level two are relieved of work but history has shown that there is value in spending time to establish the knowledge management process well.

It is worth noting that contractual support or negotiation may be required to ensure that intellectual property (IP) rights do not become an impediment to knowledge management. IP rights and contracts are discussed in more detail in Section 5.3.9. The key to the knowledge management discussion is to keep the focus on the win-win aspect of the sharing of knowledge – since everyone's cost is decreased.

3.4.2   Service catalog

The federation of services from multiple providers is not a trivial task. It is not unusual for the service catalog design process to get frozen in debates about 'taxonomy' of services and not progress much further. However the service catalog management processes are critical to defining what the customer buys and consumes – it is the plan of what services are required in the IT environment in the future, what is available today and what it is planned to remove.

Ask any person in the industry, "What is a service?" and there will be sorts of answers but they seem to fall into one of two categories. One is a description of something that is 'done' (e.g. change my password). The other is a description of something that exists (e.g. LAN service). The debate about who is correct can be passionate. This has been dubbed the 'nouns and verbs' debate and it is not helpful as both have a purpose depending on context.

There is a need to be able to support the two concepts in order to assist the communities of both end users and IT Service Providers. The simplest approach is to say that any request is based on an "action being performed on an object". To state this differently, assuming that it is a 'service' a noun (a thing), then a request will always be structured along the lines of "perform action on object". For example "Reset my password in the corporate directory" or perhaps "build me a new hosting platform".

Service designers and architects will be most concerned with the classes of services (nouns) that are available in the service catalog, including when they will be upgraded, changed or no longer supported.

> **Practitioner tip:**
> The service catalog is a key intersection of plan/build/run/monitor collaboration.

Operations people will be most focused on the actual instances of the services in operation and the requests being made in relation to them.

End users and project delivery people are most likely to be focused on the requests that are available to them.

There are other ways to present service catalogs – but regardless of how they are presented, the issues for the catalog that need to be considered are:
- How are the services presented in a coherent and consistent way across Service Providers?
- To whom are the services available – for instance a 'new production virtual machine'? This may be available to IT consumers or projects but is unlikely to be available to end users.
- Who is accountable to create and publish the services?
- Who will review the quality and consistency of the published services?

3.4.3   Configuration management

When designing the cross-provider configuration management process, there is a need to consider the "who really cares?" question. Somebody has to know the detailed configuration of all of the services. The Service Integrator has to know who knows at any time.

The difficulty lies with the fact that aggregated services span details that potentially cross multiple suppliers. How much detail is required to be held in a central location for the visibility of all? The answer will vary by organization.

As discussed in other sections, using the concept of a 'Service CI' allows the end-to-end view to be constructed without needing all of the detail. This is somewhat analogous to the revolution of shipping when the containerization of freight occurred. In a similar way that freight is very efficient to move when loaded into standard sized containers, configuration management is simplified when 'loaded' in Service CIs. The Service Providers care about the content but the rest of the parties mainly care about the Service CI 'container'. This does, however, require that Service Providers map their communications about the impact of the more granular detail back to the service container. This is a recommended approach but may require negotiation in an environment where there are existing contracts and processes in place.

3.4.4   Event management and monitoring

Fairly clearly, every service provider should have a clear understanding of the status and performance of the services they provide and be able to report that status and performance. The more interesting question is how much other Service Providers (including service desk), the Service Integrator, business executives and end users need to know.

In particular, for aggregated services not every level of service ownership should monitor all the components. It would be wasteful and likely impact the services in a negative way. This implies that some level of service impact information must be managed by the Service Integrator's role to 'collect, collate and disseminate' data.

One way intended to simplify this collection, collation and dissemination has already been discussed with respect to configuration management, and involves having the data reported against the services presented (Service CIs) rather than the technical components.

There will always be a role for the Service Integrator to correlate events across Service Providers where the aggregated data is required to perform the correlation. This enrichment could be delegated to the service desk provider. Either way the service desk will be keenly interested in the results.

4   Data and Tools

One of the biggest areas of contention between practitioners of Service Integration is that of tools and data. The two extremes of the argument being that it is impossible to hold a Service Provider accountable for their services if the retained organization provides the tools, whilst on the other hand it is impossible to integrate Service Providers if there are no common tools. The potential to have detailed and rationale discussions about a middle ground is further complicated by the lack of a consistent ontology for tools and their capabilities.

This chapter will discuss the ways to simplify the overall IT Service Management tooling and data architectures and how to achieve successful operations. It will provide some key principles for design and operation, aimed at reducing cost and complexity and then focus on the operations tools to provide some guidelines for implementing multi-source aware tools and data models. This chapter focuses on the operational service management data and tools of the COBIT enablers: Service, Infrastructure and Applications and Information.

This chapter is not intended to cover the detailed architectures or the pros and cons of internal and external integration interfaces. As Tom Le Bree notes in his article in the Guardian newspaper (Bree, 2014), the variety and capability of the technology available in the market now is not the challenge, it is ensuring that the resulting complexity is not allowed to drive our behavior. We need to stay focused on what we want to achieve with the technology, not what it is capable of.

4.1   Introduction

While processes can deliver repeatable output in an effective way, automation of those processes through tooling is the key to efficiency. The tools and the data that reside within them are therefore crucial to delivering the benefit case of IT services. They:
- provide the structure and rigor within which automation becomes a possibility – speeding up service delivery and service quality;
- provide the capability to deliver increasing levels of integration, enabling business users to take advantage of more advanced capabilities inside and outside the organization;
- provide the structure within which workflow can be embedded to operationalize processes using resources from anywhere in the world.

Hence the two key questions that need to be answered when planning a multi-sourced environment are:
- *"Which processes and data need to be mandated as consistent across all suppliers and which can be left to individual (or groups of) suppliers to manage and maintain?"*
- *"Which tools should I procure, maintain and mandate across all suppliers, and which ones are best sourced as part of the services I procure?"*

These two questions have a major impact on the balance between supplier efficiency and service efficiency and as such, make or break the business case for Service Integration.

In most cases, the decision of which tools to source is based on the existing tools landscape or a perceived potential to reduce the cost and/or service delivery risk. In reality, this approach can lead to an overall increase in the cost and complexity. The balance that needs to be struck in the design of the SIAM function is the balance between the effectiveness and efficiency of the individual services versus the overall efficiency and effectiveness of the eco-system. Complex and highly integrated tools and data architectures which span multiple suppliers are cumbersome to maintain, difficult to change and ultimately impact the ability of the organization to change suppliers as needed.

4.1.1 The Open Groups IT4IT

To try and put some level of structure around the tools which can be used in the IT Service Management environment, The Open Group is launching a new industry framework for the 'business of IT' which is intended to be more architecturally orientated than ITIL or COBIT. In IT4IT (The Open Group, 2015) the focus is on end-to-end IT value streams that are underpinned by Support Activities with an underlying data model. Using the structure of the Open Group's IT4IT framework Value Streams, these primary resource types can be placed into a high-level meta-model which covers the entire service lifecycle, see Figure 4.1.

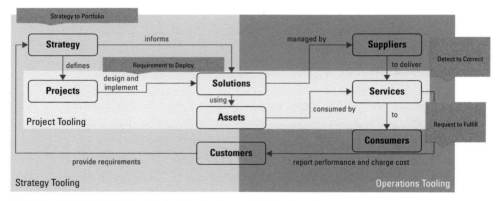

Figure 4.1   High-Level IT4IT Value Stream Mapping (source: The Open Group)

In the whitepaper 'Impact of Multi-Sourcing on the IT4IT Reference Architecture' (Davis, 2014), the IT4IT Forum discusses the impact of multi-sourcing on the framework and introduces some interesting ways to address tooling within this context. The paper introduces three patterns for tools and data integration in this environment:
- Central: all partners use the same functional component and the information is managed in a single place;
- Replicated: partners each have their own functional component and the same information is replicated in multiple places;
- Referenced: partners have their own functional component, but each is managing a different part of the information.

These three patterns are represented visually in Figure 4.2.

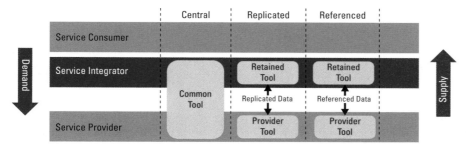

Figure 4.2   IT4IT Integration Patterns (source: The Open Group)

Since the main focus of this publication and the most challenging aspects of SIAM are in the area of day-to-day operational service delivery, the remainder of this chapter will focus on the two value streams of Request to Fulfill and Detect to Correct. Project tooling has typically been dealing with different groups of people coming together to achieve a coordinated plan of activities for many years and as such requires little in the way of specific clarification for a multi-sourced environment. Operations tooling however has in the most part been designed with single operating organization use case. In the case of an IT organization, a single retained IT organization, and with Service Providers, multi-tenant systems are a use case where there may be many customers and many services, but only one delivery organization.

These two IT4IT value steams will be used to discuss the structure of the overall tooling and data architectures required to successfully integrate multiple suppliers without unduly increasing complexity and cost:
1. Request to Fulfill – those tools required to **publish** available service requests to consumers and allow them to **subscribe** to services, **fulfill** requests and **measure** performance;
2. Detect to Correct – those tools required to **detect** issues which affect the normal operation of services, **diagnose** the root cause and make the appropriate **change** to **resolve** them.

4.2   Foundation principles for multi-sourced architectures

The scope, cost and level of integration of any service management architecture will vary greatly with the size of the organization and the level of service management maturity. However, when designing tools architectures for a multi-sourced environment, it needs to be recognized that the challenges are different. Trying to re-create the internal complexity of ITSM tools architectures using contractual requirements, cross-organizational enterprise service bus models and complex data standards can become an intolerable cost and burden over time.

Defining some core principles for the integrated components of the architecture can save time, money, blood, sweat and tears and is possibly the strongest indicator of the earlier question "What type of integrator are you?"

4.2.1   Output vs outcome

When sourcing IT services, it is often necessary to give up a level of control in the *way* that things are done in return for a level of assurance that they *will* be done. To realize the benefits of this change requires a change in focus of the retained organization, a move from *output* to *outcome*.

> **Practitioner tip:**
> To realize the benefits of sourcing requires a change in focus of the retained organization, from output to outcome.

The *output* of a service provider measures what work has been done or how many units have been produced whereas the *outcome* focuses on the impact, the change achieved as a result of doing that work. Specifically within most multi-sourced environments, the focus needs to be on the outcome of the combination of Service Providers and the retained organization. While some of the largest contracts and single-sourcing can move this accountability for output to a Service Provider, it is predominantly the accountability of the retained IT organization.

As part of that accountability, the role of the Service Integrator is to balance two perspectives:
- Make sure that the Service Providers are producing the outputs and/or achieving the outcomes that are defined in their contracts;
- Ensure that these outputs are combining correctly to deliver the desired outcome to the business;
- Address any gaps between the two.

To integrate the output of provider services in a multi-sourced environment requires a certain level of integration of the processes used to deliver those services. Certain key processes must have been designed with integration in mind. One way of mapping the components of an integrated process between provider, integrator and customer is shown in Figure 4.3.

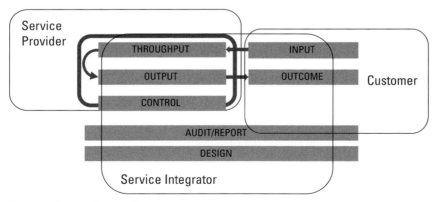

Figure 4.3   Process Output vs Outcome

Within this model:
- The Service Provider receives the input from the customer and delivers the output, and is responsible for the effectiveness and efficiency of their execution;
- The Service Integrator defines the process down to the level required to achieve integration, reports on the performance and audits the compliance. The Service Integrator is responsible for either:
  - Ensuring that the process output combines with other processes and services to **deliver the desired outcome** if they are an accountable Service Integrator;
  - Ensuring that the process and its outputs can be combined with other processes and services and is **capable of delivering the desired outcome** if they are an enabling Service Integrator.

By ensuring that the process definition is only down to the level "required to achieve effective integration", the Service Integrator can maximize not only the accountability of the supplier, but their ability to optimize. This approach can have particular benefits in the area of tooling where it can reduce the number of tools held by the retained organization, reduce the amount of integration between Service Providers and maximize the value that a Service Provider can bring.

> **Practitioner tip:**
> By ensuring that the process definition is only down to the level "required to achieve effective integration", the Service Integrator can maximize not only the accountability of the supplier, but their ability to optimize.

4.2.2   Identify the requirements for tools and data integration

Before defining multi-sourced tools architecture, first it must be understood what level and type of integration is required by reviewing the following key questions.
- **The case for integration**, "what is the value (service improvement or cost reduction) of technically integrating my Service Providers and the cost of not doing so?"
  - Across different industries, there are many examples of end-to-end services with varying degrees of integration.
    - For example, in car leasing, the leasing company has contracts with different Service Providers and is integrated in terms of booking and payments, but the driver is required to integrate the service by taking their car to different garages for windscreen, servicing or tire replacement;
    - Travel agents offer a range of services which range from a fully integrated 'package' holiday through to DIY holidays where each element is booked separately.
  - The value of integration can take many forms and it is best to clearly identify the value of integration before reviewing ways to achieve it:
    - Mitigation of risk through ensuring that any service gaps between procured services are identified and managed;
    - Integration of the experience in the eyes of the end-user. Visibility of the individual down-stream suppliers can be masked from the end-user who sees a single 'face of IT'.

- **Supplier integration** vs. **Service Integration**, "where will the balance be between the effectiveness of the aggregate service and that of the individual component services?"
  - A major part of selecting service delivery partners is assessing a potential partner's ability to deliver services in an efficient and repeatable fashion. Their price and their pedigree. This, in turn, is based on the ability to integrate people, process and tools internally within their organization to deliver the selected services better than anyone else. This internal **supplier integration** is an essential part of the business case that has led to their selection. This integration includes not only the level of integration between their tools and process, but also their ability to integrate with other parts of their own organization and any subcontractor organizations they require to deliver the service;
  - Once the partners are selected however, the end-to-end performance of any customer-facing service which is supported by two or more suppliers is, to a greater or lesser extent, dependent on the SIAM function's ability to **service integrate** those partners and any associated tools together to deliver a service end-to-end;
  - This balance becomes especially important in the tools and data discussion because where a supplier service is tightly coupled to the tools used to deliver it, it will become more difficult to integrate.
- **Level of integration**, "at what level do I need to technically integrate my supplier services to deliver best value to my customers?"
  - Depending on the amount of inter-dependency between the supplier services which make up the end-to-end customer service, integration can occur at one of three levels:
    - Reporting and management information (MI): processes are relatively autonomous, operating on different tools, but just enough data standardization has occurred to enable the resulting data to be aggregated at an ecosystem level. For example, the number and performance of service requests delivered by each supplier in the environment;
    - Process: the level of interdependence is such that activities in one service provider need to be exposed to other providers and evaluated or at least acknowledged. For example, changes made in one supplier's scope may have an impact on services delivered by another, such as infrastructure and applications;
    - Tools and data: where the level of interdependence is high and the need for efficiency is high, integrating through tools, and therefore data, may be the only option. For critical services where availability is essential, identification, diagnosis and routing of incidents are time-critical activities which will need to happen as fast as possible, this requires tightly integrated tools, data, processes and reporting.
  - The level of tools and data integration required is also somewhat dependent on the process being supported e.g.:
    - Configuration management can support many processes across many providers and its prime reason for existence is to provide common and consistent data to all of its subscribers. In this process, there will be a high-level of integration required;
    - Service request management can be very specific to a service and therefore integration may only be required at the point of request and potentially an output into configuration management to update any changed CIs. Tools developers have begun

to provide specific support to this use case with capabilities such as HP Propel and Service Flow.

The answers to these questions need to be detailed early in the planning lifecycle because different types of service that may be procured will typically come with some hidden limitations in this specific area:

- Software as a Service (SaaS) services are typically commodity-based and allow limited direct integration:
  - May contain an almost complete architecture within the solution;
  - Integration will be via limited input and output mechanisms, if at all.
- Platform as a Service (PaaS) services offer commodity application platform architectures to support bespoke application configurations:
  - Typically, the solution will contain the majority of the technical components of the solution which will limit opportunities for bespoke non-functional requirements;
  - Asset management and the platform-specific aspects of service management may be procured as part of the service; they will typically be limited to the platform scope and will have to be integrated to broader service management.
- Infrastructure as a Service (IaaS) services offer commodity infrastructure to support bespoke architectures and applications:
  - Typically, will contain a subset of the architecture focused on the operational activities of the platform; discovery, monitoring and orchestration;
  - Correlation, service management and asset management of the overall solution will remain the responsibility of the customer.

These high level requirements, defined early in the process, will enable tooling and data considerations to be included in the overall contract service ecosystem and inform the contracts and services that will be procured.

4.2.3   Principles for simplifying tools design

While the process of defining an overall Service Integration tools architecture can be daunting, by adopting some key principles, many of the pitfalls associated with overly complex integrations and data models can be avoided before they become serious issues.

Practitioner tip:

By adopting some key principles, many of the pitfalls associated with overly complex integrations and data models can be avoided before they become serious issues.

---

1. **I will integrate at the highest level possible to maximize supplier accountability and manage the total cost of delivery.**

   Integrating tools and data leads to increased cost and complexity of integration and can reduce a supplier's ability to deliver value by reducing their effectiveness and efficiency. Reducing the level of data and technology integration required, where beneficial, increases the flexibility and autonomy of Service Providers thereby allowing them to optimize within their service autonomously.

2. **I will retain the tools I need to measure and manage the experience of my users.**
   The most common failing in managing and measuring multi-sourced services is allowing the focus to be shifted away from the service being delivered to IT's customers and onto the service being received from IT's suppliers. Focusing tools, processes and data on measuring the service received from providers can lead to increased cost and complexity and serious gaps in the quality of the services provided to the business.

3. **I will minimize the set of common data elements, and their master sources, which must be the same for all services.**
   Common data elements are essential to being able to integrate services and processes together. As few items as possible must be defined and managed centrally to ensure they are common across all services. Examples include; services, customers, consumers, locations, organizations and suppliers.

4. **I will delegate the management of data elements which can be wholly contained within a single service or supplier.**
   Those data elements which can be wholly contained within a single supplier or services should remain encapsulated within that service to reduce the overall complexity of data in the environment. Examples include; individual configuration item details for fully contained solutions or services, and changes which have no impact outside of the agreed service boundaries.

The level to which these principles can be adopted will depend greatly on both the type of relationship that has been contracted (see Relationship types in Section 2.2.1) and the types of services that have been procured. However, the traditional approach of capturing everything, managing everything and measuring everything in a multi-sourced environment will not only hinder the value that suppliers can bring, but also measurably increase the cost of multi-sourcing.

4.3   Data implications of multi-sourcing

Integrating multiple Service Providers together to deliver aggregate services has significant implications in terms of data and the way it is measured, managed and interpreted. Figure 4.4 provides a framework to discuss these implications.

Within the Service Management tools architecture, there are typically four types of data that need to be managed and maintained. Key decisions must be made as to the ownership and management principles that will be applied to each data type:

- Foundation data:
  - Configuration items and assets; data about the IT estate;
  - Data that relates to the logical and physical components which make up IT services and contractual and commercial agreements associated with their cost. The scope of the data is defined by:

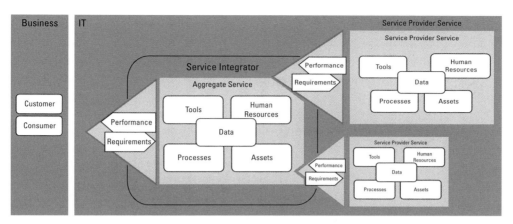

Figure 4.4 Data Elements in SIAM

- Ownership – those items which have some financial or commercial consequence for the retained IT organization;
- Function – those items which may impact the delivery of the service in a material way.

• Data about performance; service performance data includes ticket performance, systems and service performance. Data is tracked in real-time and is typically aggregated before being used for historical trending. Data is compared to customer SLA requirements to define how acceptable the measured performance is. Where process and/or tools level integration is required, this data will include process performance and compliance data specific to each Service Provider as well as the IT organization overall.

• Data about the customer, consumer and the provider. Data about the customer includes information about who they are, what their demand is and how much they pay. For the consumer it is about how much they use. Provider information will include services they are contracted to deliver, costs and performance. While consumer information typically changes on an ongoing basis (leavers and joiners), customer information is managed through defined demand cycle and provider information through a contractual lifecycle.

Each of these data types has ownership and retention parameters that need to be reviewed and agreed as part of data management within a multi-sourced environment. Industry or country specific legislation trumps all other agreements, so that must be dealt with first, but in the absence of other requirements, how can these decisions be made?

The following section discusses each of these categories of data in the context of Service Provider services being integrated into an aggregate business service and delivered to a business consumer, at the request of a business customer.

4.3.1 Foundation data

The first area of focus must be on identification, effective management, correlation and distribution of foundation data that provides a consistent view of:

- Customers: who they are, what they do, how they are referred to and which services they consume?
- Consumers: who they are, what they do, where they are located, how they can be contacted, which organization they work for, who can provide approval for them?
- Processes: the different processes which manage and maintain different aspects of the services portfolio?
- Services: what they are called, what are their service level expectations, which components are they made up of?
- Suppliers: which services do they support, who are they and how can they be contacted?
- Assets: what are they, where are they, how are they supported, how are they performing and what are the costs associated with them?
- Environmental data: what are the parallel things happening that might affect the organization and its IT services?

> **Practitioner tip:**
> Validate that the proposed integrations and transfer of data is necessary for the successful delivery of the services and sufficiently accurate and timely.

While this foundation data needs to be consistent across the services being delivered, care must be taken before building complex interfaces and a full master data management capability across all suppliers. By using the principles defined in Section 4.2, it should be validated that the proposed integrations and transfer of data is necessary to the successful delivery of the services and sufficiently accurate and timely. One example of how this can be achieved is through encapsulation, where any foundation data items that are wholly encapsulated within the service do not get managed within the central service knowledge management system, just the service CI and those components which have a direct external impact.

This foundation data will provide the common keys required to link context sensitive tools and process data created within each system to enable them to be brought back together so as to provide a consistent taxonomy or classification of data to provide the structure required to support the reporting perspectives discussed above.

For an IT organization to demonstrate that it is delivering the services, as specified to the business, it is essential to be able to measure end-to-end performance of these services. For the same IT organization to ensure that it is receiving the services it has contracted for, it will need to be able to accurately measure the services that they are receiving from suppliers. These are rarely the same thing. Even when all suppliers are delivering exactly the level of performance that has been specified in contracts, unless contracting with both parties has been done from the ground up and every nuance has been considered, there will be gaps between the services procured and the services delivered:

- Cross-supplier dependencies lead to exclusions in service performance measurement; e.g. infrastructure dependencies on application performance;
- Dependencies on the retained organization or other third parties; e.g. approvals or fixes to application code;
- Dependencies on the user; e.g. additional information, or confirmation of incident resolution.

All of these (and many more) can and will impact the perceived quality of the service received from IT and therefore may need to be measured in the tools ecosystem.

The traditional 'sea of green' phenomenon of outsourcing describes a situation where all of the suppliers' SLAs are green and yet the end-to-end performance of the service still fails to deliver. While gaps like those described above contribute to this picture, the thing that makes it difficult to diagnose where the problem lies is in the consistency and correct classification of data.

Where possible, the desired outcome should be a single consistent set of data, a 'single version of the truth' from which all the perspectives can be generated, as represented by the 'data triangle' as shown in Figure 4.5. This is the data required to inform governance decisions. Perspectives include:
- Location, how well are services delivered to a particular location;
- Supplier, how well is each supplier performing against their specific SLAs;
- Performance of the service (and service provider);
- Performance of the process.

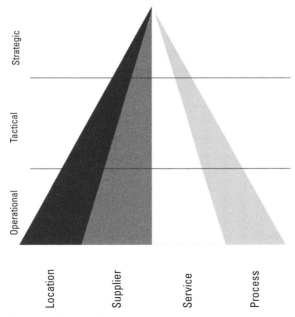

Figure 4.5   The data triangle

It should be a requirement that all of the reporting which underpins the operation of IT can be traced back to this single consistent data set at operational, tactical and strategic levels.

While there will be challenges to implementing this model due to the inevitable differences between both contractual definitions and the interpretation of contractual definitions, it must be considered a foundational element to success in the implementation, operation and continual improvement of an effective multi-sourced environment.

Practitioner tip:

It should be a requirement that all of the reporting which underpins the operation of IT can be traced back to this single consistent data set at operational, tactical and strategic levels.

Configuration item data

Configuration item data can be considered as a virtual representation of the real world, it attempts to reflect the complexity of, in this case, the IT landscape with all of its intricacies and integrations. One of the foundational elements of the multi-sourcing business case is that some of the complexity for managing and maintaining this data should be removed from the retained organization. Typically, this results in contractual clauses that require Service Providers to maintain the currency of the CMDB to X% accuracy and ensure that it is updated within Y hours of a change. In practical terms, unless the data models and processes were well established prior to sourcing the service, the result of these clauses is of little benefit and results in a significant increase in workload. Over time, the retained organization begins to lack this insight to validate the accuracy of the data.

To begin to simplify this picture, first look at the ownership of the data. One view is that the customer needs to have visibility and control over all information about anything used to deliver their services. This level of detail should only be captured if the physical assets are the financial accountability of the retained organization. If a service is procured which includes certain assets to deliver, by aggregating the configuration item information to the level of service, the accountability remains clearly with the Service Provider and the level of information required to be managed and maintained by the retained organization is significantly reduced.

Practitioner tip:

By aggregating the configuration item information to the level of service, the accountability remains clearly with the service provider and the level of information required to be managed and maintained by the retained organization is significantly reduced.

4.3.2 Performance data

While there are many ways of measuring supplier and service performance, the only ones that matter are the ones the underpin commitments made between the retained organization and its customers, and the retained organization and its suppliers. This is more often than not a consolidated view of many different elements of 'telemetry' type data which measures each and every aspect of service performance.

Many customers in the past have sought to replicate this vast quantity of rapidly changing data in an attempt to be able to see every aspect of supplier performance. In practice, a far more effective result can be achieved by setting some basic data management principles and then allowing the Service Provider to capture, collate and interpret the data, only presenting the rationalized view back to the customer in terms of reports with appropriate commentary and analysis. Only when the trends and management information indicate that further investigation is required should direct investigation of this data be required. While there may be requirements for a level of access to data for forensic or legislative purposes, these are relatively few and, in the main, clearly understood and documented in contracts. For the rest of this data, setting retention periods after which the data can be automatically deleted will reduce the size of the overall haystack when the searching for needles begins.

As with any performance measurement system, care needs to be taken in defining KPIs, in many cases a simple average that may make sense for a Service Provider, may hide significant issues for an aggregated service. For example, in many infrastructure services outsourcing contracts, a common KPI is the average availability of a certain type of server. Where there are a large number of servers, even major outages for a small number of servers may have no impact on the Service Provider performance but will have a major impact on the affected services.

4.3.3 Customer and consumer data

Information about the business customers and consumers of the IT organization, and the relationship between them, is one of the fundamental data types in IT service delivery. This information includes:
- Organizational structure, to relate departments and users;
- Geographic placement, to identify physical location of assets and consumers;
- Demand, to understand current and forecast demand for IT services;
- History, previous history of consumption and satisfaction of IT services.

4.3.4 Service Provider data

Information about the organizations, the contracts, the services delivered and the service level expectations of each. This data is owned by the retained organization typically through a SIAM type function. The data is only valid for the term of those agreements. For the Service Integrator role to be able to optimize the environment, the relationship between procured services and delivered services is one of the most critical elements. Being able to relate supplier performance to service performance is the most crucial role of a Service Integrator.

4.3.5 Summary

While the typical discussion with regards to data in a multi-sourced environment is focused on the tools within which the data is maintained and the level of technical integration required, the focus in multi-sourcing should be very different.

> **Practitioner tip:**
> Rather than thinking about how to replicate the existing data landscape, ask if that level of complexity is necessary in the first place. Think about how to realize the benefits of using Service Providers and which data elements can be encapsulated within their services.

Maturity in this area requires some bold, but basic decisions to be made early in the planning lifecycle and enforced consistently throughout the contract term. There may be times when an additional piece of data could have been used, but experience has shown that the problems of maintaining and synchronizing far too much data between organizations is far more likely to disrupt the delivery of high quality services to our joint customer.

4.4 Operational tool landscape definition

As discussed already in this chapter, in a multi-sourced environment the recommended approach is to minimize the amount of retained tooling and integration required to only those aspects which add direct value to the aggregate services delivered from IT to the business. Across a number of different industries a common approach to defining tools architectures in a multi-sourced environment is based on one key question; "What tools do I have when I plan to outsource and how do I retain them in this new environment?" However, not only does this approach limit the value of the sourcing, by compromising the foundation principles defined at the beginning of this chapter, it also has significant potential to limit the services procured by forcing them to use (or integrate with) sub-optimal tools. The more efficient and effective solution is to plan from the top-down based on a clear understanding of the role of the retained organization, the aspects of service which directly impact the user experience and those required to deliver consistent and integrated reporting.

4.4.1 Defining a top-down architecture framework

Fundamentally the role of the retained organization in a multi-sourced IT environment can be thought of as balancing five different types of resources to deliver services to customers and consumers:

1. Assets: all the different types of resource that are required, including; compute, storage, network components, human resources, skills and time. These include the processes which manage and maintain different aspects of the services portfolio;
2. Suppliers: suppliers and partners who operate solutions or deliver services to the IT organization;
3. Services and solutions: the business outcomes delivered through the use of IT solutions by a Provider;

4. Customers and consumers: the people and organization units who are procuring and consuming the services of IT;
5. Projects: activities which design and implement new IT solutions and/or services, or changes to existing IT solutions and/or services.

In a simplified architecture framework model, the overall Service Integration tools architecture can be broken down into three levels which map to four key resource types, see Figure 4.6.

Assets	Suppliers	Services and Solutions	Customers and Consumers	
How many asset of which type do we have and are they being utilized? How much are they costing us and are we utilizing them efficiently?	How are our suppliers performing against their contractual commitments?	How are our services, suppliers and partners performing to support our customers?	How are our services, suppliers and partners performing to support our customers? How is that service perceived by our customers and consumers?	REPORT & EVALUATE
What changes do we need to make to our assets? Are our assets under contracted support and maintenance?	How do our suppliers work together to meet the needs of our customers and consumers? How do we measure their performance and value?	What do we need to do to deliver the service and how do we ensure our success? How do we deliver against the commitments in our Service Level Agreements?	How do our customers interact with us when they need help and support? How do we deliver against the commitments in our Service Level Agreements?	MANAGE & INTERPRET
What assets are we using? Where are they? Who is using them? Who owns them?	Which internal and external suppliers are we using? What are their commitments and scope? For which period have these commitments been agreed?	What events are happening within our IT landscape? How do they affect the services we are delivering?	How do we communicate the events are happening within our IT landscape? How does the criticality of our services change over time?	SENSE & RESPOND
Assets	Suppliers	Services and Solutions	Customers and Consumers	

Figure 4.6   Reference Capability Framework

- **Sense and respond**
  - Discover: discover the physical and logical CIs that comprise the IT environment, including their attributes such as capacity and cost;
  - Monitor: discover events which impact and define the delivery of end-to-end services, including performance, availability, satisfaction, demand, risk, security;
  - Orchestrate: automate actions in other systems to deliver requests and/or initiate corrective actions.
- **Manage and interpret**
  - Applies structure, process and automation to the configuration items to orchestrate their availability and operation in order to deliver technology and business services;
  - Manages required configuration items as assets by linking them to contracts and licenses and tracking them through their lifecycle;
  - Coordinates and tracks the activities of operational support teams and ensures that they execute in line with the service and contractual expectations defined in Service Level Agreements (SLAs);
  - Correlate: compares the discovered and monitored perspectives with the expected outcome and identifies gaps which indicate required actions;

      – Integrate: connects to other systems to transfer information and automate specific tasks to drive efficiency and effectiveness;

      – Interface: connect to users of the IT services to provide access into the support resources for communication, knowledge sharing and self-service capabilities.

- **Report and evaluate**
  - Turns data into the information required to manage the end-to-end delivery of IT;
  - Provides access to:
    - Real-time information via dashboards;
    - Near real-time analytics;
    - Historical and trend reporting;
  - Includes cost and service performance.

Having established a framework for all of the capabilities that are required, the next step is to begin to overlay the tools capabilities required and assess the current and proposed tools against these requirements to identify gaps and overlaps. See Figure 4.7.

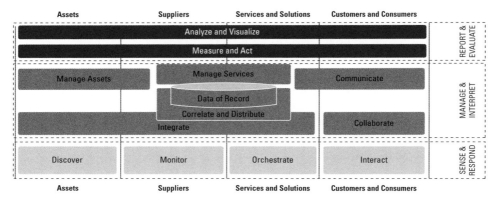

Figure 4.7   Reference Architecture Framework

This framework can then form the basis for the evaluation of tools usage and sourcing.

4.5   Tools configuration

While there are many tools that can fulfill the fundamental functional requirements of IT Service Management, none have been designed specifically with a multi-sourced environment in mind. Where multi-tenant models have been developed, they are aimed at a single supplier serving multiple customers, rather than multiple suppliers delivering to a single customer. However, with a small amount of careful configuration, large steps can be made in improving the tools support to a multi-sourced environment.

Incident management routing and resolution: one common model for incident management tooling is through the use of 'bridging' or 'e-bonding' the incident management systems of service provider and customer. In this model, an appropriate messaging interface is used to transfer tickets from one system to the other and updates are channeled back. Where the level of interdependence between services is low and the configuration items within each service are closely aligned to the Service Providers, this model can work well. When these are not true, this model becomes challenged.

For example; a single service that requires collaboration between an infrastructure provider, application provider, network provider and desktop services provider, may need to go to all teams for diagnostic activity before successful diagnosis. This process will be further hampered if these teams don't have a common view of the affected components and their dependencies, whilst inconsistent naming conventions and classifications will add further confusion. Consistent configuration items require further integration and validation. In one example, a single transaction had approximately 276 mappings, validations and corrections of the fields between two ticketing systems and the resulting orchestration interface could therefore process 7-8 transactions per second, rather than the 3,000 in the original specification.

Incident management SLAs: the typical scenario in incident management is that there is an end-to-end SLA that has been agreed with the customer and more than one downstream provider may be required to collaborate to resolve a reported incident. The typical challenges are that:
1. Each provider has specific exclusions to the measurement of their SLA – typically the scope of services which are provided by other organizations;
2. For the SLA clock to start requires some level of acknowledgement from the receiving supplier, often resulting in incident tickets spending more time 'between' providers than actually being worked on a fix.

By configuring individual supplier and end-to-end service level objectives (SLOs), both the performance of the aggregate service and each Service Provider service can be measured. Problem investigations can then be focused on the appropriate area; either the integration of the Service Providers to meet the aggregate service performance levels or discussions with an individual Service Provider if they are failing to meet their contracted SLAs.

The complexity of most environments and supplier ecosystems makes it difficult hold a single Service Provider accountable for the aggregate service levels and so it should be left to the SIAM function to measure and take appropriate improvement action.

Service request management: in the area of service request management, typically the first stage of maturity will be to add provider-specific items to the service request catalog. As maturity grows however, it becomes essential to build 'aggregated' catalog items that span multiple Service Providers. In this case, as with incident management, measurement is key. By creating the service request models using tasks, it becomes possible to measure both dimensions:
• The time taken (against a target) by any specific Service Provider;
• The time taken by IT as an organization to fulfill a request, including any time lost in the transfer between Service Providers.

Although it is difficult in contractual terms to make one Service Provider commercially accountable for another's performance, giving each service request a delivery owner makes the solution self-monitoring and enables the identification of any bottlenecks simpler and more straightforward. This approach avoids the need to create volumes of 'cross- supplier procedures' that need to be managed and maintained and allows the providers and the Service Integrator to focus on delivering the needs of the customer.

Change management: change management modules in most tools are already configured in a way that supports multi-sourced environments because the division of tasks is typically at the support team level which tends to naturally align. However, to operate effectively in a multi-sourced environment, change management does need to be planned effectively:
- Contractual definition of change needs to be clearly defined so that items which can be undertaken as a standard change vs minor or major enhancement are clear and do not introduce delay;
- Each supplier's scope of change must be clearly defined, for example; does a change to a piece of infrastructure wholly encapsulated within the supplier's service, that is predicted to have no impact to the performance or availability of the service, require a change to be made in the common systems;
- What are the delegated approvals for change? Are retained resources always required to approve any change? How will the process ensure that they have sufficient knowledge to fulfill that role? A single change can often have an impact on multiple Service Providers and because of the additional boundaries created by contracts and organizations, cross-discipline knowledge which would exist in a wholly retained organization is less likely to catch inconsistencies.

The tools area that does need specific focus though, is in the definition of change scope. Due to the typical structure of a change, the multi-sourced model makes it more difficult to define the scope of a change such that it achieves the end-objective but does not traverse any of the supplier boundaries:
- If changes are raised at a level that does not achieve the whole of an objective – there is an additional role which is required to sequence the individual changes to ensure that they are all completed as specified and are correctly sequenced;
- If changes span multiple providers, approval models can become overly complex and the time taken to complete, review and approve changes can become extended.

At this time, there does not appear to be a single perfect answer to these challenges.

Problem management: as with incident management and service request management, the effective use of a model whereby each supplier is performing specific tasks and one supplier takes the overall lead for each problem record enables effective cross-supplier collaboration and supports the objectives of multi-sourcing. This works well for reactive problem management.

Proactive problem management at an individual Service Provider level should be part of base-services in each contract, with the SIAM function owning cross-provider proactive problem management investigation and identification. As with other environments the effective use of cross-provider knowledge management and CSI can be used to help delivery of corresponding improvements:

- Known errors logged against specific services can be reviewed as part of supplier and service governance to drive investment planning and supplier interlock meetings;
- Appropriate creation of continual service improvement (CSI) opportunities, if managed correctly, can drive further opportunities for collaboration amongst suppliers. More details on this are included in Chapter 7 Continual Service Improvement (CSI).

Knowledge and configuration management: knowledge management is often overlooked and yet is crucial to successful delivery of the Service Integration vision. Depending on the organization, 'knowledge' can be considered to be a number of different things, each of which have different ways of being managed and different benefits associated with them. The role of knowledge management is to identify where each of these types of knowledge are stored in the environment and identify which need to be made available to more than one group; consumers for self-service, the service desk for first-level resolution or other support teams for incident diagnosis and change impact assessment. A key success factor for SIAM is to ensure that while the encapsulation of processes and tools can be an effective way to reduce complexity, data and knowledge should be explicitly required to be shared across the environment to support decision-making and knowledge-sharing across IT.

- Knowledge of the environment – typically considered to be 'configuration management' and managed within the service knowledge management system (SKMS). This data gives context to configuration items managed by each supplier in terms of their relationship to services, customers and other providers. Typically managed to a reasonable level of maturity, in a specific tool, but often too much focus is placed upon the details of each item rather than their relationship to the things around them. This approach will encourage supplier focus to be inward and the SIAM focus to be on the suppliers. This includes information about the service portfolio and the service level expectation placed upon it, which define the expectations of the service. The focus of the SIAM function should be on 'how does each item relate to a service and therefore a customer?'
- Knowledge of the service – typically considered as service provider documentation; run books, design documents, procedures etc. This data explains how each service is configured and how it is operated. Since a significant part of the multi-sourcing value proposition is the portability of services between providers, this area *should* be one of considerable focus. However, experience shows that this is very rarely the case. Lack of focus in this area results in limited knowledge transfer between Service Providers when service transition occurs, impacting the quality of service and often leading to incidents for an extended period of time afterwards as all the 'known errors' are rediscovered. The role of the Service Integrator in this area should be to define a set of minimum standards which need to be met in this important area, ensure that processes include steps within them to maintain this documentation and identify the impact of gaps in it (root cause analysis in problem management). In instances where work-instructions are considered

the intellectual property of the Service Provider, the customer-facing documentation may not contain the specific details of how; nevertheless the Service Provider should record that the task is performed. The master set of this documentation is best stored within the retained organization infrastructure to ensure reviews can be conducted as required and the knowledge is retained.

- Knowledge of the service operation – information about the performance of the service over time, both technical performance and service performance, sets expectations and benchmarks which should be available to identify events that need to be addressed. This information should cover the change history of the service (and its related components), previous incidents and problems.
- Knowledge to enable others – within a multi-sourced organization, the boundaries between the different suppliers will tend to become natural barriers to knowledge sharing. However, to achieve operational efficiency requires that knowledge be shared not only with the customer, but also with functions and services delivered by other providers. One common approach is to work on a 'shift-left' strategy for knowledge in a multi-sourced environment, with each provider being contractually incentivized to shift 'work' one step closer to the end-user. See Figure 4.8 for more information. Within this model:
  - Support teams provide information to other teams to support incident resolution and change management impact analysis;
  - The delivery organization enables the service desk through provision of decision trees, frequently asked questions and standardized and simplified processes;
  - The service desk enables the user by making information and processes even more accessible, so encouraging self-help and self-service for the user;
  - In more advanced environments, this concept has been taken even further, introducing autonomic (or self-healing) systems which fix issues before the user is impacted, and use advanced analytics with sensitivity analysis to identify end-user satisfaction issues before they get to the point of becoming a complaint.

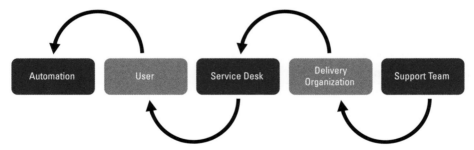

Figure 4.8   Shift Left Knowledge Management

Reporting: reporting is a capability which should be an outcome of every process and in a multi-sourced environment this approach can lead to a federated approach to data maintenance and report creation. The process for producing reports and the consistency of the data used to report them is a critical success factor for Service Integration, as all the reports will ultimately be feeding aggregated data which will be used to govern the IT portfolio.

> **Practitioner tip:**
> Encapsulation of processes and tools can be an effective way to reduce complexity but sharing of data and knowledge should be explicitly required.

One IT organization that had become focused on the output of their suppliers rather than the outcome for the business had taken it a step further and delegated the majority of their service reporting to the individual delivery teams. While the service level reports being produced by their providers showed green SLAs across the 7,000 open incidents and service requests, further investigation showed that there were in fact, four times as many tickets (incidents, service requests, and problems) 'lost' in the system. A combination of gaps between Service Providers, poor system implementation and no double checking was causing a massive impact on the services being received by the end-user.

In a multi-sourced environment, there are plenty of opportunities for discrepancies to appear in reporting before even considering any attempts to cloud the picture:
• Gaps between Service Providers through differences in scope;
• Gaps between Service Providers in the routing of tickets;
• Differences in exclusions between Service Providers; waiting for another Service Provider or third party supplier is often excluded from SLA measures, waiting for the customer is almost never included.

Having a consolidated view of service and ticket performance against which the different provider views can be assessed helps to identify these gaps and address them. Gaps in reporting can often be the difference between customers being satisfied or not and are a big opportunity to identify contractual enhancements and continual service improvement opportunities.

> **Practitioner tip:**
> Gaps in reporting can often be the difference between customers being satisfied or not and are a big opportunity to identify contractual enhancements and continual service improvement opportunities.

4.6 Common tools governance and sourcing

There are two factors which need to be reviewed when evaluating which tools to source versus which tools to own internally, these being:
1. Who requires the tool functionality to deliver the services for which they have been contracted? Typically, this would be either one or more suppliers in the ecosystem;
2. Who requires access to the data contained in, or produced by, the tool to deliver the services for which they have been contracted? Typically, this would be either one or more suppliers in the ecosystem.

Where more than one supplier uses the tools, to execute their contracted services, these tools become a candidate for retained ownership as **common platforms**. The same is true if multiple suppliers are required to interact with the data in the tool in near or real-time. If the tools' functionality is required by only one supplier and the data is only required for reporting or evaluation, then the tools should be sourced as part of a broader service.

> **Practitioner tip:**
> Where the tools are used by more than one supplier to execute their contracted services, these tools become a candidate for retained ownership as common platforms.

Due to the brownfield nature of most corporate IT environments and the diverse types of service which can be consumed from the market (from staff augmentation, through 'as a Service', to business process outsourcing), there can be many exceptions in any environment. For example, there may be one or more providers who have their own tool that integrates to the centralized standard to deliver as closely as possible to an integrated solution. Where these exceptions exist, end-to-end service performance should be evaluated against SLAs to assess whether that situation should be permitted to continue or if some other action is required.

4.6.1   Owned versus sourced common platforms

While at face value, the question as to whether to own or source the tools is a very simple one, there are a number of complexities and implications which need to be considered as part of this decision. Ownership can be based on ownership of the assets, the data or the governance of the platform and the services required to operate the platform can be sourced individually or as part of a single 'platform as a service' type model. There is also the question of funding, who pays and who receives the benefit is not as simple as it might seem at first glance. This section will highlight some of the lessons learned in this area and highlight the areas that need careful consideration.

The 'ownership' of any tools platform can be broken down into six component parts, see Figure 4.9:

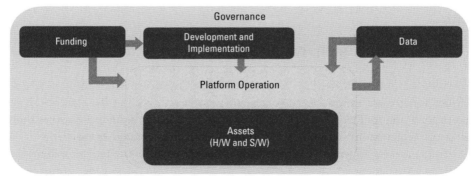

Figure 4.9   Tools Delivery Components

- Governance guides the overall direction of the platform and typically holds the organizational responsibility to ensure that the tool is capable of meeting the functional and non-functional requirements placed upon it;
- The same organization that owns governance typically controls the funding and investment in platform change and operation;
- Data refers to that which is pushed into the tool (see Section 4.3.1) as described above and that data which is managed and maintained within the tool;
- Development and implementation and platform operation (including maintenance) refer to the services associated with changes to the platform and general day-to-day operations;
- Assets are the hardware, software and human (staffing, skills and experience) assets required for the platform to operate, including associated support agreements.

Using this model, there are three common archetypes for service management tooling in a multi-sourced environment.

1. Wholly sourced tools:
   a. These are tools which are sourced as part of a larger service and are predominantly encapsulated within that service with little usage by other parties, apart from as a consumer;
   b. Examples: monitoring, discovery or orchestration tools which are specific to the in-scope services. Although other systems may request activity or receive data – they are reasonably independent and best delivered by the service-specific expertise.
2. Wholly owned tools:
   a. These are tools which are wholly owned and delivered by the retained organization. They are typically tools which need to be used by all Service Providers in a way which is required to be consistent to support Service Integration;
   b. Example: the primary IT Service Management tool which is required to be consistent across all Service Providers. The level of integration required between individual supplier operations and data is high and the data needs to be consistent to facilitate integration.
3. Tools 'as a service':
   a. These are tools which are owned by the retained organization in terms of data, governance and funding, but the services required to operate and enhance the platform and the hardware and software assets are procured from another organization 'as a service';
   b. Example: there is an increasing array of service management, reporting, event correlation and visualization platforms available 'as a service' which reduces some of the resourcing, hosting and integration challenges for the retained organization.

In all of the 'owned tools' models, the retained organization would typically retain the data, governance and funding. The reason for this becomes evident when beginning to discuss the cost and benefit equation of developing and enhancing these cross-supplier tools.

Due to the nature of these cross-supplier tools, the benefits and impacts of change need to be considered above the individual supplier level, so the decision regarding platform development priorities can only be made by the retained organization. Changes that would benefit one partner may have implications for another, or all others, and that benefit needs to be assessed against the costs involved. Likewise with the cost of change, since there is no easy way for one supplier in an environment to pay another, the cost of change will fall on the retained organization. Again, this situation requires a maturity in the supplier relationship model to ensure that:

- An improvement or increase in efficiency for one or more suppliers is recognized as being a benefit to the retained organization;
- Where appropriate, the benefits derived from tooling change can be reflected in commercial or service improvement benefits back to the retained organization.

4.6.2   Common tools governance

In the case of these common tools, it also becomes necessary to integrate the governance of change to ensure that the changes requested by one supplier do not have a detrimental impact on the services provided by another. An effective change management process should prevent any direct impact on operating services, but it will not manage the negotiation and, at times, compromise is necessary to get the best from shared tools. An effective and collaborative governance process will be required to find the optimal balance of functional requirements for each tool. One example is in the area of cumulative impacts such as ticket classification. While it makes sense at an individual provider level to implement deep levels of detail, when viewed at a system level, or from the perspective or reporting or a service desk, creating a classification system of hundreds of different types will inevitably impact the overall usability.

> **Practitioner tip:**
> An effective and collaborative governance process will be required to find the optimal balance of functional requirements for each tool.

A common mistake is failure to consider usability as an important non-functional requirement. This needs to be taken into account from the start, as complexity at the user interface will inevitably lead to non-compliance, invalidating chunks of system functionality. More and more often in outsourcing contracts, the Service Provider is able to deliver at a lower cost due to leveraging resources in lower cost countries (either off-shore, near-shore or landed resources). It is therefore essential to recognize that in such instances people can work on multiple projects and will very rarely have the same natural language or the same level of experience of using IT systems. Thus the usability of both tools and processes are more important than in a traditional IT organization and must be judged across the entire range of those using them.

A model that has proven popular across multi-sourced organizations in the financial services and oil and gas sectors is to have tiered governance around these complex tools involving representation from all impact suppliers in a Community of Practice model as shown in Figure 4.10.

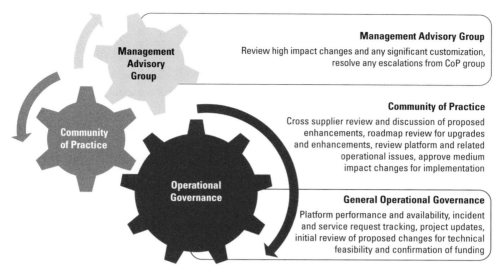

Figure 4.10   Example of Common Tools Governance Framework

In addition to the standard governance considerations in tools of this kind, such as the level of customization, impact on upgradeability, cost etc., the Community of Practice (CoP) also brings the views of the multiple suppliers into the decision-making process encouraging not only ownership, but also shared best practice and collaboration.

To assist in the decision-making process and ensure sufficient control, it is recommended that the terms of reference and delegated authorities are agreed up-front using a matrix similar to the example included in Figure 4.11. Since the Service Providers themselves cannot directly fund initiatives with the team that manages the tools, whether they are retained or sourced, the funding approval has to come through the retained organization service owner type role.

Scope/Cost Impact	Small (less than $x, agreed funding)	Medium (between $x and $y, agreed funding)	Large (greater than $y, or not agreed funding)
Individual Team	**Low** • Impact limited to the requestor's support groups/service requests • Cost impact low and funding agreed with requestor	**Medium** • Impact limited to the requestor's support teams/service requests • Cost greater than clipping level but funding agreed	**High** • Impact limited to the requestor's support teams/service requests • Cost is greater than the clipping level and/or funding is not agreed
Multiple Teams	**Medium** • Impact is broader than requestor's scope and affects multiple groups • Cost impact low and funding agreed with requestor	**Medium** • Impact is broader than requestor's scope and affects multiple groups • Cost greater than clipping level but funding agreed	**High** • Impact is broader than requestor's scope and affects multiple groups • Cost is greater than the clipping level and/or funding is not agreed
System Wide	**Medium** • Impact is system wide, operational/upgrade impact low • Cost impact low and funding agreed with requestor	**Medium** • Impact is system wide, operational/upgrade impact low • Cost greater than clipping level but funding agreed	**High** • Impact is system wide, operational/upgrade impact high • Cost is greater than the clipping level and/or funding is not agreed

Figure 4.11   Governance Decision Making Example

In this example the decision to proceed and implement would be part of operational governance for low items, medium items would be decided at the Community of Practice level and high impact items would need to be ratified by the Management Advisory Group. The objective of the model is to delegate increasingly to the CoP group over time, balancing supplier decision-making power with measurable benefits to the services.

5 Sourcing Service Providers in the Multi-Sourcing Framework

5.1 Introduction

The world of IT services is highly competitive, with a large number of organizations delivering hardware, software, services or complete outsourcing partnerships. Many Service Providers focus on a particular niche and aim to be considered as 'best-of-breed', while other Service Providers offer a broad set of capabilities that enable them to commit to end-to-end outcomes. As a result there are very few enterprises today that do not use outsourcing or out-tasking as part of their IT services supply-chain. The result is an ecosystem of Service Providers; it is the level of collaboration required between these Service Providers which drives the need for Service Integration.

Figure 5.1 is a schematic overview of such an ecosystem in its context of serving the business. It may contain dozens of companies, each with their own role and contract. There are hardware and software suppliers, and the Service Providers can be divided into minor and major. The Service Integrator provides the coordinating entity towards the retained IT organization, which is supporting the business.

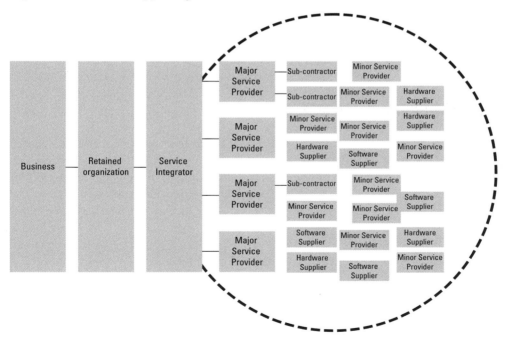

Figure 5.1   Overview of multi-service provider ecosystem for IT services

In the previous chapters we have discussed what a Service Integration function is and how it could be designed. This chapter will focus on sourcing strategies to ensure that the business requirements will be translated into IT service requirements which can then be sourced using a mix of internal and external resources that are working in the Service Integration space in order to provide optimal business outcomes. The requirements that must be placed upon other services if they are to exist in an integrated environment will also be discussed.

Sourcing has been a complex element of IT strategy for many years, and in our opinion, the rise of multi-sourcing has introduced even more complexity as the dependencies between partners have become as important as the services themselves. Therefore the experience with regard to this topic, specifically related to Service Integration, will be shared.

The sourcing process will be covered in detail, and ideas and experiences shared on how to cope with the challenges. When an organization has decided on a multi-sourcing strategy, what are the requirements that must be put in the RFP for the major Service Providers? And what is required from potential Service Providers for the Integrator role? And how can it be ensured that all Service Providers will work effectively in the multi-sourcing ecosystem?

As a next step the content of the outsourcing contracts will be discussed. There are multiple elements that need special attention in a multi-service provider context and, although the authors do not have a legal background, some of their lessons learned will be shared.

This chapter will conclude with some advice on managing an outsourced contract and will discuss how to keep control and suggest how to organize performance management in a multi-service provider environment. The impact of cloud services will also be addressed.

5.2   The sourcing process

Selecting and contracting Service Providers is a complex process in itself. It is an essential part of implementing a multi-service provider ecosystem, whether the Integrator role itself is outsourced or not. In this section some practicalities around the sourcing process will be shared. Please be aware that this process is focused on selecting major Service Providers. The specific procurement of other elements of the ecosystem such as hardware and software are not covered in this book.

5.2.1   On getting third party advice
Buying a house is something most people don't often do. Getting a real-estate agent to help is a good example of outsourcing because of a lack of skills. Outsourcing Service Integration is an activity that most organizations have not done before and will not do often, so getting third party advice is a good move in general, and it represents a sourcing decision in itself. When planning the sourcing of a Service Integration function, the extent to which external advice is taken is a crucial first question.

> **Practitioner tip:**
> Third party advisors can only be as good as the questions they are required to answer.

What value can third party advisors bring? Experienced third party advisors will provide their intellectual capital on Service Integration, which will consist of templates for RFI/RFP questions, statements of work and contractual terms and conditions. They can gather the requirements and customize the demand for services to be put on the market. They can bring external resources with hands-on experience in implementing and delivering Service Integration in a multi-sourcing context. They can also facilitate the process by providing project offices, handling Q&A sessions with potential Service Providers, scoring RFI/RFP answers etc. In addition they can customize their consulting offering depending on the specific needs of their customers and where skills are lacking. Typically, the IT procurement department will include people with experience in selecting and contracting IT services. There may have to be multiple other talents in-house to drive and support the process as well.

5.2.2   Cost drivers of the sourcing process
There are many cost drivers to influence the throughput time and cost of a sourcing process. Amongst these are the size and complexity of RFI and RFP, number of parties invited, customization of requirements, complexity of contract negotiations etc. Third party advisors can influence the cost drivers of such a process significantly by guiding their customers through the best options for each of these drivers.

The number of Service Providers invited to the process is the most important cost driver. A low number will have the disadvantage of lack of choice. A large number of Service Providers, however, will result in a lot of work in reading, reviewing and scoring proposals and listening to Service Provider presentations. It is not uncommon to witness sourcing processes where more than 15 Service Providers were invited to bid. The solution presentations alone took six weeks! One can only wonder how to remember – let alone differentiate – the value propositions of the individual Service Providers.

5.2.3   Service framework
"What to outsource?" is the next question, considering also the scope of services. This should be based upon a business service catalog, which is defined between the business and IT. The business service catalog defines the way IT services will be delivered to the business. It will mainly consist of aggregated services (e.g. business applications or a mobile workplace), which need to be decomposed into smaller service elements in the technical service catalog. The technical service catalog can have multiple layers and in each layer there may be multiple alternatives to use (e.g. different brands of smartphones, different hosting platforms, different types of cloud services, etc.).

The usual approach to prepare a sourcing exercise is to group the services of the technical service catalog into service bundles. A requirements register can be used to assign each requirement to a service bundle; in this way any overlap of scope of services can be avoided. Defining the bundles can seem straightforward to a large extent, but there will always be a portion of the services that is arbitrary.

As early as 1975 Stevens, Myers and Constantine stated principles for good structures in the context of system development for IT. One of their statements is "A structure is stable if cohesion is strong and coupling is low" (Stevens, Myers, & Constantine, 1975). This statement applies to IT services as well, so define the bundles in such a way that they adhere to the 'minimal coupling, maximal cohesion' principle. For example, consider the backend servers that are supporting the end user computing environment. They could be part of the end user computing services, but for stronger cohesion one could also consider including them in the data center services bundle.

However, it is always possible that potential Service Providers may have a slightly different approach to their service portfolio and are not happy with the defined service bundles. Therefore it can be useful to ask, as part of a Request for Information (RFI), whether the Service Providers have suggestions on changes to the presented service bundles.

Practitioner tip:
Keep an open mind as far as suggestions from Service Providers are concerned.

The edges of the service bundles need to be clearly defined. Therefore a demarcation of activities between two bundles is needed to establish further clarification on the boundaries of the service bundles. As an example, let's consider the data center network. This is the local area network that connects all of the equipment in the data center. Managing this LAN can be part of a 'network services' bundle or a 'data center services' bundle. If it is considered to be part of the data center service bundle, demarcation with the network bundle will be needed in terms of which of the bundles will include the switches between the WAN (which is included in the network service bundle) and the data center LAN. Both Service Providers will be capable of doing it, but you do not want to outsource this activity twice, or leave it out of the scope of both contracts resulting in a gap in service.

And what about the gaps that arise in this example when a WAN change results in a configuration change requirement for the switches to be updated and vice versa – how is this catered for across Service Providers? Will the Service Integrator coordinate things and take ownership of such a change, or will the Service Integrator let the Service Providers sort it out amongst themselves?

5.2.4 Scope
The scope of services expected to be part of a bundle can be defined by means of a specific statement of work. This statement needs to be crisp and clear and limited to the exact responsibilities of the Service Provider, and where necessary the customer responsibilities are to be included as well. Demarcation between customer and Service Provider, as well as

demarcation of a service bundle with other bundles, can be documented by adding clarifying appendices to both bundles. A widely used technique to document and clarify demarcations is the RASCI table. It lists detailed activities with the party being: accountable for the result, responsible for the deliverables, supporting the activities, informed or consulted. Apart from demarcation of scope this technique is also used to clarify process responsibilities as part of an end-to-end OLA. In the latter case, the end-to-end process manager, being part of the Service Integration function, will manage adherence by the Service Providers to the RASCI table. Beware, though, that RASCI tables pose a risk of providing a false sense of accuracy. The devil is in the detail and discussions between parties often occur on a more detailed level than is reflected in the RASCI table. Table 5.1 is an example of a RASCI table, where the Integrator role is not outsourced.

Table 5.1 RASCI table example for retained Service Integrator

	Activity	Service Integrator	Application Management service provider	Infrastructure service provider	Network service provider	Service Desk service provider
Incident Management						
1	Define and manage the incident management process	R/A	I	I	I	I
2	Provide and maintain the ITSM tool for incident management	A	I	R	I	I
3	Incident Logging (triggered by event management)	A	I	R	R	I
4	Incident Logging (triggered by end users)	A	I	I	I	R
5	Incident Classification	R/A	S	S	S	R
6	Incident dispatch to resolver group	A	S	S	S	R
7	Monitor overall incident status during its life cycle	R/A	I	I	I	RS
8	Escalate critical incidents to service integrator when encountering problems with incident resolution across multiple service providers	I	R/A	R/A	R/A	S
9	Coordinate service provider internal investigation/resolution/escalation	I	R/A	R/A	R/A	S
10	Coordinate investigation/escalation across service providers	R/A	S/I/C	S/I/C	S/I/C	S/I/C
11	Chair incident management meetings and review s and resolve Incident management related issues	R/A	S/I/C	S/I/C	S/I/C	S/I/C
12	Managing exceptions of rejected & unaccepted incident records	R/A	C/I	C/I	C/I	S
13	Monitoring process metrics	R/A	I	I	I	RS
14	Initiating and review ing the Service Improvement related actions based on incident management reports	A	R	R	R	R
15	Coordinating the Service Improvement related actions based on incident management reports	R/A	C/I	C/I	C/I	C/I
16	Close the incident	A	S	S	S	R
17	Publish overall daily report	A/R	S	S	S	S

When outsourcing the Service Integration function, the Service Integrator will be part of the service framework. Therefore a statement of work for Service Integration will need to be developed. In this statement of work the sourcing model and service framework, as described above, should be reflected. The RASCI table in Table 5.2 would have an additional column to split the responsibilities of the retained IT organization and the Service Integrator.

Table 5.2   RASCI table example for outsourced Service Integrator

	Activity	Customer Retained IT	Service Integrator	Application Management service provider	Infrastructure service provider	Network service provider	Service Desk service provider
Incident Management							
1	Define and manage the incident management process	R/A	S	I	I	I	I
2	Provide and maintain the ITSM tool for incident management	C	A	I	R	I	I
3	Incident Logging (triggered by event management)	I	A	I	R	R	I
4	Incident Logging (triggered by end users)	I	A	I	I	I	R
5	Incident Classification	C	R/A	S	S	S	R
6	Incident dispatch to resolver group	I	A	S	S	S	R
7	Monitor overall incident status during its life cycle	I	R/A	I	I	I	RS
8	Escalate critical incidents to service integrator when encountering problems with incident resolution across multiple service providers	R/A	I	R/A	R/A	R/A	S
9	Coordinate service provider internal investigation/resolution/ escalation	I	I	R/A	R/A	R/A	S
10	Coordinate investigation/ escalation across service providers	I	R/A	S/I/C	S/I/C	S/I/C	S/I/C
11	Chair incident management meetings and reviews and resolve Incident management related issues	C	R/A	S/I/C	S/I/C	S/I/C	S/I/C
12	Managing exceptions of rejected & unaccepted incident records	C	R/A	C/I	C/I	C/I	S
13	Monitoring process metrics	R/A	S	I	I	I	RS
14	Initiating and reviewing the Service Improvement related actions based on incident management reports	R	A	R	R	R	R
15	Coordinating the Service Improvement related actions based on incident management reports	I	R/A	C/I	C/I	C/I	C/I
16	Close the incident	S	A	S	S	S	R
17	Publish overall daily report	I	A/R	S	S	S	S

A common approach to determine the scope of the Service Integration function is to use the ITIL process framework as a checklist. For each process it should be decided whether end-to-end process ownership should be retained, outsourced as part of the Integrator role, or delegated to each service provider separately. For each of the processes it is evident that it will also be part of each Service Provider's scope, creating a 'matryoshka dolls' effect of process implementations.

For example, end-to-end demand management is a process that many organizations are likely to keep in-house, because it concerns the relationship between the IT organization and the business units. So, while some organizations would like to see it as part of the retained Service Integration function, others will prefer to keep it within their retained organization, as part of their strategic IT function.

End-to-end incident management is a process that could very well be part of the Service Integrator role, as incidents can originate from every Service Provider and restoring normal service often requires detailed operational coordination.

Asset management, meanwhile, is an example of a process that could be delegated to each Service Provider, in case each Service Provider retains ownership of the assets in their own scope.

5.2.5 RFI and RFP

One way of getting additional ideas on how best to structure the service and supplier portfolio, and in fact make decisions about whether or not to source the Service Integration function, is to submit specific Requests for Information (RFI). The purpose of an RFI is to get a better understanding on what the market has to offer. As part of the RFI several consultative questions can be asked, to which the Service Provider will be invited to provide advice. For example, a typical RFI question could be: "Considering our organization, which parts of the Service Integration function would it be advisable for us to retain, and which parts would you (as a supplier) be willing to take into the scope of your offering?" The answers to such questions will provide the customer organization with a lot of food for thought with regard to the optimal demarcation and sourcing of the Integrator role.

Keep in mind, though, that questions like these and their answers, will take considerable time to digest. Therefore, the number of potential Service Providers invited for an RFI should not be too high. Five or six should be more than enough. In order to get to this shortlist, it is quite common to create an initial list of 'knockout'-criteria. If a Service Provider does not qualify against one of these criteria, it is immediately out of the race and will not be invited to bid for the RFI.

> **Practitioner tip:**
> Any service provider added to the 'short list' will have a significant impact on the time and
> money spent on the sourcing process.

It is important that all stakeholders of the future service contract are involved in the RFI process. This includes procurement, legal, finance, HR as well as technical competences, service management and security. Where the initiative for an Integrator role is taken by an IT infrastructure department, the application management department should become involved – and the other way around. Depending on the scope of processes and functions included, the role of the Service Integration function can (and in our view should) span beyond service operations, as it needs to cover the full lifecycle of all services and their ongoing improvement. In the case of a retained Integrator role, it is expected to be an independent department reporting directly into the CIO office – not as a part of either the application or the infrastructure services department.

There are differences between providers in terms of how easy it is for them to become integrated. Therefore, requiring a proven track record and ongoing relationship are valid inputs into the selection criteria. These factors may also have a direct impact on the cost of the Service Integration function and the amount of transition work that needs to be done. Be aware that the field of Service Integration is not a mature one. Gartner Outsourcing Trends 2013 highlights that Service Integration services are entering the 'Trough of Disillusionment' (Gartner, 2013). This would imply that it could be considered a maturing field by now. However it is good practice to ask for specific experiences and references: has the provider done this before – and what were the results, and which lessons were learned?

The answers to the RFI will provide the customer organization with a wealth of ideas on how to design and implement the Integrator role. The added value of such an RFI is the two-step approach: by digesting the RFI answers the design will be sharpened and perhaps even the scope will be finalized.

The results and lessons learned from the RFI process will be used to detail the requirements for the Request for Proposal, or RFP. Table 5.3 provides some insight into the key differences between RFI and RFP: each has their value in the process and should be used at the right moment. It is good practice to send such an RFP to fewer Service Providers than the RFI. In that case there is a 'down-select' to two, maybe three Service Providers. It is not a wise thing to down-select to only one Service Provider in this phase, for obvious procurement reasons. However, there may be a 'favorite' already, in which case the other Service Providers can be used to benchmark the number one candidate. And of course an open eye for every offer that is made in response to the RFP should be kept.

Table 5.3   Differences between RFI and RFP

Request for Information (RFI)	Request for Proposal (RFP)
Initial stage of sourcing selection	Later stage of sourcing selection
Customer is unsure about what is required and what is available on the market	Requirements are clear
Limited customer information shared	Much customer information shared, for example in a virtual data room
Five to six Service Providers	Two to three Service Providers
Open, investigative questions	Focus on comparability of proposals
Standard approaches requested	Specific solutions requested
Limited investment from Service Provider needed	Large investment from Service Provider needed
Indicative pricing required	Detailed pricing sheet required

The questions in the RFP should be more closed in nature, focusing on the comparability of the proposals. There are several ways to enforce this comparability:

- Be specific in the structure of the answers expected. For example, when asking for a description of the technical solution, provide a template with a table of contents along with an expected maximum number of pages per chapter;
- Ask for compliance to the most important requirements by demanding a 'yes' or 'no' answer;
- Provide volume baselines in the pricing sheet with which every Service Provider needs to work;
- Provide draft contract schedules and demand feedback from the Service Provider;
- Follow-up on the experience with Service Integration by demanding reference calls or reference visits.

Selecting the best Service Provider is not a topic that will be discussed in detail here. Best practice is to work together with the business stakeholders to define the business objectives of the sourcing process, and translate those into IT objectives and sourcing objectives. Be sure to define the decision criteria aligned to these objectives, so that every Service Provider knows what their offer will be measured against. The decision process should be defined as well, as part of the overall planning of the sourcing process.

Although RFPs are very useful instruments, do not make a decision based on factual RFP answers alone. Personal preferences of stakeholders and past experiences with Service Providers will play a role in any case. As IT services is a people business, make sure that the delivery leadership as well as the sales team of potential Service Providers are introduced. Are these people capable of making the objectives happen?

5.2.6   Contract negotiations and signing

For the establishment of a multi-service provider ecosystem that is consistent and aligned, the contract negotiations need to be orchestrated in a mature way. Deviating from standard service parameters in any way will complicate the overall Service Integration. Therefore the customer sourcing professionals must act as a single team and hold alignment sessions on a regular basis. For example, it is best practice to ensure that the contract terms of the major

Service Providers and the Service Integrator are equal, so that they have the same service commencement date. This will ensure a clear set of roles and responsibilities and avoid a fuzzy period where old and new contracts and responsibilities are mingled.

> **Practitioner tip:**
> Contract negotiation is an important step in relationship building and gaining mutual trust. It is not a battle that one party must win and the other party will lose.

Whenever there is a tough subject to discuss (e.g. service levels and associated penalties) the customer should reach an agreement with the Service Integrator first and then present that to the other parties as the overall framework with which every Service Provider needs to comply. Make sure that every Service Provider commits to reaching an agreement on operational level agreements with the other relevant Service Providers before the service commencement date.

A further word of caution needs to be raised here about the focus of the negotiation phase. In far too many cases, the focus of negotiations is to drive the last ounce of cost out of the deal before final signature.

When possible, celebrate the contract signings with multiple Service Provider representatives to kick-off the collaborative culture in a positive way.

5.2.7   Transition and transformation
In order to change from the existing service delivery to the new, multi-service provider/service integrated model, multiple projects need to be executed in a controlled way. There is a distinction between transition and transformation.
- **Transition** is the program to change responsibilities from the incumbent (internal or external) Service Providers to the new Service Providers. This may include people changing jobs: HR transition of employees to the new enterprise. The principle of 'person follows job' is applied here. But transition could also mean the take-over of hardware and software assets as well as projects and third-party contracts. Typically this will be in the first six to twelve months of the contract.
- **Transformation** relates to the projects that the new Service Providers will undertake to establish the target-operating model in which they can execute according to the contractual commitments. This can include implementing new technology, moving work to off-shore locations etc. Transformation is typically executed within the first half of the agreement (for example, in years one to three of a five year agreement).

Let's now zoom in on the kind of projects one could expect when implementing an Integrator role. Ideally the SIAM function will be set up while the other services are relatively mature so that they are stable, and then the Service Providers will be re-contracted into the new structure rather than trying to do it all in 'a big bang'. The less certain the processes and service level achievement is – the more commercial risk the Service Provider for Service Integration will load into their cost and the less certain the delivery outcome would be.

The implementation of an umbrella ITSM tool suite is very likely to happen as part of such a transformation. Along with it, the process framework can be deployed and Service Providers will need to start using the new tool or to build automated interfaces to interact with the tool. Most Service Providers will opt for automated interfaces, because their preference will be to standardize their own internal architecture to serve multiple customers and contracts in order to be as efficient and cost-effective as possible.

When the old contract is monolithic (major Service Provider type) the multi-service provider ecosystem needs to be implemented as a whole, including OLAs, cross-service provider procedures, multi-service provider governance, new or changed service levels, consolidated reports, etc.

With multiple Service Providers running transition and transformation programs in parallel, a multi-service provider steering committee will also be needed to facilitate all the dependencies between the Service Providers. The retained organization will either take the lead or delegate this to the major Service Provider/Service Integrator.

5.3   Contractual aspects

Apart from the specific scope of services there are multiple other elements that need to be addressed as part of any outsourcing contract – and it is no different for a Service Integration contract. Some specific elements for Service Integration will be covered, assuming that the reader either has the experience in 'traditional' outsourcing contracts or will be able to get this information elsewhere.

Although details may differ as a result of contractual negotiations, the legal basis to every service contract should be similar for all Service Providers. If the plan is to outsource the Integrator role, make sure that the requirement for every Service Provider to acknowledge and accept this role from a third party is included. Requirements include acceptance of authority of the Service Integrator, transparency of data (except for commercial data), exchange of data via automated interfaces, as well as the commitment to establish OLAs.

The overall contract, or master service agreement will usually be written under the law of the country where the headquarters of the business are situated. In case of international service delivery there can be a requirement for local invoicing for local subsidiaries of the business that will be the service recipient. For these countries local service agreements will need to be agreed, which will refer to the master service agreement.

5.3.1   Reversibility and exit plans
Service Provider lock-in is a risk that every outsourcing customer must acknowledge. It refers to the situation where a retained organization has become so dependent on a Service Provider that it becomes nearly impossible to switch to a different Service Provider. This

can be caused, for example, by a lack of knowledge or skills with the retained organization, combined with specialist knowledge and a lack of documentation provided by the Service Provider. Also the sheer scope and size of a specific service bundle can be the cause of supplier lock-in.

For Service Integration contracts the risk of Service Provider lock-in is also a factor because of knowledge and skills. The Service Integrator will have a good insight into the end-to-end service delivery, which will not be transferrable overnight.

> **Practitioner tip:**
> The concept of reversibility provides the business with a risk mitigation strategy.

Reversibility is implemented in the form of contract clauses that demand that the Service Provider is able to transfer its knowledge, as well as any assets and operational data back to the retained organization. In order to make this actionable, an exit plan can be required as part of the contract. Such an exit plan describes how the Service Provider will transfer its services back to the retained organization or to a different Service Provider. The exit plan must be updated and renewed on a regular basis, for example once or twice a year. A typical exit plan should contain elements like:
- A timetable with milestones and deliverables for the transfer of services;
- A list of assets, third party contracts and documentation to be returned to the customer;
- A list of running projects, their status and expected end dates;
- A list of Service Provider employees who are critical to deliver the transfer of services and who should remain committed to finalize the transfer;
- Any dependencies on the business, the retained organization or third parties, for the transfer of services, including expected resources;
- A plan on how to return all data owned by the business.

Beware that external Service Providers are usually not very keen to lose a contract and then have to transfer their knowledge to a competitor. Such an action plan looks nice on paper, but when a relationship ends in a less than positive fashion, close control will be needed to ensure proper and professional execution of the agreed exit plan.

In any case, the risk of supplier lock-in can be reduced by keeping more control, retaining architecture skills, maintaining end-to-end process ownership or owning assets. Most standard contracts contain additional protection clauses as well, for example that the customer will retain ownership of all data produced while performing the services.

For Service Integration, the authors have yet to come across situations where a business has moved from one external Service Provider to the next; however, as Service Integration will become a more mature service offering, the same risks will apply. The examples which are currently known are either long-term relationships, in which a limited Service Provider lock-in is accepted due to the partnership; or the Service Integration is being insourced as a result of strategic reconsiderations with respect to managing and controlling end-to-end services. As a result of the second scenario there have been employees who were in a Service Integration role working for the Service Provider, and have subsequently been offered a job at their customer in order to continue doing what they had already been doing for some years.

5.3.2 Definitions

Most contracts have a separate contract schedule with definitions. Make sure that this schedule is the same for all major Service Providers. Ensure that the definition of 'Service Integration' and 'Service Integrator' in included in this schedule to create a common understanding.

> **Practitioner tip:**
> Crafting the definitions schedule should be a combined effort of subject matter experts and contract managers.

5.3.3 Statements of work

This is the contractual description of the service framework as described above, detailing the scope of work for each and every service bundle. This should be supported by alignment of definitions, service levels, service windows, maintenance windows, change plans, release plans, IT continuity plans etc. The easiest way to do this is to work with a common requirements database as well as a service and contract framework as described above.

5.3.4 Service catalog and service request catalog

Create transparency by providing the complete service catalog to every potential Service Provider. This will enable them to get a good idea of the context in which they may be operating. In many cases, the provided service may be encapsulated within an aggregated service in the catalog so they will also need to understand their upstream and downstream dependencies. And when the retained organization has a standard tool and standard process established already – they can be added as an attachment to the contract as well, as they provide an excellent context of the services and will stimulate further standardization amongst the major Service Providers. The orderable items of each service of the various Service Providers will need to be consolidated in a service request catalog, which should be implemented using the umbrella service request tool. As part of the contractual framework, there should be a single consolidated service request catalog, where each line item is assigned to a single service bundle.

5.3.5 Pricing and chargeback

As there is limited experience with the outsourcing of Service Integration, the authors have not yet seen a convergence of resource units that can be used to put a price on a managed service contract for Service Integration. The known examples of contracts are based on either a fixed price or on a time and material basis. With fixed price, the risk of variations in the workload is with the Service Provider, who will likely put a premium on its offer as a result. For time and material, however, this risk is entirely for the customer organization. Key to successful collaboration would be to introduce some element of shared risk into the contractual relationship.

An approach that contains the best of both worlds and has successfully been used is a capacity-based deal, in which the Service Provider's solution is based on a fixed amount of FTE for the activities in scope. However, in order to remain aligned with the actual need for Service Integration services, one should consider building in a regular joint assessment of the existing capacity versus the actual need. This could then lead to a correction of the resource capacity, resulting in less or more FTEs provided by the Service Provider. Such a discussion should take place at least every three months in the first year – and depending on the stability of the environment, with less frequency in later years.

Such a discussion demands partnership; but it should be fully understood by now that partnership is the kind of relationship that is needed to make the outsourcing of an Integrator role successful.

5.3.6   Invoicing and chargeback

Where services are aggregated, it has to be decided what the invoice is going to look like and how the costs are being distributed amongst the business units of the enterprise. There are many options here and it is beyond the scope of our book to discuss them in any detail. The Service Integration service framework adds complexity to this already complex field.

Be aware that the retained organization will ultimately remain responsible for performing chargeback to the business units, its internal customers. Therefore, for a retained Integrator role, it makes sense to combine the invoices of the various Service Providers into a consolidated invoice using agreed chargeback keys with the business units. The costs of the Integrator role would then be put on top of the integrated invoices to create a price for the aggregated service.

For an outsourced Integrator role this is a less likely activity to be in scope since Service Providers will typically be reluctant to share commercial information between each other. They may collaborate for this particular customer, but for the next customer contract they are likely to be competitors again.

The prices (and invoices) that are required from the Service Providers must include data that enables the chargeback mechanism. Depending on the pricing mechanism, this needs to include a level of granularity that is based on a lot of consistent foundation data. Consider for example project hours from multiple Service Providers (with different hourly rate structures) that need to be invoiced to the sponsor of the project. A common tool with a 'single truth' will establish this management information.

5.3.7 Service levels

In each and every service agreement, be it internal or external, there will be a schedule on service levels. COBIT provides both the context and structure on how to arrive at a concise and complete set of metrics that can be used as service levels. It is based on a cascade of goals. Starting with the enterprise goals, the IT goals can be derived and from the IT goals, the goals of individual IT processes as an enabler can be identified.

For our discussion on Service Integration, the most relevant COBIT process is APO09 Manage Service Agreements. Table 5.4 provides the details from COBIT on how the IT-related goals and process goals of this process lead to a set of metrics that can be used as a template for developing a service level framework.

Table 5.4 COBIT context of metrics to be used to manage service agreements (ISACA, 2012)

	Area: Management
APO09 Manage Service Agreements	**Domain: Align, Plan and Organize**
Process Description Align IT-enabled services and service levels with enterprise needs and expectations. Including Identification, specification, design, publishing, agreement, and monitoring of IT services, service levels and performance Indicators.	
Process Purpose Statement Ensure that IT services and service levels meet current and future enterprise needs.	
The Process supports the achievement of a set of primary IT-related goals:	
IT-related Goal	**Related Metrics**
07 Delivery of IT services in line with business requirements	• Number of business disruptions due to IT service incidents • Percent of business stakeholders satisfied that IT service delivery meets agreed-on service levels • Percent of users satisfied with the quality of IT service delivery
14 Availability of reliable and useful Information for decision making	• Level of business user satisfaction with quality and timeliness (or availability) of management information • Number of business process incidents caused by non-availability of availability information • Ratio and extent of erroneous business decisions where erroneous or unavailable information was a key factor
Process Goals and Metrics	
Process Goal	**Related Metrics**
1. The enterprise can effectively utilize IT services as defined in a catalogue.	• Number of business processes with undefined service agreements
2. Service agreements reflect enterprise needs and the capabilities of IT.	• Percent of live IT services covered by service agreements • Percent of customers satisfied that service delivery meets agreed-on levels
3. IT services perform as stipulated in service agreements.	• Number and severity of service breaches • Percent of services being monitored to service levels • Percent of service targets being met

In order to manage and control a Service Provider there must be an agreement on how the performance is measured and what the consequences of under- and over performance will be. Service levels are the most widely used mechanisms of performance measurement and they come in a number of varieties.

> **Practitioner tip:**
> Use existing measurements and recent performance reports as input for the service level discussions.

It is very important that service levels (and service hours) are standard in each major IT services contract. Inconsistencies will create multiple issues in service delivery where multiple parties are involved. After all, Service Providers tend to organize and behave as directed by the service levels. By definition, alignment of Service Providers will be very hard if they do not work according to the same service level definitions. When the Service Integrator needs to resolve incidents (end-to-end) within four hours, it cannot be that one of the other Service Providers has six hours to resolve the same type of incidents. This may seem an open door, but there have been situations like these.

An example of how small differences in definitions can lead to significant frustration between Service Providers is illustrated in a story on the service levels for problem management based on one of our case studies.

Service Providers A and B both agreed on a contract with the same customer, although the contract with Service Provider A was negotiated a little later. As a result, within the contracts there was a small change in the definition of the service level for implementing a solution for a problem (see Figure 5.2).

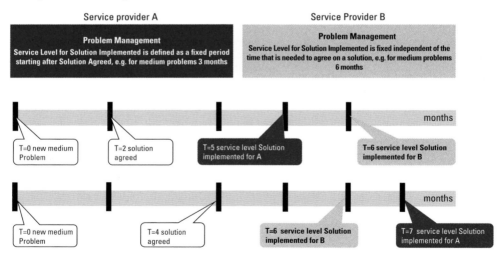

Figure 5.2   Inconsistencies in definitions can lead to operational frustration

For Service Provider B, solutions for medium priority problems had to be implemented within six months after the problem was identified. The customer then negotiated the same service level with Service Provider A, but a different approach was agreed: the service level target time for an implemented solution was not measured starting from the day the problem was identified, but instead from the day the solution to the problem was agreed.

There was no right or wrong in these solutions, they were just different. This led to some serious discussions in practice, where Service Provider A and Service Provider B had to work together to implement any solution for the problem. The reason for this is evident in Figure 5.2. For Service Provider B the deadline for implementation was always six months. In the upper case, the solution was agreed after two months and consequently the deadline for Service Provider A was actually one month before Service Provider B. In the lower case Service Provider B had an earlier deadline. As a result, there was always a perceived difference in the urgency and priority of implementing the solution.

This issue was solved only at the contract renewals stage, when a standardized service level regime was contracted with both Service Providers.

The root cause can be a lack of centralization for IT procurement, resulting in inconsistent terms and conditions for different Service Providers. Coordination of requirements could result in a minimum set of mandatory requirements that are common for every contract and may not be altered. This could result in shared SLAs. The only other way to address this is to have contractual SLAs for the individual scope of services and less formal KPIs for the end-to-end services.

Generic best practices for service levels include:

Service levels should be aligned with the business outcomes of the service.
There can be conflicting interests here, because different stakeholders can have different objectives. Typically, from a senior management level, low cost and stable service are very important, while at a tactical level more importance is placed on things like high process quality and end user satisfaction. These conflicting interests should be well-balanced, because a Service Provider cannot be forced to offer the lowest price and the highest quality at the same time; distinguish between critical and non-critical service levels to reflect every stakeholder's perception of what is important in terms of the service in a consistent way.

Service levels should be defined crisply and clearly.
A vague description of a service level in a contract can be the cause of a lot of frustration, when the actual perception of the performance differs from the measured performance.

Example: "incident resolution for on-site support measured as an average for all incidents" can raise dissatisfaction in two ways:
1. For senior executives, because their expectation of the service is much higher. This has resulted in VIP support services, where quality of on-site support is much higher for a premium price;

2. If remote locations are included in the measure, performance for remote locations can be very bad, while the overall performance remains within the agreed boundaries.

Another good example is average server availability. The owner of an application whose server is the only one in a thousand that is down for a week is very likely to be unhappy, while the average availability will be reported 'green'.

Service levels should be SMART
It is a widely accepted view that quantitative objectives should be SMART (Doran, 1981):
- Specific – target a specific area for improvement;
- Measurable – quantify or at least suggest an indicator of progress;
- Assignable – specify who will do it;
- Realistic – state what results can realistically be achieved, given available resources;
- Time-related – specify when the result(s) can be achieved.

Service levels are not different. When a service level is agreed, it must be clear how this is going to be measured. Trying to work out how to measure a service level after an agreement has been signed can become a big challenge, especially where service level penalties are at stake for the Service Provider. Using standard measurements with standard reports from existing and already implemented tools will be much simpler and cheaper than creating add-ons to tools using customized reporting. The realistic perspective of service levels must also represent a level of business judgment as to possible impacts from unforeseen circumstances and deal with them as part of the ongoing governance processes

Service levels should be under the control of the provider
If the score of a service level is significantly influenced by actors and/or stakeholders outside the control of the Service Provider, an underperformance cannot be blamed on the Service Provider. For example, a data center Service Provider is not likely to accept a service level on the response time of an application, if they do not have control over the network architecture. Another common issue is where the service level is dependent on information to be provided by the retained organization (which they cannot provide) or has a dependency on the retained organization (for review, approval or funding) that they cannot meet. This results in exclusions that open up gaps between the contracts and issues with end-to-end service.

Service level targets should be fair and make sense
Service level targets that prove to be very hard to achieve in practice, even when both parties agree that a good service has been delivered, are suboptimal and counterproductive. A way to mitigate this is to introduce the concept of self-adjusting service levels, which:
- Can be changed relatively easily within the context of the contracts
- Evolve with the organization
- Can be different per customer set.

Taking these generic guidelines into consideration, how can service levels for the Service Integrator role be defined? First, a clear distinction needs to be made between service levels that are measuring the service delivery performance of the individual service bundles, and the service levels that are measuring the performance of the Service Integrator. For simplicity, let's call them SD service levels and SIAM service levels respectively.

Now consider the Service Integration sourcing models that were introduced. For the 'retained SIAM' sourcing model (shown in Figure 5.3) the retained Service Integrator can be held accountable for both SIAM service levels and SD service levels. The Service Providers will only have SD service levels as part of their contract.

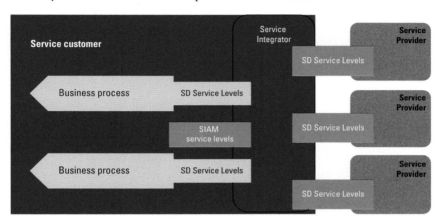

Figure 5.3   SIAM service levels and SD service levels in retained SIAM sourcing model

A Service Guardian Service Provider (Figure 5.4), could argue that it would not be fair to be penalized twice for the same underperformance. That would not be the case when the Service Integration services would only be measured against SIAM service levels. On the other hand, when the Guardian Role Service Provider is accepting accountability for the end-to-end performance, there is little need to have additional SIAM service levels defined and contracted.

An independent operational Service Integrator (Figure 5.5) will most likely not take accountability for the end-to-end performance, thus SIAM service levels need to be defined here. The SD service levels will be the service levels that the Service Integrator is measuring; the SIAM service levels are the service levels that the Service Integrator is measured against.

SD service levels can be determined from the contractual agreement with the Service Provider. A set of service levels and objectives may already be in the contractual agreement with that Service Provider and therefore would be used as a basis for the Service Integrator to measure per Service Provider performance.

SIAM service levels should be aligned to the scope of services and the mandate and accountabilities of the Service Integrator.

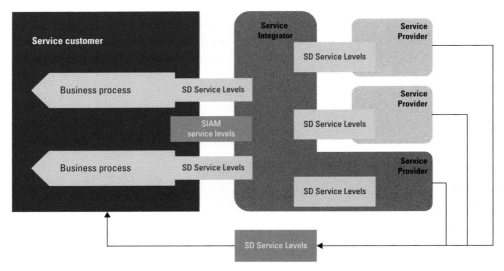

Figure 5.4 SIAM service levels and SD service levels in a service guardian sourcing model

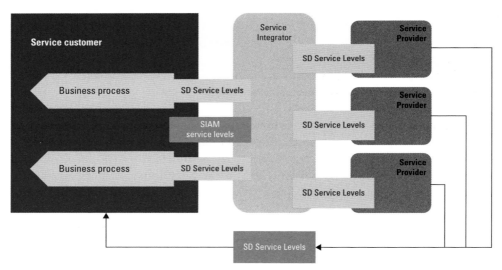

Figure 5.5 SIAM service levels and SD service levels in an independent SIAM sourcing model

When the Service Integrator does not hold end-to-end accountability, possible SIAM service levels could be:

SIAM service levels (Service Integrator only):
- Number of issues/disputes between Service Providers that are escalated to the Service Integrator;
- Attendance at formal multi-supplier governance meetings by all internal and external Service Providers;
- Number of achieved outcomes by multi-service provider service improvement initiatives;

- Combined retained organization and Service Provider satisfaction – this is a satisfaction survey taken from representatives across the organizations of the ecosystem.

When the Service Integrator has end-to-end responsibility over all internal and external Service Providers, the following service levels will be possible candidates to implement, but probably not with penalty clauses:

End-to-end (all service bundles):
- Business application availability;
- First call resolution;
- Percentage of decrease in the number of incidents and/or problems;
- (Major) incident resolution;
- Multi-service provider problem resolution;
- Percentage of successful multi-service provider changes;
- End user satisfaction;
- Multi-service provider project success (in time, within budget, all deliverables).

5.3.8 Management of operational data

In any IT outsourcing environment, it should be a principle that the customer 'owns' the operational data for the environment with rights to assign access to that data. However, with the introduction of the Service Integrator (as an 'agent' of the customer) some more granularity of ownership of data is required.

The multi-service provider ecosystem will only be effective when a single truth can be established and shared between the (major) members of the ecosystem. Therefore both Service Providers and the Service Integrator need to commit to a reasonable level of data transparency.

Clearly, the overall collection of operational data, aggregation and dissemination back to Service Providers is a necessary part of the Integrator role. However, a lot of very useful information can be gleaned by the analytical reporting of that data. As a consequence, care must be taken that commercially sensitive data is not inappropriately shared between Service Providers.

For instance, project prices and other rates from one Service Provider cannot be allowed to leak to another when they are in a competitive scenario. However, when a service catalog is published the 'retail' pricing must be available. This is particularly the case when building aggregate services from multiple Service Providers. There have been cases where the Integrator role was outsourced and the customer was required to aggregate the pricing of component services to alleviate concerns about commercially sensitive rates becoming available.

Similarly, while it is essential to be able to share service level and performance details across teams in order to allow work to be done, service credit allocations or negotiations that might occur as part of a corrective action should not be shared.

> **Practitioner tip:**
> Do not share the commercial data of Service Providers with their competitors.

One effective mechanism is to include a set of policies on data management within the contract appendices. Of course this should be a standard set of policies for all parties – otherwise management of the policy is difficult.

Broadly, there needs to be a simple classification scheme for data that describes the breadth of publication permitted. A default policy for each data category can then be applied, which is used for overall management of collection, collation and publishing of data. When it gets to the tool implementation this greatly simplifies access policies.

As an example, please consider the policy as specified in Table 5.5.

Table 5.5   Example of Classification scheme

Classification	Description	Examples of default classifications
0	Public information	Any information that was publically released e.g. press releases.
1	Available to customer, Service Integrator and any current Service Provider	Most operational data, e.g. service availability, capacity, all ITSM system tickets (read access). This is the default classification of ITSM data.
2	Available to the customer, Service Integrator and the originating Service Provider	Contract scope information, service credit weightings etc. (write access to ITSM data).
3	Available to the customer and originating Service Provider only	Financial information, contract values etc.
4	Customer and Service Integrator only	Rarely used. Could include Service Provider performance management plans.

In Section 5.3.7 on reversibility and exit plans the accessibility of operational data for the business has already been briefly discussed. In the uncomfortable event of a contract dispute it may become a challenge getting access to the data in a timely fashion. Having the right to something or the right to access something does not necessarily mean having the ability to access it as and when you require it. Contractual agreements should also provide for the regular collection of data and the storage of that data off-site where the span of control of the external service provider is limited.

5.3.9   Intellectual property

Customers should ensure that any intellectual property (IP) required for the ongoing support of their business and/or IT environment is retained. However, the legitimate rights of Service Providers to hold market-differentiating information and tools as their IP should be recognized. The value that these things bring should be enabled.

There will be no dispute where the extant environment and tools and processes required to maintain it are agreed to be the property of the customer. But when this IP is declared as property of the Service Provider, leaving remediation or ongoing license fees as a legacy, it must be closely negotiated.

As an overriding principle, clauses are recommended that declare data, systems and tools used to support or manage the extant environment become either the property of the customer, or that the customer is granted perpetual rights to use the IP or product. A contract appendix then supports this clause where the service provider can propose:
• Any IP they wish to claim as retained;
• The remedial action required during unwind (remove, sell, license etc.);
• Any associated fees for the remedial actions.

In order to protect the customer's right to have access to use the IP or product, an escrow agreement is sometimes defined, for example to deposit the source code of a business-critical piece of software with a third party. Under special conditions (e.g. bankruptcy of the Service Provider) the customer then can get access to the IP.

That way, the risks associated with the use of the IP are clearly stated and may be accepted as required. This appendix is then maintained under standard contract change control clauses. It is always better to avoid IP battles than to fight them. For an interesting insight into IP management, please see the 'Art of IP War' reference (McKenzie G., 2015) which uses Sun Tzu's 2,500 year old 'Art of War' as an analogy.

5.3.10 Miscellaneous multi-sourcing specifics

There need to be very specific contract clauses developed to enable an effective multi-service provider ecosystem. Although the authors do not have a legal background, a few of these topics need to be pointed out. Some aspects to pay attention to are:
• Accountability and control. Service Providers will not be happy to take accountability for something that they cannot control. So when outsourcing the end-to-end accountability for a specific service (and putting a price on that by using service level penalties), it needs to be ensured that the party assigned the end-to-end accountability will be able to execute control over the end-to-end scope. For other Service Providers that are not subcontractors of the selected Service Integrator, this is not a given. Therefore, it will need to be facilitated by the contract. An alternative approach is to ask for a 'softer' kind of accountability and ask them to report on the end-to-end service level and have a target set against it without any penalties attached. So long as the target is set at an achievable level and then improves over time, the business will get the best of both worlds. This can be done by getting the Service Providers to commit to the following:
  – Let them acknowledge that provider X is the Service Integrator provider, which, on the customer's behalf, has the mandate to manage and control their service delivery;
  – Let them commit to jointly develop and agree on a series of operational level agreements in which they mutually acknowledge the scope of services and commitment towards their customer.

- Exclusiveness or not. Whether or not multiple Service Providers will be allowed to bid on a specific project during the term of the contract is something to clarify at the start. If a specific project budget is included, associated with the delivery scope in the contract, that piece of work is exclusive by default. If not, the decision can be taken to make it exclusive or not.
- Multi-sourcing governance. Invite the Service Providers to collaborate by introducing multi-service provider governance structures. For example a common board for continual service improvement with a KPI on joint improvement proposals could be a suggestion here. See Chapter 7 Continual Service Improvement (CSI) for more guidance on this.
- Tooling integration. Let the providers commit to either use, or automatically connect to, the central service management tool, where required. More details on this can be found in Chapter 4 Data and Tools.

5.4   Managing outsourced contracts in a multi-service provider environment

The Service Providers have been selected and the contracts have been signed; transition and transformation is well underway. The service commencement date is the start of a new service framework: the multi-service provider ecosystem.

5.4.1   The contents of the ecosystem

A closer look at the various entities that play a role in supplying IT services to a business will reveal the fact that there are different categories of companies. Each play their own role, some very large and critical, others small but very useful. The Service Integrator must be aware of all contributors to the service and the way these contributors need to be integrated. Such a categorization can be visualized in Figure 5.6.

The Service Integrator will have the closest relationship to the retained organization. Then there will be a group of major Service Providers. They will have multi-year outsourcing contracts, and hold full responsibility for one or more service bundles. And then there is a large group of companies that either act as a minor Service Provider (e.g. by having a software as a service contract for one specific business application), a hardware supplier or a software supplier. Each of the categories require a specific approach.

5.4.2   Managing the Service Integrator

Managing an outsourced contract in a multi-service provider service framework (Archetype C or D) has some specifics to be taken into account compared with managing a 'regular' outsourcing contract (Archetype A or B). This has to do with the unique position of the Service Integrator as a (semi)-independent partner between the retained organization and the Service Providers. The exact relationship depends on the demarcation of roles and responsibilities; there are multiple possibilities here. Normally, the retained organization

Figure 5.6   Central and peripheral sourcing relationships

will work more closely together with the Service Integrator in a 'special' relationship rather than a 'transactional' one (see Figure 2.3 on the Henderson Portfolio of Relationships).

> **Practitioner tip:**
> All Service Providers are equal, but the Service Integrator is more equal than the others.

We have already established that the Service Integrator will be controlled against different service levels. There will also be separate, bilateral governance between the retained organization and the Service Integrator. In these meetings, topics with regard to the performance of individual Service Providers can be discussed. Escalated disputes between Service Providers must be discussed. In general, Service Providers should resolve any disputes that arise between them by themselves, when necessary mediated by the Service Integrator. Therefore, escalation to the retained organization should be limited and probably related to commercial discussions only. It is important that these disputes are resolved quickly and in a controlled way. Unresolved disputes can harm the relationship between Service Providers and will hinder end-to-end performance.

5.4.3   Project and changes

There should be agreed processes and procedures for projects and changes. Each Service Provider will have arrangements in the contract on how to deal with minor and major enhancements of the service. Parts of these enhancements can be included in the base contract, as they are expected to happen and budgeted for. Examples might be standard changes, security patching, capacity upgrades, and technology refreshes etc. Most of these changes will also be contained within the scope of the Service Provider. However, some changes may not be anticipated and will need additional funding.

Larger enhancements and non-standard changes are more likely to be implemented as a result of (application) projects; these are typically multi-service provider by nature and the changes can have a business impact as well, e.g. when the functionality of an application changes.

Whenever changes are not included in the agreed services, it is common practice that the Service Provider is asked to provide a proposal for the change or the project (if the change requires significant effort). In a multi-service provider environment, such a proposal will need the cooperation of multiple Service Providers. Who will take the lead? It can be the retained organization or the Service Integrator by default. One could also decide to have a lead Service Provider based on the activities and scope of the project. For a network upgrade, the network provider could be the lead Service Provider.

The involved parties will need to come up with their respective proposals for the project. They will share their activity plan, the milestones and the resource requirements as well as their interdependencies. Most probably, however, they will not share their price. This commercially sensitive information will go to the retained organization directly – and the business will decide whether to continue with the project. Having a lead Service Provider assigned will limit the project management overhead for the other Service Providers. A project office could be shared with resources from multiple parties in order to provide an effective project portfolio management support.

5.4.4 Step-in

Step-in refers to the situation where a retained organization overrules the existing hierarchy and governance in order to take control of part of the execution of the outsourced services.

Note that, in the event of disaster recovery or major incident, cooperation between the business, the retained organization and the Service Providers is not regarded as a step-in so long as both customer and supplier remain active in their respective agreed roles and responsibilities. It does become a step-in, however, when for example a major incident owner from an external Service Provider, assigned by regular governance to resolve an incident, is replaced by a customer manager who takes over the Service Provider's responsibilities from that moment onwards. The retained organization should always be prepared to take such a step when needed to secure their business objectives.

Step-in may occur at two different levels: the retained organization takes over from the Service Integrator and the Service Integrator takes over from a Service Provider. Both are uncommon, should be avoided and used as a last resort only. The risks of step-in are multifold:
• Does the party taking over have the knowledge and skills to do a better job?
• If the situation does not improve after step-in, who is liable for the damages?
• When and how is the original situation restored – and what about trust?

Mature outsourcing contracts have specific clauses for step-in situations.

5.4.5   Onboarding

Onboarding refers to the introduction of new Service Providers into the multi-service provider ecosystem. This can be any new minor Service Provider or supplier delivering hardware, software, SaaS or other cloud solutions. For a new major Service Provider the onboarding will be their responsibility and the retained organization as well as the Service Integrator will need a transition and transformation plan to get them on boarded. Minor Service Providers and other new suppliers often get introduced as part of a project – sometimes very visibly, sometimes almost without anyone noticing. However, the services framework that is actually running the services once they have become part of the production environment needs to know. Therefore, the service design package as introduced in ITIL needs to contain a full list of suppliers that have delivered part of the solution for the service package. The Service Integrator can then analyze these suppliers in a structured way using an onboarding procedure. This procedure will check the importance of the new supplier within the ecosystem and, as a result, will decide upon the relative importance and status of the supplier.

> **Practitioner tip:**
> Check the possibility of onboarding of any new third party with every project.

It is the project's responsibility to ensure that new suppliers get onboard according to the instructions received by the Service Integrator. As a typology of suppliers one could distinguish between major Service Provider, minor Service Provider, private cloud provider, public cloud provider, hardware supplier and software supplier. Each of the categories demands a different level of data to be shared in the service support structure and therefore the onboarding procedure should be different.

For minor Service Providers, the contact details of the Service Provider will be enough to ensure that the service desk knows who to call for second line support. But when a major Service Provider is added to the ecosystem, it must be decided whether or not an OLA is necessary with the other major Service Providers and how this new Service Provider will use or connect to the central service management toolset. These decisions will be based on an analysis of their scope, configuration items, contracted SLAs, resolver groups etc. The larger the impact to the overall service support structure, the more likely it will be that this onboarding procedure will result in a set of transition and/or transformation projects.

For software suppliers the license management details are important as well as who will be the owner of the licenses. For hardware providers the maintenance contracts will be important. And, of course, all new Service Providers will need to align with the service structure (service windows, maintenance windows, service levels) and any exceptions will need to be documented.

5.4.6 Subcontracting

Apart from the sourcing of individuals – subcontractors - the term 'subcontracting' is also used for third-party contracts that are managed by the IT Service Providers. It is a common approach for Service Providers to outsource some of the niche capabilities to partners for whom such capabilities are core business. Examples of such subcontracting areas are wide area network providers for network services, mobile carriers for telecom services, data center facilities for infrastructure services or on-site support for end user services. The business should provide guidelines to the Service Integrator as to what can and what cannot be allowed with regard to subcontracting, and under what conditions. This should be part of the contract as well. Consequently, the Service Integrator must control whether the Service Providers comply with these guidelines.

> **Practitioner tip:**
> A Service Integrator must completely understand the contract structure of the services that are provided, including the use of subcontractors.

The sourcing technique used by Service Providers for this kind of services is 'back-to-back' contracting. The requirements of the business are part of the main Service Provider's contract, but are copied into the subcontract. In this way the main Service Provider delegates its responsibilities within the contract to its subcontractor. Such a subcontractor may do the same thing and a chain of subcontracts can be the result. The risk of this is illustrated by the following example.

An outage due to planned maintenance from a network provider unexpectedly caused a whole data center to go down, resulting in a major incident. When analyzing the root cause of this incident, it turned out that the maintenance was communicated upfront and analyzed for its impact by the data center Services Provider. The impact was considered low, due to the fact that the network connection to the outer world was duplicated: one line was subcontracted with network provider A, the other line was subcontracted with an entirely different network company B. This was considered best practice from a continuity management point of view. In this case, it turned out that network provider B had leased its line with network provider A, resulting in both lines going down at the same time – and according to plan. So in this case the root cause was not technical, it was lack of transparency in the multi-service provider ecosystem.

Lesson learned from such an example are that a Service Integrator must completely understand the contract structure of the services that are provided; this includes transparency with regard to the subcontractors.

5.4.7 Performance measurement in a multi-service provider environment

In a multi-service provider environment each and every contract will have their own service levels defined. Now the most quoted issue on Service Integration is having a low end-to-end performance, where every individual Service Provider reports a green service. Having Service

Providers pointing the finger at each other is one of the main reasons for becoming aware of the need for Service Integration in the first place!

Typical issues in multi-service provider outsourcing include:
- There are no end-to-end service levels; by default it is the informal Service Integrator role which will be accountable in this situation;
- One Service Provider does have end-to-end service levels, however it does not have control over the end-to-end service delivery. This is likely to result in a troubled relationship with that Service Provider if the root cause of the underperformance is not found;
- Service Providers have similar service levels, but either the definitions or measurements or service windows or targets are not aligned. Consider the situation where a Service Provider needs to resolve an incident within four hours on a Friday evening, where they have a dependency with a third party. The Service Provider needs to deliver 24x7, but the third party has contracted 8x5. Such a situation would cause frustration with the first Service Provider and the retained organization alike.
- There are end-to-end service levels, but underperformance leads to a 'blame game' – multiple Service Providers accuse each other of the root cause of the underperformance in order to avoid penalties or even more serious consequences for the relationship with their customer. Each end-to-end service chain has its weakest link.

Companies have struggled with these issues, some for years. There can be many causes for these kinds of issues and some of these can take a lot of time to resolve. Let us give a few examples.
- Contract terms and contract change processes. Many outsourcing contract are multi-year commitments with fixed scope, performance and price elements. Changing the contract is not done on an overnight basis;
- Contract terms are determined historically and may not be aligned. In a green field approach one would like to have one Service Provider management department agreeing all outsourcing contracts in parallel, based on the same performance management framework and with the same service commencement date. There are companies who have made this huge effort, with a lot of assistance from third party advisors. Other companies struggle from having distributed procurement and Service Provider management departments, which work together on a limited basis, ending up with a mixed bag of contracts and a resulting lack of integration.
- Reporting lines. Especially in large organizations, IT infrastructure services and IT application services can each have their own reporting line, which converges at CIO level. This puts pressure on the alignment and integration of application and infrastructure services. Lack of cooperation and communication can be the result. The impact can be suboptimal change and release management; there are too many incidents after project go live and a backlog of unsolved application incidents.

5.4.8 Best practice example: multi-service provider common KPI model
The European bank from **Case study 3 – European bank** in Section 1.9.3 struggled with some of the multi-service provider performance management issues as stated in the case

studies and therefore added a new element to the performance management framework in its outsourcing contract renewal cycle in 2010: a multi-service provider common KPI model.

The idea is simple: define metrics where each of the major outsourcing providers can be held accountable. These metrics should be defined based on KPIs derived from the strategic objectives of the retained organization in supporting its business. In this way everyone is in the same boat together. If there is over performance, there can be a bonus for both the retained IT leadership team and each of the providers; if there is underperformance, every Service Provider needs to pay a penalty, regardless of the root cause of the underperformance. Typical metrics that could be part of such a framework include end user satisfaction, business application availability and project performance.

There are some critical success factors for the implementation and management of such a framework:
- Obtaining Service Provider buy-in. It is unnatural behavior for Service Providers to sign up for penalty-based service levels, where they are dependent on third parties. The risk appetite of the Service Providers will be tested as a result. Therefore, time is needed in the outsourcing engagements to explain and 'sell' the concepts of the framework in order to get a buy-in from the Service Providers. The Service Providers that would enter such a framework need to have a significant 'wallet share' of the business' IT budget. This will give them more control over the performance and the business will be an important customer for the Service Provider. These two elements will help the Service Provider's sales teams get their internal approvals for such a framework.
- Alignment of targets with business targets. Sharing common KPIs and objectives with the main Service Providers only makes sense when the targets of the metrics are aligned with the overall targets of the retained organization in their support to the business. This improves the overall contribution to the business targets and creates a collaborative culture between customer and Service Provider: "if we work together in a productive way, we will both benefit". The more the sense of purpose for the Service Providers is improved, the more they understand that their performance is linked to the performance of their customer, which is linked to the business outcomes of the customer. It does make a difference to the perception of an IT operator if they are operating, for example, an infrastructure service which is crucial in running an airline, as opposed to operating an anonymous infrastructure server.
- Internal resolver groups will need to act and perform and be treated in a similar way as external Service Providers. In an ecosystem of Service Providers it should not make any difference whether a Service Provider is internal or external. This may be tricky for some organizations since the way internal Service Providers are normally managed is not as formal as external Service Providers. This is of course due to the lack of a commercial agreement, which necessitates the need for formal performance reviews. For internal Service Providers the performance is on a 'best can do' basis and any underperformance is seldom challenged.

- Multi-service provider governance. The common KPI model encourages the Service Providers to collaborate in multi-service provider governance which aims at measuring and improving the actual scores of the common metrics. Typically there will be three levels defined:
  - Strategic, executive level where the metrics and targets are agreed and the resulting financial impact is discussed and decided upon;
  - Tactical, management level, where measurement reports are discussed, joint improvement efforts are initiated and executive decision-making is prepared;
  - Operational, subject matter level, where the detailed measurements are defined and managed, the results discussed and improvement projects proposed and executed.
- End-to-end Service Integrator. It is evident that one party must take the lead in the common KPI model. This is, by definition, the operational Service Integrator. Whether retained or outsourced, this is the role that should chair the common KPI meetings and resolve any issues that occur.
- Measurable, achievable targets. What is applicable for individual service levels is just as important for the metrics of common KPIs. There must be an objective, collectively approved way to measure them and target setting must be fair for all parties involved. Setting a target too low will result in happy Service Providers, but the business will not get the most out of its services. Setting the target too high will result in frustration. One could consider defining a high 'stretch' target, with a (higher) bonus attached, but this will only make sense if this high target is based on a business requirement. The phrase 'good is good enough' will certainly apply for metrics such as low priority incident resolution. One could consider defining a 'pilot year' in which all measurements and results are operational, except for the financial consequences. This enables parties to gain experience with the framework and, at the end of the year, evaluate the target setting before defining the new targets for the fully operational framework in the next year.
- Stake in the game. Service Providers will need to be asked to put a percentage of their revenue at risk in support of this common KPI framework. In return the business should also free up the budget in order to have a fund to reimburse bonuses for overachievement, should they occur. A CIO whose own individual variable pay is dependent on the performance of the Service Providers should be ready to make such a commitment in spite of Service Provider management considerations.

The bank that started to work with this framework in 2011 has found that the collaboration with their major Service Provider has improved significantly over the years. And so have the end user satisfaction, the business application availability and the project performance.

5.4.9 Contract changes, renegotiations and renewals
Most outsourcing contracts have a multi-year term of at least three years, but for larger contracts the duration is usually five to seven years. For the IT industry, and also for many businesses, five to seven years is a very long time and a lot can happen, which may result in the obsolescence of part of the contract. Companies can merge or become divested – and the same can happen with Service Providers within the ecosystem. The result is a strategic need for proactive contract management.

Outsourcing contracts are large and complex and liable to both large and smaller changes. The small changes are usually combined in a new release of the contract. Larger changes will be handled on an ad hoc basis. Both parties will have a contract manager assigned who will, under normal circumstances, sort things out amongst themselves and provide the joint executive committee with an advice to be decided upon.

When reality is very different from the intentions and/or expectations, parties can decide to renegotiate parts of the contract. This may be caused by underperformance of a Service Provider, new requirements by the retained organization, benchmark results triggering commercial discussions, new technologies (such as cloud in the last couple of years) and the like. The Service Integrator can play a facilitating role in the analysis that precedes a decision for renegotiation. After all, it is the Service Integrator who reports performance to the retained organization and facilitates discussions around new technologies and innovation.

Although renegotiations require a lot of energy, it is not a rare practice. Particularly in good relationships, renegotiations often occur about a year before the end of the contract term. The reason for this is that a win-win renewal could be the result:
- For the business a new solution with newer technologies, better aligned with changed business needs and probably more efficient and thus less expensive – and this being performed by a well-known Service Provider with good knowledge of the enterprise;
- For the Service Provider a confirmation of the relationship, securing revenue for the future in a non-competitive bid and extending the term beyond the existing commitments of the business.

During these renegotiation/renewal discussions the business can always put the RFI/RFP card on the table to open the services in scope to the market again.

5.5   The impact of cloud services

Cloud services have become a significant part of the IT services ecosystems in the last few years. There are multiple types of cloud service models: public versus private, Infrastructure as a Service, Software as a Service, and Business Process as a Service. How are all these relatively new ways of sourcing services affecting the Service Integration aspects described in this book?

First let's differentiate between public cloud and private cloud. Private cloud services are dedicated for one specific service customer. In some instances large private cloud farms can be customized and will then follow the Service Integration principles, enablers and sourcing aspects as described in this book, as they are typically part of archetype C (please see Section 2.4 for a detailed description of the archetypes). Other private cloud services, as well as public cloud services, are definitely archetype D kind of services as they are by no means meant to be customized towards a specific Service Integrator. This raises the question of how easy it is to integrate these services. In general cloud services are easier to procure and deliver, but harder to integrate. It makes sense to use cheap and flexible public cloud services for isolated IT services with limited interactions and interfaces towards the other IT services of the enterprise. Examples can be test environments, specialized business applications and websites.

If the cloud service is Infrastructure or Platform as a Service (IaaS or PaaS) it needs to be integrated in the overall IT architecture. This should be done by defining minimum acceptable criteria on service quality and service levels before procuring such a service. If it is a Software as a Service or a Business Process as a Service (SaaS or BPaaS) it needs to be easy to integrate into enterprise information and still deliver all of the functional and non-functional characteristics.

The ease of procuring public cloud services creates an opportunity for every line of business in the enterprise to procure their own IT services, thereby possibly ignoring the central IT department or the Service Integrator. As with every opportunity, there is a threat, especially in the areas of security, data integrity and regulatory compliance. These three management objectives are and should remain the accountability of central IT in the enterprise. The role of the Service Integrator should be to create and manage policies and best practices on how to procure and use cloud services in the business environment. Similarly, these policies should be part of the requirements for major Service Providers in the sourcing process described in Section 5.2 The sourcing process. The reason is that major Service Providers will be increasingly likely to use cloud services as subcontracted services.

An additional option is that the Service Integrator can elect to take on a cloud service broker role. In this way, the usage of cloud services can be optimally coordinated: knowledge and skills with regard to cloud services will be combined in a central center of expertise, which can serve the enterprise's demand for cloud services in the most optimal way, continuously monitoring the agile cloud marketplace and enabling the flexible transfer of workloads from one cloud provider to the next when this is economically feasible.

5.6   Conclusion

Managing outsourcing contracts in a multi-service provider ecosystem demands more than just managing contracts and managing Service Providers. It has more to do with the orchestration of a group of Service Providers, facilitating optimal collaboration while taking into account the objectives of every organization; all subject to the business objectives of the customer organization.

6 Strategies for Governance and Management

As discussed in Chapter 1 Introduction, the purpose of SIAM capabilities is to ensure that the value promised by the organizations delivering the services is in fact realized. Put simply the intent is to ensure that all parties:
- Are fully aware of their outcomes, expectations and accountabilities;
- Are enabled to deliver those outcomes;
- Are held clearly accountable for these outcomes.

In this chapter we show that success in this area is doing the right things, the right way, doing them well and measuring the benefits. However, what is critically important to enable this advice to be realized, is to make sure that the 'right people' are doing them.

Underpinning much of this book is the very basic principle (perhaps 'meta-principle') that accountability is the basis of authority. To make outsourcing work beyond the 'your mess for less' approach, it is necessary to have the ability to hold the Service Providers to account for the required services. The meta-principle says that it is not possible to tell them *how* to do their jobs without taking at least some accountability for the results. On that basis it needs to be decided *what, when and to what standard* and have the maturity to allow the Service Providers to decide *how*.

Clearly the governance of IT is a part of the governance of the total organization. The technology does not exist for any reason except to support the organizational outcomes. In several organizations there has been an expectation that the SIAM function only affects the service management or operations management parts of the organization. When looking at the end-to-end supply chain of IT inconsistencies typically exist far more broadly across the plan/build/run parts of the IT organization (and potentially the enterprise more broadly) that must be addressed, including the linkages back to the raison d'être. The Open Group's work on the IT4IT Forum clearly demonstrates this end-to-end view of the supply chain.

There are a series of challenges and associated critical success factors that have proved to be good indicators of success. Conversely when these are ignored there is a high correlation with sub-optimal outcomes – in some cases outright failures.

6.1 Formalizing SIAM governance

Governance – it has many definitions and whole frameworks. In this context COBIT definitions are preferred but with a slightly different lens. The typical view of COBIT governance and management is hierarchical with governance above management. In a singular environment, this is quite intuitive. However where there are multiple parties interacting within the ecosystem then it must be understood that there will be layers of governance within *each* of the parties within that ecosystem. This means there is not a single waterfall flow of governance to management levels. It is better viewed as a recursive model – where COBIT-like hierarchies contain Service Providers with their own hierarchy. The parties in the model all have their own internal governance and management and this 'cell' in the ecosystem must be linked to the overall governance and management regime.

What this means in practice is that the enablers for governance will be – to some extent – federated outcomes rather than monolithic outcomes. So the COBIT enablers will exist in multiple parties (customer and supplier) and the SIAM implementation must enable those to work together in a collaborative way.

Shouldn't all governance be formal? Probably not – four sole trader partners working together could have a weekly meeting over coffee and be adequately governed. This should not be confused with having unclear contract agreements. At the very least there should be written agreement between these hypothetical partners that talk about the basis for working together, what happens when a party wants to leave the arrangement (or the others do!) and who owns intellectual property. Once that is done, the contracts can stay in the bottom drawer until needed. The governance of such a small arrangement can be quite informal – yet rigorous. Contract support for SIAM arrangements can be an enabling factor or create a strait jacket constraining the parties. This was discussed in Chapter 5.

In a collaborative environment this decision-making process must be transparent, effective and timely to allow all parties to act in accordance with the intent. 'Commanders intent' will be discussed later in this chapter.

Any SIAM contract should have formal governance and that formal governance should be used to drive any dispute or disagreement to resolution. Whatever the outsourcing environment, unresolved disputes will cause deterioration of the working environment. The authors have known examples of contracts where transition risks and issues have remained unresolved for more than five years into the contract operation. These risks and issues create daily friction between the parties and it is almost always the case that the first step to improving the outcomes is to finally resolve these long standing concerns.

> **Practitioner tip:**
> Clean the slate of old issues up-front – don't allow 'historical enmity'.

In a multi-supplier environment the required resolutions are very often multi-party. In several SIAM implementations the authors have used a three level model with tactical and strategic management and executive level governance with very clear escalation criteria and triggers. This has proven to work well.

Figure 6.1 shows an alignment of this three-layer model to the COBIT view of governance and management. Ultimately the customer retains the strategy and governance accountability.

The SIAM function acts as an agent of the customer. The figure also shows the engagement with the various parties at the three layers but the primary accountability changes. Typically, the SIAM function is accountable for the strategic and end-to-end operational management. Suppliers are accountable within their Service Provider scope.

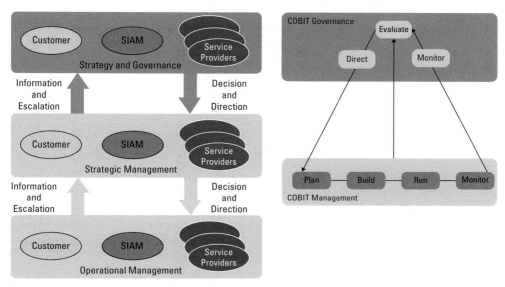

Figure 6.1   Three Level Governance Model aligned to COBIT

The recursion idea allows us to visualize a COBIT-like structure inside each of the suppliers and (potentially) the Service Integrator. Overall governance and management should embrace and align those cells rather than ignore or fight against them.

Using three levels allows simple operational decisions to be managed with low overhead at the level of team leaders or operational forums. Where there is a more intractable concern, this usually relates to contractual obligations and funding, and should be escalated to a more senior level for resolution. In all cases the issues are proactively managed and recorded.

Starting at the bottom of figure 6.1, there is an operational level labeled 'Operational Management'. There will be a joint operational forum that meets regularly – likely to be weekly – with all supplier representatives. This typically takes the form of an escalation-clearing meeting for the day-to-day operational challenges that occur in any environment. This is a working-level forum that allows peers to interact. The expectation is that the standard processes and peer-to-peer communications deal with the non-controversial events. The Service Integrator chairs this forum. The purpose of the meeting is to quickly clear any impediments to the smooth operation of the aggregated environment.

The next level of Figure 6.1 shows Strategic Management forums. There is likely to be more than one. They are typically on a monthly basis, but this is not a hard and fast rule. There will be a joint review of performance and service levels but it is not uncommon for Service

Provider by Service Provider meetings to also occur to deal with specific supplier matters that may not be appropriate in front of other suppliers. Matters related to commercial negotiation and specific corrective action reviews are examples. These may happen only on exception, although typically they are regular events in newly established implementations.

The strategic management level meetings are typically focused on end-to-end performance and management of escalation from the operational levels. It is normal for executive level delivery managers to attend.

The top level of Figure 6.1 is an executive forum. The focus of these forums is management of overall relationship and any matters escalated from the management level. There is usually a joint partnership meeting and also individual Service Provider scorecard meetings. These are commonly quarterly.

Most important to these layers of governance and management is that they drive matters to a resolution. Where matters cannot be resolved for any reason, they should be rapidly escalated. As a rule of thumb, where an action or decision has been stalled for two cycles at any level (e.g. two weekly meetings) then there should be an automated escalation of the action or decision to the next level. If there is an agreed resolution in progress then the action is not stalled.

This automated escalation can be applied in all meetings where risk and/or issues are discussed. If the risk or issue has been noted for two meetings of that forum without an agreed action plan then it is considered to be intractable at that level and escalates to the next level.

> **Practitioner tip:**
> Escalation should be rapid and automatic where resolution is stalled.

Given the goals of a SIAM implementation as stated at the beginning of the chapter, it should be fairly obvious that the governance of the SIAM arrangements is a critical success factor. The goals and benefits of COBIT are very closely aligned to providing the role clarity, enablement and accountability that SIAM is designed to achieve.

Looking back to the 'Are's' of governance that COBIT has long espoused:
1. Are we doing the right things?
2. Are we getting the benefits?
3. Are we doing them well?
4. Are we doing them the right way?

In the SIAM construct the very important additional question becomes "*Are the right people doing them?*" Arguably, in a SIAM environment, if the wrong people are performing the task it is almost inevitable that the four 'Are's' listed above will fail. In 'The McKinsey Way'

(Rasiel, 1999) he states "MECE (pronounced "me-see") stands for 'mutually exclusive, collectively exhaustive' and it is a sine qua non of the problem-solving process at McKinsey." In short, no gaps and no overlaps. Experience in managing roles and responsibilities in SIAM indicates that if the solution is not 'MECE' or someone is doing another party's job then the gaps become issues and the overlaps become gaps, and then issues.

> **Practitioner tip:**
> Role clarity is key to good governance in a SIAM environment.

Of course measurement of the outputs and score-carding the various KPIs is also important to the maintenance of governance. There needs to be fact-based discussion in governance and management forums for them to be effective. Nothing is likely to be resolved if the parties simply state and restate opinions in the absence of verifiable data.

Later in this chapter the concept of model driven design is referred to, looking at the assignment of responsibility and accountability based on principles rather than slavishly enumerating use cases. This has proven to be effective in managing exceptions using what one organization called "commander's intent". By describing the goals required of the collaborative organization, it allows people to act intelligently when they interpret the current situation.

Commander's intent is a term borrowed from military planning. It is a statement of 'what success looks like'. The commander's intent recognizes that the best-laid plans may require improvisation and the intent provides a yardstick to measure tactical actions against the strategic outcome. Helmuth Karl Bernhard Graf von Moltke, a Prussian Field Marshall summed up the need for a commander's intent with his famous quotes:
- "No plan of operations extends with certainty beyond the first encounter with the enemy's main strength";
- "Strategy is a system of expedients".

This approach is characterized today in the German army doctrine commonly called Auftragstaktik ('mission command') although more correctly, Führen mit Auftrag ('leading by mission'). A commander's intent is based on an approach of assuring self-induced action rather than assuring control. This has clear implications for the approach to SIAM governance – managing assurance aligns to the outcome-oriented philosophy rather than a 'command and control' approach.

Wikipedia states:

"For a mission-focused command to succeed, it is crucial that subordinate leaders:
- Understand the intent of their orders;
- Are given proper guidance;
- Are trained to act independently.

The obverse of this is the implicit requirement imposed on superior commanders:
- To give their subordinates no more orders than are essential (every order given is regarded as an additional constraint upon its recipient);
- To be extremely rigorous, absolutely clear, and very succinct in the expression of their commands."

This is a key observation and will challenge the leadership and service provider culture in many organizations. This is a more 'mature' approach to outsourcing management and may take time to nurture.

When Service Providers and enterprises want to deliver 'as-a-Service' and consume that way – in particular when consuming cloud services – the role of the 'commander's intent' and the maturity to allow Service Providers to choose how to meet their mission is essential to avoid SIAM becoming a shadow IT organization. The interactions of service ownership in an environment with aggregated services constructed with components from multiple parties requires clarity of roles and formalized governance. Chapter 3 People and Processes for Service Integration discusses the value of service ownership and its key role in the development of the service catalog. It will be no surprise that the governance of 'services' is important in delivering IT Service Management in a collaborative and federated way.

6.1.1 Management of SIAM

Moving from the establishment of governance in a SIAM implementation, the next topic to discuss is management. How do the ITIL (and other) processes work across the plan, build, run, and monitor management layer? How do the mission statements get articulated? The answer is to some extent "it depends…". It depends on how the organization is structured and the current processes used, and it depends on the modeling used to create the Service Provider bundles. For instance:
- Is the organization structured around plan/build/run competences or does it expect those functions to exist in location-based or line of business units?
- Have the Service Provider bundles been structured around lines of business (application and infrastructure support within one Service Provider) or is it competence-based (hosting, network, application management in bundles)?
- Are there cloud-based services to be integrated – if so are they integrated via a Service Provider or managed directly via the Service Integrator?

All of the variations above – and many more – have been observed.

The goal of SIAM management is to standardize that which can be and manage the variability effectively. On that basis the Service Provider outputs can be abstracted to 'services'. Each service has the usual warranty and utility specific to that service but the roles and responsibilities associated with managing them can be standardized. The roles and responsibilities of the ITIL processes can (and should) be standardized. This may not always be possible in dealing with existing contracts. However most suppliers will understand that the savings associated with the standardization are savings for all parties and there are case studies where the processes were standardized without resorting to wholesale contract changes.

Experience shows that RASCI charts are very useful in capturing the differing roles and responsibilities. Why is the 'S' added to the more familiar RACI? The 'S' stands for 'Supports'. It is really a placeholder for 'more specific detail is required'. So why use it at all? The answer is that practical experience shows it is very useful in development. It allows the 'parking' of a very detailed debate until the higher level of the roles is completed.

For example, for an application provider to undertake root cause analysis of a serious incident for their application, they may require the support of other providers for specific information – perhaps they need capacity data from the hosting service provider or the network service provider. If a RACI chart is attached to the cross-functional scope of work (CF-SOW) then the provider might argue that without that support they cannot be held accountable and responsible. Not using the placeholder 'Supports' for other Service Providers causes a need to drill down quite a long way to get agreement. Using the 'Supports' allows a high level of the chart to be agreed first and to then drill down as required. The 'Supports' allows a 'breadth first' rather than a 'depth first' algorithm which has been found to be successful because it get the high level intent agreed without having to have hundreds of lines of detailed tasks.

The concept of 'generic roles' can be used in combination with the RASCI charts to establish the playing field without excessive detail, which can obscure the intent. Generic roles might include 'service desk', 'client business unit', 'Service Provider 1', 'Service Provider 2' etc. The intent is that any transfer of control in a process is standardized regardless of which supplier is involved – greatly simplifying the process descriptions. The ability to use generic roles, rather than having to name each contract bundle or delivery organization explicitly in the swim lanes (potentially with different responsibilities for each) greatly simplifies the development and maintenance of the processes. It also has significant implications for the automation of the processes. This is why the standardization of cross-functional responsibilities and interactions is so important. Ideally this standardization is encapsulated within contracts but otherwise as far as possible by negotiation.

The practical implementation of generic roles involves the Service Integrator defining how the parties interact. A useful way to think of this process is *codifying the transfer of control*. The Service Integrator defines how control in the process transfers from party to party but not what happens in the execution of the process within that party. If the process is codified using swim lane diagrams, there is a simple visual clue to the transfer of control. Very simply, where a line crosses a swim lane between sub-processes there is a transfer of control. Defining these transfers and ensuring the fidelity of this transaction is the role of the Service Integrator. Where the sub-process executes within a swim lane it is the role of that party to define *how* the sub-process is executed.

The diagram in Figure 6.2 shows one implementation of the method to define the transfer of control between the parties. In many cases the transfer of control was through a tool interface hub (see Figure 6.3), but in some cases transfer of control was a phone call or file transfer. The lane crossings (representing transfer of control) are enumerated. For every enumerated swim lane crossing there was an entry in the procedure documents to describe:

• Source;
• Destination;
• Method of transfer (e.g. via tool hub, phone call etc.);
• Any applicable standards or interface references.

These interactions can also be used to define the use cases for the automation of technical interfaces for transactions and tickets. Note that the process flow is enumerated where it crosses the swim lanes. Where it does not cross a swim lane, the assumption is that the process remains within a supplier. This methodology does allow for sub-processes to span swim lanes at lower levels of drill down but it is best to minimize this as much as possible by coherent responsibility modeling at the top level of process design.

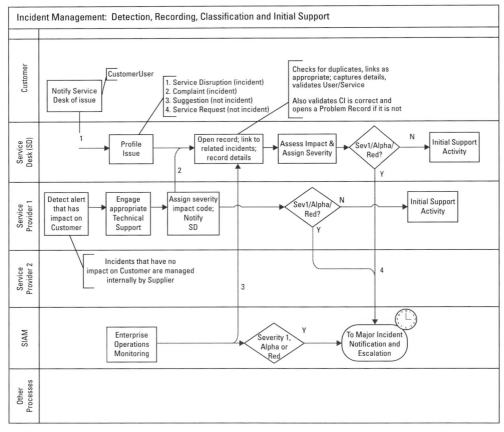

Figure 6.2   Example of a Swim lane Diagram showing Transfer of Control

Figure 6.3 shows the high level interactions between the executive governance and the Service Integration capability. The executive governance must be a retained accountability of the business. Ultimately it is this executive governance layer that must bear the responsibility for the delivery of the IT service to the organization.

The Service Integration layer is shown at the next layer. It can be insourced or outsourced to some level. There are a number of different approaches to defining what should or should not be outsourced. To a large extent the answer will depend on the circumstances of each business. It does take a very mature consumer of outsourcing to significantly outsource the Service Integration layer. Consensus amongst the authors of this book is there is no 'one size fits all' answer to the question of sourcing the Service Integration function.

Next a 'process and tools hub' is depicted. This is not an organizational function but a logical one. It represents the flow of information between parties when working together. The processes will expect the parties to interact on a peer-to-peer basis but the interaction will be based on the Service Integration rules. Where tool bridges are built, the recommended model is a hub or operations bus architecture operated by (or on behalf of) the Service Integrator. This is discussed in Chapter 4 Data and Tools. The use of a single (or tightly integrated) tools hub allows the simplest implementation of the 'single source of truth' service management data.

At the bottom of the figure the delivery teams are shown who are performing the delivery roles as per the bundling strategy. Whether the delivery teams are retained or outsourced is not material to the overall model.

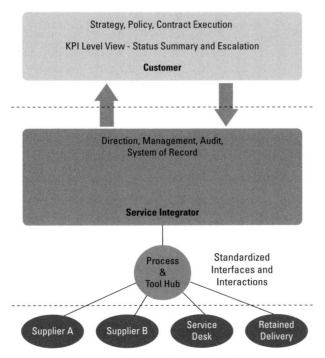

Figure 6.3   Service Integration Tool and Process Context

6.2   Practical lessons for SIAM implementation

6.2.1   Organizational change and sponsorship

The introduction of a SIAM function *will* change job roles and responsibilities for both the delivery teams and those assigned to the SIAM function. There are many good references on organizational change. Whether using John Kotter's little penguins (Kotter, 2005) or Karen Ferris' book on Balanced Diversity (Ferris & itSMF, 2011) or the many other published approaches, there is a need to make this activity a significant part of the plan.

Whenever there is a change to an organization, there is an aspect of organizational change. While this seems like a statement of the obvious, simply transitioning work from one provider to another is a very expensive way of achieving little or nothing at all. To realize the value of the investment requires a successful transformation as well. As a business representative very succinctly said - "Why spend money to change if you don't intend to change anything?"

The work required to implement the organizational change will be proportional to how big a change is being attempted. In the case of a mature organization, working with mature suppliers and good cooperation, then implementation of SIAM is really an incremental improvement. On the other hand if the current state is an organization that is not a mature consumer of outsourcing or is implementing outsourcing of functions for the first time then a fundamental shift may be required.

It should not be surprising that there will be an emotional response from retained people when sourcing changes are executed – notably a very natural tendency for those people to perceive the new partner as an adversary. Preparing people for the change and supporting them through the change is essential.

Where there are adversarial relationships with low levels of trust, this can become a self-fulfilling prophecy. The goal state is to have the retained IT organization and all suppliers (regardless of sourcing) looking for win-win scenarios. This will not happen if even one party has a mindset of 'getting the upper hand'. There are many references from the field of game playing theory related to the 'Tragedy of the Commons' scenario. The key message is that win-win can be a stable state. Win-lose is an unstable state and is typically a transition to lose-lose. It is far easier to manage behaviors to avoid lose-lose than it is to remediate that sort of relationship.

It is certainly possible to assist staff through the emotional adjustments as part of a well-implemented organizational change program. No successful change will happen without active management. What experience has clearly shown is that where IT organizations have tried to short cut necessary organization change programs, there have been some poor outcomes, with many requiring rework of the entire plan.

> **Practitioner tip:**
> Include organizational change in the implementation plan.

The breadth of the change that must be planned will depend on the implementation scope within the organization. Broader scope of optimization (i.e. including more of the organization in the change) will potentially yield better overall results but it is not always possible given the organization constraints as already discussed. The axiom "you cannot help people who do not want to be helped" most certainly applies. Experience shows that constraining the change to the scope that has executive sponsorship is necessary. In some cases, it may also be required to take guidance from another axiom "if you cannot change your people, then you will need to change your people".

There is value in providing Service Integration and process orchestration across specific services, just as a primary provider would over subcontractors. However, to ensure the success of the overall model, it needs to be planned in a way that is extensible across the broader organization to avoid rework if (and when) the rest of the organization recognizes the value and gets on board.

This brings us to an important topic, which is where the mandate to change comes from. While a single clear sponsor simplifies the stakeholder management and can have significant benefits, improvement opportunities will cross organizational boundaries.

There is a need to make a pragmatic assessment of the level of support that exists for change. As an example, in one early case implementations were observed that were limited to 'infrastructure teams only'. There was no mandate to even involve applications delivery teams – there were significant political barriers to engagement across teams. Even so, there was an expectation that the change and release processes were to be included in the Service Integration scope. Quite predictably, the initial implementation was not very successful. Subsequently there was a mandate to implement the Service Integration function more broadly and the results were significantly more successful. That IT organization is now a mature Service Integrator.

> **Practitioner tip:**
> Negotiate the mandate for change as part of the SIAM planning.

In achieving the goal of cross-organizational collaboration, it becomes essential to break down the barriers between the retained and supplier organizations. There is often quite a heated debate when they are confronted with the suggestion that internal teams are held to the same level of accountability and are managed to the same outcomes and measures as external suppliers. (See also 'Separation of Duties' and 'Sourcing Independence'.) Service Integration implementation is a cultural change more than a technology or process change.

> **Practitioner tip:**
> Focus on change readiness and resilience for staff.

Of course, as part of any good change plan there will be skills and behaviors education to be delivered to all parties. It is a culture change – but the best way to change culture is to manage behaviors. 'Good behavior' is encouraged and rewarded; conversely there is active discouragement of 'bad behavior'.

6.2.2 Separation of duties

Key to the modeling of the multi-sourced environment is separation of duties between the Service Integrator and the roles of a performing supplier. It is important to ensure that where the Service Integration function is outsourced (wholly or partially) this separation avoids conflict of interest. Interestingly, a similar concern arises if the Service Integrator is retained and there are some delivery functions that are also retained. If there is any chance that the Service Integration layer will be outsourced in the future it is worth considering this principle in the planning. (See also 'Sourcing Model Independence'.) It is always easier to include the separation of duties up-front than to try to retrofit them later. In fact separation of duties between the plan/audit and implementation functions is just good governance practice anyway. Implementation of this separation of duties requires specific rules, data isolation and staff training.

There is quite a lot of discussion in the industry about what aspects of Service Integration capability can (or should) be outsourced. This principle of separation of duties is a key enabler for more flexible approaches to sourcing. As discussed above, this separation is less important where the IT organization retains the Service Integration role *and* does not retain delivery roles. However for a more resilient implementation over time, separation of duties should be considered a design constraint. Separation of duties and recognition of the role of the Service Integrator as the 'agent of the customer' should be encapsulated in the contract structures.

The most successful practice – and a key differentiator between Service Integration and prime contractor models – is that the retained IT organization maintains the commercial relationships, not the Service Integrator. This means that the roles performed on behalf of the retained IT organization to manage service delivery (the Service Integrator) and the role of service delivery must be quite distinct. The enabling factor is that the SIAM function is contracted to act as agent of the retained organization and this is recognized in all contracts.

Where a supplier is not only the Service Integrator but performs one or more contracts as a performing supplier, it is crucial that the Service Integrator is seen as being separate from delivery. It is also important that the information being supplied is treated with appropriate security and probity. In short, all suppliers need the confidence that they are not disadvantaged as a result of the sourcing decisions.

> **Practitioner tip:**
> Design should include separation of duty to allow management of conflict of interest as sourcing changes over time.

Because the Service Integrator is in the chain of escalation and is also the party that monitors performance of the suppliers, the areas of management of operational data, intellectual property and conflicts of interest should be specifically reviewed.

6.2.3 Management of operational data and intellectual property

The information that can be gleaned by the aggregation of operational data is very powerful. The use of a single source of truth (or system of reference) for the operational data aggregated from the Service Providers creates a data set that can provide not just end-to-end performance information but comparative information and exception reporting for each Service Provider.

As a general principle, the customer should own all operational data and all configuration and support information that is required to run the operating environment. There should be a practical and timely way to access the information if and when required. The customer has to be able to operate even if a supplier suddenly 'disappears'.

It may be that there are legitimately commercially valuable assets being used by a Service Provider to support their customers – indeed that is a value proposition of outsourcing. However customers cannot allow a situation where the operation of the business stops if a supplier disengages. This is particularly true of cloud providers. Where the services are provided on-site or with dedicated assets, a level of control can be secured. Where the assets are shared this is less likely. There is more detail associated with the management of intellectual property in Chapter 5.

As an aside, it should go without saying that the *business* data must be owned and available to the customer. Where cloud services are used and the data is off-site for the customer they *must* own the data and have either on-site copies or escrow arrangements in place. It is inappropriate to rely solely on a cloud provider for business continuity when one of the disaster modes is loss of economic viability of the cloud provider.

6.2.4 Conflict of interest (CoI) management plan

Even if the plan is to have an insourced Service Integration layer it would be wise to make sure that there is a conflict of interest management plan. It is easier to have the necessary policies in place as part of the framework than to try to retrofit them later if circumstances change.

As mentioned above, even if the Service Integrator is insourced there is nothing wrong with making sure there is clarity of roles between the Integrator function and any other functions that may be retained – or outsourced in the future.

In short, the magistrate cannot also be a defendant. This is key to the separation of duties. It should be quite clear that when performing root cause analysis or post incident review – which may have cost or service credit impacts – the parties feel that there is no 'favoritism'. Some of the mechanisms that can be used include:

- Separation of lines of management. The line of management for the Service Integrator is different from that for delivery teams from the same organization. Obviously they will come back together somewhere but the key is that this should occur above the level likely to be motivated by the tactical internal KPIs (such as monthly targets). A senior account executive is far more likely to take the longer term view required to support the separation of duties.
- Training modules for staff from all organizations to understand the way the separation of duties should work as part of the context of the Service Integration framework. This should be included with the overall framework training aligned to both organizational education and other education. This has been covered in more detail in Chapter 3 **People and Processes for Service Integration**.
- Specific executive messages when training integration staff. The staff of the Service Integrator need to know they have 'air cover' to (politely) reject requests from more senior people if they are making requests that are not appropriate. In one example, laminated cards were issued with words to the effect "That request will need to be approved – I am very happy to escalate the matter for you." The staff were instructed that they were immune to sanction if they played the 'escalation' card.

On the basis that proactivity is always better than reactivity, it is better to avoid the perception of conflict of interest than it is to attempt to manage the suspicion and distrust later. On the flip side, a breach of the trust by the Service Integrator should be dealt with promptly. Working with one supplier, there was concern that the Service Integrator was asking for costed project proposals to 'review' for the customer and then submitting competing proposals. Based on the separation of duties and most certainly based on any reasonable conflict of interest management plan, this is unacceptable. The advice should be to escalate the concern and seek assurance that financial data would not be inappropriately used.

Without the separation of duties implemented, the risks associated with perceptions of conflict of interest related to managing the environment over time are high. With the clear separation, the design is much more resilient to the impact of changes – particularly sourcing changes.

6.2.5 Output/outcome oriented management

It has been discussed how the alignment of accountability and authority is a basic management tenet. It is, however, a consistently ignored tenet in many IT management regimes. Perhaps it is that people drawn to roles with deep technical knowledge like IT personnel are naturally inclined to want to know how things work.

When it comes to the management of suppliers in a Service Integration model, it becomes important to understand that *knowing* how it works does not imply the authority to *change* how it works.

> **Practitioner tip:**
> Any time the customer tells a party <u>how</u> to perform their role the customer becomes partially – if not completely – responsible for the outcome.

In the early days of outsourcing, the concept of outcome-oriented management was not well developed. Deals were colloquially referred to as 'your mess for less' or similar disparaging terms. This implied that there was little transformative benefit planned. The service levels agreements (SLAs) were typically based on component level availability and even then often utilizing 'base lined' service levels. Base lined service levels were effectively whatever the actual SLAs were during the transition phase. Whilst this is an effective way of negotiating a contract in the absence of valid service level data, it will not serve well in today's multi-supplier, outcome-based world of IT management.

The principle of outcome-oriented management is to focus on the outcomes that are wanted from the delivery organizations. It does *not* attempt to manage the methods they use to achieve the results beyond the compliance with standards and policies. The basis for utilizing a multi-sourced model is to allow us to orchestrate best of breed or highly efficient organizations to deliver services. Therefore it makes little sense to instruct them on how they should perform the job.

Ideally – and certainly in any 'greenfield' implementation – these inter-contract interactions should be standardized and contractually supported by the cross functional scope of work. In greenfield builds, there is an opportunity to model the roles and responsibilities to allow standardized interactions. Where there is a constraint to work in an extant implementation this is a goal state but it may take time – and contract renewals – to finally enact. In the interim, there will be a need to deal with the party-by-party customization where standardization cannot be negotiated. At the very least, there is a requirement to document these anomalies so they can be managed.

The compliance with the policies of the customer is a key outcome that must be captured contractually. This implies that the policies will be under change management and suppliers should be bound to comply with them. These policies may include:
- Security policies;
- Privacy policies;
- Policies related to legal compliance (e.g. workforce legislation, worker's compensation insurance etc.);
- Social policies (if applicable – e.g. ethical sourcing).

If all suppliers are not contractually required to support these policies, there will be a need to become involved in managing their supply chain – which breaches the principle of outcome-oriented management. For example, if a Service Provider is not contractually obliged to support a corporate ethical sourcing policy, then comprehensive audit of the compliance becomes an overhead for the customer. With the contractual support it is a diligence activity not comprehensive audit. If they are contractually committed to support the policies then compliance becomes a verification activity. Of course, should policies then change there is requirement for contract change but such a change is appropriate if the policies are changed.

6.2.6　Model driven, service-based design

Over the last 10 years since the large global automotive manufacturer started on their multi-sourcing journey of outsourcing, work has been done to build some 'model driven' approaches that can be used as a theoretical basis for discussion. Theory is wonderful but is best when it drives practical outcomes. So, not too much time will be spent on the theory but it may be of some use to those who want to extend the body on knowledge on the topic.

It has already been explained that the Service Integrator should be the person bringing clarity of engagement – but what is the basis? In one case study there was a very mature consumer of outsourcing. They had decided that they wanted to model the outsourcing bundles in a "greenfield" way. Once they had done that, they designed the high-level end-to-end processes and operational roles. Then they went to market for the suppliers to deliver the outsourcing bundles.

As part of this engagement, the Service Integrator was outsourced. The retained IT organization always kept control of the governance and right to direct strategy but as a mature consumer of outsourcing, they were happy to rely on an outsourced partner. They extended significant trust to this supplier but (quite rightly) demanded that the trust was not misplaced.

As part of this engagement, the Service Integrator also had the role of managing end-to-end infrastructure architecture.

The original modeling had infrastructure bundles as organizational resource pools. The applications development and support was aligned to business units with application Service Integrators assigned to each business unit. Being the service *and* infrastructure Service Integrator the integration across all services needed to be developed holistically. The methodology known as Model Driven Architecture was adopted and an IBM extension (Brown) used to create a modeling approach that aligned the technical approach to cross supplier aggregated services to the contract and service operations models. This alignment was used to great effect in terms of role clarity, simplified Service Integration and reduced costs.

The approach to aligning service, system and contract integration was further developed in a paper presented to the Open Group conference in Sydney in April 2013 (McKenzie

& Murphy, 2013). A diagram from this is shown in Figure 6.4. The left hand column is a high level description of Model Driven Architecture, which is a methodology developed by members of The Open Group. The columns in the center and on the right represent the analogous Commercial (contract) and Operational Architectures proposed at the conference. These collectively are the responsibility of Service Integration.

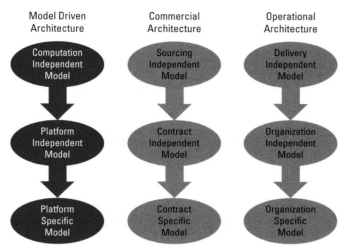

Figure 6.4   Extensions of Model Driven Architecture

Example artifacts that can be represented in this model include the following:

Architecture	Model	Example Artifacts
Commercial Architecture	Sourcing Independent Model	• Cost models/charts of accounts • Benchmark data • Chargeback models
	Contract Independent Model	• Standardized terms and conditions • Standardized cross functional SOW
	Contract Specific Model	• Specific scopes of work • Service specific SLAs
Operational Architecture	Delivery Independent Model	• End-to-end processes • End-to-end service catalog design • End-to-end SLAs and KPIs
	Organization Independent Model	• Standard engagement mechanism/multi-supplier engagement model • Standardized supplier escalation procedures
	Organization Specific Model	• Supplier-specific performance review reports • Supplier-specific SLA measurements

So what is the practical implementation of this approach?

A very important implication is that the way in which services delivered to the business are modeled will, inevitably, affect the way that contract bundles are defined. For example, in the case study above infrastructure and hosting was modeled (and contracted) as a corporate pool. Applications were modeled as business unit aligned. If the strategy is defined differently, there would be a change to the contract bundles. For instance many enterprises model the hosting infrastructure as aligned to the applications – the hosting is considered inherently part of the service. This would change the way the contract scopes were considered. Software-as-a-Service, for instance, would be modeled that way.

The approach can, for example, help develop a standard cross functional scope of work to be used across all contracts in order to define the interaction of the roles between contracts. This artifact is in the 'sourcing independent model'. The modeling ensured that the contractual obligations were closely aligned to the agreed operational processes. This was a key to the automation of those interactions, reducing both cost and complexity.

6.2.7   Sourcing model independence
It has become apparent that sourcing does not impact the operational modeling of a Service Integrator.

This means that the underlying principles and methodologies will work regardless of whether the Service Integrator role is outsourced and whether the 'performing' roles are insourced, outsourced or mixed. Once there is an established service strategy and implemented role clarity there will be flexibility in sourcing.

The key learning from this principle is that during the establishment of the SIAM environment, it is best not to short cut the rigorous definition of the process transfer of control and service level expectations because some of the SIAM capability or service provision will remain part of the retained IT organization. These short cuts will limit future flexibility and will very likely result in ongoing governance issues, as Service Providers will not all be held to the same level of accountability.

6.2.8   Standardization of roles and responsibilities
One innovative organization used a very powerful technique that allowed suppliers to engage in designing the high level processes before the tender process started. This ensured that commercial positioning did not skew the process design. More importantly they standardized the roles of performing suppliers. This was encapsulated in the standardized cross-functional scope of work, which was included in every contract. This cross-functional scope of work defined all the ITSM accountability methods for interaction with suppliers.

Standardizing the interactions and cross-functional scope of work has profound implications in terms of reducing the complexity of SIAM environments:
• Standardized expectations – regardless of suppliers, reduces gaps and overlaps in the roles and responsibilities;
• Standardized interactions reduces the complexity of the process documents and reduces the required training;
• Automation and tooling is simplified because the interfaces and data can be standardized.

When implementing the Service Integrator systems, SOA principles can be used to standardize the automation of the transfer of control and data in the process. In particular, the recommendation is to avoid point-to-point tool interfaces. The preference, leveraging standardization, is to create hub (or bus) based process-to-process interfaces. This is covered more fully in Chapter 4 Data and Tools.

The combination of standardization with abstraction of the interface from any Service Providers' internal processes and tools allows continual improvement within Service Providers and means changes in any supplier should not impact another supplier. This enables the Service Providers to deliver their services with minimal unnecessary constraints.

There is also an implication for sourcing changes. If a supplier is changed, the standardization of interfaces should insulate the other suppliers from the transition. With our early, innovative organization minimizing the disruption resulting from a transition was a design constraint that had to be overcome. The standardization of roles and interfaces and the use of a hub-based approach to automation was the solution to the constraint.

7 Continual Service Improvement (CSI)

In every IT organization, change is the only constant; change in market conditions, change in markets and resulting changes in priorities. As a result, any long-term business relationship requires innovation and continual service improvement as 'business as usual' behavior. But how to enter a contract without knowing the prerequisites of the future? It is possible to enter into a contract for the delivery of an analytics platform that will identify new markets or ways of delivering services more effectively, but how do you turn that opportunity into reality in a rapid and sustainable way?

This chapter will discuss various common approaches for managing CSI and their application in a SIAM context. It uses one potential framework model to introduce the key elements of aligning CSI and innovation, organizing and contracting for CSI and establishing an improvement culture.

7.1 CSI methods

ITIL V3 introduced an entire publication and a renewed focus on CSI, the emphasis of which is "evaluating and improving the quality of services, overall maturity of the ITSM service lifecycle and its underlying processes". The '7-Step Improvement Cycle' is a closed-loop feedback system, based on the Plan-Do-Check-Act (PDCA) model introduced by the Deming Cycle.

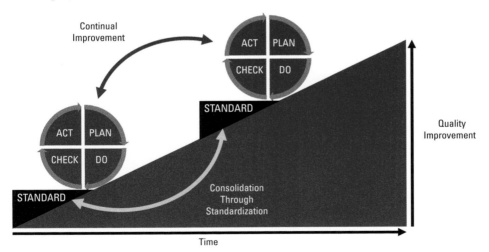

Figure 7.1   CSI through the Deming Cycle

There are many other methods for driving continual service improvement that are applied to IT including Lean and Six Sigma, both of which have their roots in manufacturing:

- Lean manufacturing or lean production, often simply 'lean', is a systematic method for the elimination of waste ('Muda') within a manufacturing system. Lean also takes into account waste created through overburden ('Muri') and waste created through unevenness in workloads ('Mura'). Working from the perspective of the customer who consumes a product or service, 'value' is any action or process that a customer would be willing to pay for (Wikipedia, 2015);
- Six Sigma seeks to improve the quality output of process by identifying and removing the causes of defects (errors) and minimizing variability in manufacturing and business processes. It uses a set of quality management methods, mainly empirical, statistical methods, and creates a special infrastructure of people within the organization ('Champions', 'Black Belts', 'Green Belts', 'Yellow Belts', etc.) who are experts in these methods. Each Six Sigma project carried out within an organization follows a defined sequence of steps and has quantified value targets, for example; reduce process cycle time, reduce pollution, reduce costs, increase customer satisfaction, and increase profits (Wikipedia, 2015).

Each of these approaches provides a method or set of tools to drive continual service improvement but each to varying degrees relies on the basic context that the parties involved in production are aligned in their overall goals and objectives. Manufacture takes place in a tightly controlled environment designed to facilitate the required outcome as effectively and efficiently as possible. The fundamental approach to delivering the process/product/service will remain the same over time, thereby making improvement over time valuable.

In today's IT environment, neither of these precepts are true:

- The parties involved will change over time, and their priorities are not going to naturally align to the overall service:
  - A commodity cloud service provider used as a component in a service will have different improvement priorities to total service;
- In many IT projects, the service deployed is required to fit into the existing operational environment with non-functional requirements sometimes left to the service transition processes to validate;
- Innovation may change the fundamental cost vs value dynamics or the delivery mechanism of services.

These concepts are tailored to the IT environment through the introduction of Lean IT (www.lean.org), most famously detailed by Orzen, 2010. Lean IT is based on enterprise Lean principles, as applied to the development and management of IT. In their book Lean IT Partnering (Zee, 2015), the authors discuss the application of Lean IT principles to a multi-sourced environment and suggest effective ways to apply these principles to strategic service provider relationships.

The foundational element that is common to these approaches, and transfers easily from one industry to another is culture. As Frederick Winslow Taylor said in his Principles of Scientific Management, (Taylor, 1911):

"And whenever a workman proposes an improvement, it should be the policy of the management to make a careful analysis of the new method, and if necessary, conduct a series of experiments to determine accurately the relative merit of the new suggestion and of the old standard. And whenever the new method is found to be markedly superior to the old, it should be adopted as the standard for the whole establishment".

Practitioner tip:
The cultural perspective of continual service improvement is fundamental, it does not matter where the suggestion comes from, if it is better, it should be adopted.

This puts the emphasis on everyone becoming a champion of improvement.

Another phrase from Taylor's words in 1911 that should inform IT organizations looking to deliver successful SIAM states that:

"...after a workman has had the price per piece of the work he is doing lowered two or three times as a result of his having worked harder and increased his output, he is likely entirely to lose sight of his employer's side of the case and become imbued with a grim determination to have no more cuts if soldiering (marking time, just doing what he is told) can prevent it."

As a result, CSI and innovation in a multi-sourced IT environment need to be closely integrated and constantly evaluated and re-assessed, Service Providers must be positively motivated to succeed. Each of the methods of CSI have value, in reducing cost and/or improving service, but they must be used in the context of multi-sourced IT and integrated with the innovation process so that innovation supports the objectives of CSI and CSI executes with awareness of pending innovation.

7.2   CSI and Innovation in SIAM

While the basic premise of continually improving through the repeated use of this method is relatively straightforward, the practical application of these philosophies in a multi-sourced environment needs some additional 'help' to deal with improvements that span more than one service or supplier. For example:
• Improvement for one party often means a loss of revenue for another;
• What is the process to decide who invests in the 'plan' phase when the benefit may be accrued elsewhere?

Previously, from an outsourcing perspective, this type of challenge has been resolved by establishing contracts that contain measures such as benchmarking clauses, stepped improvements in service levels and/or stepped reductions in cost. While these measures can often have an impact within a Service Provider, none of them can require, drive or reward collaboration across Service Providers, and this is often where the most significant benefits exist. Changes in technology and delivery models are not constrained to conventional contract boundaries and neither are new markets. CSI should also be dealt with as a source of innovation. The concept of innovation as the domain of strategists and technologists needs to be re-written as new ways of delivering services and linking data can now create new markets and opportunities that never existed before.

> **Practitioner tip:**
> Recognize the unique aspects of driving improvement in a multi-sourced environment and lay a foundation within which CSI becomes an everyday activity.

In most environments today where multi-sourcing has evolved (planned or not), the first step cannot be predicated on contractual change, it has to be achievable in the current contractual landscape. As such, a staged approach that can be adopted and adapted to each unique situation must be used:
• Establish a framework for innovation and CSI;
• Create the appropriate functions to coordinate, measure and manage improvement activities;
• Establish the culture and values within the organization;
• Contract for innovation and continual improvement.

In a complex multi-sourced environment, it is crucial to understand the winners and the losers. Where there is a total reduction in spend, there will be (in most cases) a corresponding reduction in revenue for another party and this behavior impacts the organizations involved and needs to be understood.

This chapter will review one potential framework for delivering an integrated innovation and CSI framework as a way of illustrating the key challenges of continual improvement in a sourced model. It is not a framework that will apply to all environments, but an example of the ways these challenges can be addressed.

7.3   Framework for innovation and CSI

Within most IT management frameworks and therefore most organizations, there is structure around the management of innovation (strategic improvement) that is owned within some form of strategy and architecture group. What is often less clear is how that relates to tactical and operational improvements which need to align and integrate with their loftier cousin.

> **Practitioner tip:**
> Improvements in the way to deliver something can often result in innovations that are as profound as the changes in the services delivered.

Who would have imagined the impact of cloud service delivery models 20 years ago? Operational and tactical decisions about the way things should be done can also help (and hinder) individual innovations, as well as the process of innovation itself.

Firstly this picture must be understood from a retained organization perspective, looking at what is the value and the cost required to deliver it. The first pass should be to look at the domains of value:
- Business value – is the proposal delivering business value, enabling new markets or capabilities, or creating new revenue streams?
- Business cost – does the proposal reduce the overall cost to the business of delivering the existing services or enable them to be funded in a more flexible way?
- IT cost – does the proposal reduce the cost of IT to deliver the services in its portfolio or enable them to be funded in a more flexible way?

A common pitfall is to prioritize those proposals that reduce IT cost and miss the greater value available from the other two categories – or worse, optimize IT at the cost of the business.

Once the value is known, the process of evaluating proposals can begin which will give an indication of the costs associated with achieving that value. As with the value domains, the investment domains also need to be understood to ensure that the case for change can be created and sustained. An investment domain is an area of the organization in which investment is required to realize value:
- Business;
- Retained IT;
- Sourced IT – will this have an impact on the revenues of our providers? Which will increase and which will reduce? How do I manage the communication to them to ensure I get the engagement I need?

Bringing these two elements together enables us to understand the differences between cost and value sufficiently to evaluate the proposals. Note that the cost of contract change (if required) can be an inhibitor to the success of a proposal mid-way through a contract cycle and that this is just as much a valid expense as any of the others.

One of the additional challenges created in a SIAM environment is the organizational and contractual boundaries. Using a domain analysis matrix (see Figure 7.2) can help to assess the benefits and costs to each of the parties involved and identify any gaps. If the cost-value

equation is not balanced in all of the domains, in a specific Service Provider's contract, this gap needs to be understood and addressed. There are many ways to address the balance:
- Awarding additional scope to a Service Provider who has sacrificed revenue in support of a broader improvement opportunity;
- Using the strength of the relationship to motivate a Service Provider to reduce cost or revenue;
- Helping the Service Provider realize savings or service improvements in other areas.

Each of these approaches may be used sparingly to deal with specific situations, but they must always be used in balance to maintain the relationship.

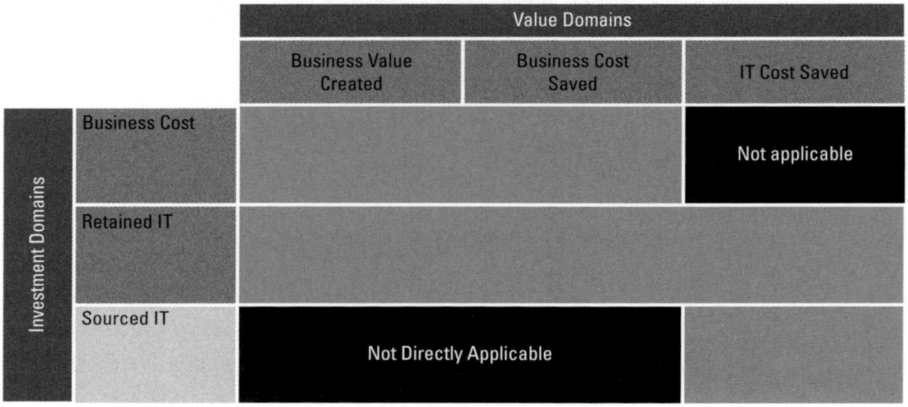

| | Value Domains | | |
	Business Value Created	Business Cost Saved	IT Cost Saved
Business Cost			Not applicable
Retained IT			
Sourced IT	Not Directly Applicable		

(Investment Domains)

Figure 7.2   Domain Analysis Matrix

Once this analysis has been completed, the proposals can move forward as candidates into rationalization, delivery domain-specific execution and then ongoing operation, evaluation and CSI. An overview of this end-to-end framework can be seen in Figure 7.3.

This framework also introduces the differences between *operational* and *tactical* CSI; these terms are introduced to highlight the variances in the approach required:
- Operational CSIs are those improvements that can be delivered within a single service or supplier with little or no impact on other suppliers or services;
- Tactical CSIs are those which require coordination across multiple suppliers to deliver the end-to-end value.

While this model represents only one way of integrating innovation and CSI, it does nevertheless provide a framework for discussing some of the key components:
- Identification: candidates for innovation can come from a number of different drivers and must be evaluated in each of the domains of cost and value.
  The potential to create business revenue, save business cost or save IT cost, has to be assessed against the implementation costs and disruption to those areas. In a SIAM context the IT cost/value must also be understood within each Service Provider. Other processes,

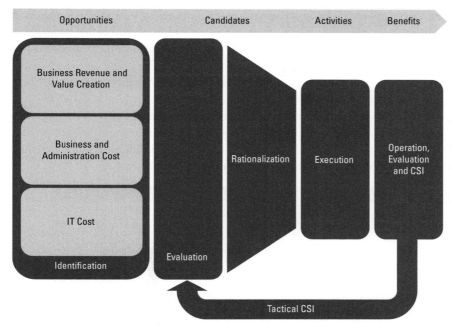

Figure 7.3   Innovation and CSI Framework

such as demand management, business relationship management and service portfolio management will also identify opportunities for improvement and innovation.

- Evaluation: evaluation of potential candidates for innovation must be assessed against the candidates for tactical CSI to ensure that the cases for 'implement new' have been assessed against the cases for 'improve what we have'.

  With the increasing coupling between service and Service Provider in areas such as cloud provision and 'as a Service' offerings, decisions which require a change in Service Provider or integration of another Service Provider need to be considered as an influencing factor.

- Rationalization: rationalization of candidates for innovation and improvement has to be considered in terms of the boundaries of Service Providers.

  One benefit of having discrete services and Service Providers is the ability to isolate the disruption of change activities – potentially increasing the possible volume of change. Changes that affect multiple Service Providers will need to be carefully planned and may take longer to execute due to the organizational and contractual boundaries.

- Execution: execution roadmaps should be visible to all stakeholders and include the impacts and benefits to their specific IT services.

  Improvement actions should deliver value to one or more of the services that IT delivers to the business and it is essential that these benefits are communicated. Likewise, any dependencies or impacts should be communicated to stakeholders to ensure they are understood.

- Operation, evaluation and CSI: once improvement activities are completed, the expected benefits should be evaluated and CSI should continue to operate on an ongoing basis.

Benefits realization not only measures the results of the innovation or CSI activity, but acts as a calibration and lessons learnt on the whole innovation and CSI process. As such, it not only needs to verify if the benefits were realized, but to which organization. Opportunities for ongoing CSI can be split into two categories:

- Operational CSIs – those that can occur within a single Service Provider or delivery team and are covered by operational costs;
- Tactical CSIs – those that require the collaboration of multiple Service Providers and need investment. Tactical CSIs should be evaluated as part of the overall innovation and CSI process.

7.4 Organizing for CSI

A basic driver of human beings is that they want to do a good job. The challenges that arise in terms of driving improvement, made more complex in a multi-sourced environment, are:

1. Agreeing what 'good' looks like to ensure that people are driving towards it in a coordinated fashion;
2. Multiple teams and organizations being aware of what is being done to prevent wasted effort through different teams pulling in different directions.

To address this requires governance around improvement that is lightweight enough not to stifle creativity while being strong enough to prevent redundancy and waste. This governance needs to recognize the 'cascade' nature of improvement. Improvements executed within an individual service or Service Provider does not drive improvement elsewhere in the ecosystem unless it is brought up to the Service Integrator level and cascaded back down to all.

> **Practitioner tip:**
> Very often, cross-supplier improvement initiatives are where most of the value lies.

A model used successfully within a number of different companies and industries is to have a central team that can communicate operational CSIs and coordinate tactical CSIs through collaborative working across the suppliers in the ecosystem. This is achieved through having some form of tracking and communicating system where CSI items are tracked as small scale projects with requirements, objectives and milestones. This same solution provides a mechanism for communication by sharing the details of ongoing activities. In the same way, the number of CSI milestones met and missed can be used as an organizational KPI.

For tactical CSIs, the picture is more complex. One successful approach is to allocate a resource pool for leading and coordinating these improvements on a quarterly basis. In one multinational oil and gas company, this process was deployed successfully focusing on outcomes as the primary KPI, e.g. reduce the number of P1 incidents by 20%, reduce the percentage of failed changes by 5%, increase customer satisfaction by 10%. Within this model – the critical success factors were:

1. Outcomes (or shared KPIs) are not contractually binding for the suppliers in the ecosystem. They are mutually agreed targets that would benefit most, if not all of the suppliers in the environment. This is how the supplier investment in the process is 'funded', by being confident that they will achieve some level of increased operational efficiency. The quarterly outcomes are agreed by the representatives of all suppliers as: outcomes they can commit to achieving and from which they will receive benefit.
2. Governance is cross-supplier. To drive successful change in a multi-sourced environment requires collaboration with suppliers at multiple levels. In the context of CSI this requires representation at:
   a. 'Working group' level from the resources who can actually affect operational change in the individual organizations;
   b. 'Steering committee' level from the leaders of each supplier's account team, these people can commit to invest the required resources and act as an escalation point.

By having representation at both these levels, it becomes possible to affect change and motivate change. The leadership resources are measured as much on customer satisfaction and new business development as they are on delivery.

Just like in our previous skydivers' example, success concerning outcomes is recognized at an organizational and individual level. While engaging at an organizational level, work is done and the ideas come from individuals, so this needs to be recognized. A commendation from a customer is one of the more powerful tools for a supplier's internal promotion case.

Having identified the tactical CSIs and put in place a function to manage and deliver them, it is important to recognize their impact on more strategic improvements and innovation. By sharing the proposals for tactical CSI initiatives as part of the architectural innovation governance, it is possible to identify additional opportunities:
- For multiple teams or suppliers within the organization to collaborate on common improvement priorities;
- Identify potentially conflicting improvement initiatives early e.g.:
  - One team investing time in getting tickets through the service desk as quickly as possible – catch and dispatch;
  - While another is investing time in increasing first call resolution and asking the service desk to take a little longer to analyze issues before passing them on.

7.5   An improvement culture

To have a 'culture of continual improvement' is something that can be found in the vision and mission of almost all IT organizations. However, to deliver that culture in a multi-sourced environment is a more complex challenge than many appear to believe. Establishing a set of contracts with year-on-year cost reductions or incremental increases in service levels can achieve part of the goal, but it is not a sustainable model for the longer term. Relentless pressure on cost can lead to a "do more with less" approach from suppliers and partners that affects levels of service and will lead to the retained organization having to deliver more whilst the overall cost remains flat. Continual increases in service levels, if not driven by true improvements in the efficiency of the service will lead to better and better management of exclusions to meet the more stringent targets, thereby reducing efficiency rather than improving it.

Developing and delivering a true culture of continual service improvement requires trust and leadership. Those resources in the retained organization must lead by example and support improvement in and across the partner ecosystem. Accepting that this responsibility is shared requires a recognition that multiple parties need to be successful, and that at some level, success may mean different things.

Practitioner tip:
Developing and delivering a true culture of continual service improvement requires trust and leadership.

One of the most common pitfalls is the perception of the relationship between supplier and customer as one of conflict where each party is trying to force the other to do more for less, or trying to get away with doing less for more. In large organizations where multi-sourcing is now the de facto standard, this is very rarely the case and assuming that the worst case is always true is in fact similar to the assumptions made in the prisoner's dilemma.

Studies of behavior have shown three very interesting points using the iterative forms of Game Theory (Fischbacher, 2003):
1. In reality, humans display a systematic bias towards cooperative behavior in this and similar games;

The **prisoner's dilemma** is a canonical example of a game analyzed in game theory that shows why two purely 'rational' individuals might not cooperate, even if it appears that it is in their best interests to do so. It was originally framed by Merrill Flood and Melvin Dresher working at RAND in 1950. Albert W. Tucker formalized the game with prison sentence rewards and gave it the name 'prisoner's dilemma' (Poundstone, 1992), presenting it as follows:

Two members of a criminal gang are arrested and imprisoned. Each prisoner is in solitary confinement with no means of speaking to, or exchanging messages with, the other. The prosecutors do not have enough evidence to convict the pair on the principal charge. They hope to get both sentenced to a year in prison on a lesser charge. Simultaneously, the prosecutors offer each prisoner a bargain. Each prisoner is given the opportunity either to: betray the other by testifying that the other committed the crime, or to cooperate with the other by remaining silent. Here is the offer:

- If A and B each betray the other, each of them serves two years in prison;
- If A betrays B but B remains silent, A will be set free and B will serve three years in prison (and vice versa);
- If A and B both remain silent, both of them will only serve one year in prison (on the lesser charge).

It is implied that the prisoners will have no opportunity to reward or punish their partner other than the prison sentences they get, and that their decision will not affect their reputation in the future. Because betraying a partner offers a greater reward than cooperating with him, all purely rational self-interested prisoners would betray the other, and so the only possible outcome for two purely rational prisoners is for them to betray each other. The interesting part of this result is that pursuing individual reward logically leads both of the prisoners to betray, when they would get a better reward if they both cooperated.

Source: Wikipedia - http://en.wikipedia.org/wiki/Prisoner's_dilemma

2. In iterated versions of the game, the total number of rounds in the game needs to remain unknown to promote constructive behavior
3. Axelrod's 'The Evolution of Cooperation' (Axelrod & Hamilton, 1981) demonstrated that altruistic strategies consistently outperformed greedy ones.

So, how to translate that into some rules for multi-sourcing?
1. The chances are in favor of a potential partner *wanting* to collaborate, and starting with that assumption will prove to be right most of the time;
2. There should always be a number of rounds (contract renewals, new contract awards) kept open so that there are tangible reasons to collaborate and recognize that, while corporate relationships are typically multi-year, individual performance goals can be annual or quarterly;
3. Collaboration is far more likely to be successful than confrontation and rules need to actively discourage 'bad behaviors' (see Section 7.5.4).

Empirical evidence for point 3 is covered in Chapter 2 of this book.

"Recognition within the retained organization that collaboration will bring greater rewards for the organization is only one piece of the jigsaw. This must be reinforced through more proactive changes in the behaviors of each individual. The team made a proactive choice to stop rewarding 'heroes' who wade in to fix a crisis and start rewarding those who made CSI differences. This same approach was applied to retained and sourced teams to demonstrate consistency, but it was very effective in changing behavior. It must be done in consultation with the outsource team management but all organizations sending a clear message that recognition is based on "what you did to make the things better" is a powerful positive step."

An alternative lever to motivate suppliers to collaborate is to incentivize them based on joint KPIs. This will lead to a natural 'win-win' situation. This has been described in Chapter 2 on sourcing strategies.

7.5.1   Interactions within interactions

It is essential to remember that, in this situation, as well as a set of contractual relationships played out between the organizations involved, there are individual human interactions taking place every day that impact the overall success of the system.

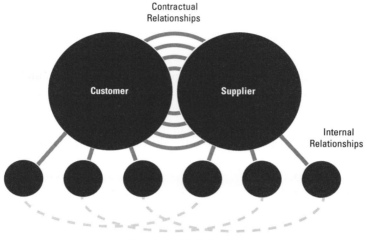

Figure 7.4   Relationship Categories

A common misconception is that sourcing reduces all of this relationship and resources management complexity to a single measurable relationship, that between customer and supplier. In fact, in developing and maintaining an improvement culture – all of them need to be considered:

- Contractual:
  - What provisions have been made in the contracts to encourage and recognize CSI?
  - Are the people that manage and maintain the contractual relationship reinforcing those commitments with their behaviors?
- Internal:
  - What is each organization doing and saying to its people to encourage and motivate them to improve?
  - Are those activities aligned to the improvement required? Do they recognize mutual success or focus on in-organization goals only?
  - Are both organizations discussing collaboration and openly discussing mutual success?
  - Do both organizations have a common view on which individuals to focus when reviewing performance? Is the internal process recognizing and rewarding the same behaviors and people?

- Cross-organizational:
  - How is each person ensuring that the working relationships are good?
  - Does the customer organization recognize the need to attract, retain and promote the best resources within their partners? Remember that resources on both sides can request to work elsewhere.

> **Practitioner tip:**
> Many of these relationship practices are second nature to good leaders and recognizing that a sourced relationship does not remove the need to lead is a key element of success.

7.5.2   Five successful strategies for CSI

- Look for win-win scenarios – improvement initiatives that deliver benefits to multiple partners encourage teams to collaborate for success. For example, collaborate in 'shift left' by moving work to the service desk, enabling them through knowledge and automation drives collaboration, cost reduction and service improvement;
- Allow partners to reap the rewards – share the investment, including time and resources as well as cost, and share the rewards by not expecting cost reductions in contracts for every success;
- Reward the right behaviors – ensure that the improvement successes are communicated widely, both internally and externally, to ensure that individuals and organizations see maximum benefit for their investment. Citations and commendations can be as valuable to organizations and people as additional revenues;
- Recognize and report on the impact of CSI – a significant proportion of the benefits available through improvement can come from cross-supplier initiatives, but in most cases this will result in a reduction in revenue for one or more parties. Be ready to recognize this impact and understand the need to mitigate the impact through increased scope or other reward mechanisms;
- Require cross-supplier collaboration – engage all delivery teams in identifying, developing and delivering improvement, and set up forums for sharing best practice between teams. This will not only set benchmarks of behavior and performance between teams but also identify opportunities for small changes in one team that can deliver significant benefits to another.

7.5.3   CSI facilitators

The uncertain nature of the items in the CSI category mean that they cannot form contractual deliverables in themselves, but there are proven ways to contractually facilitate and motivate these activities to occur. In a multi-sourced environment where one of the main contributors to cost is human resource, and every service is focused on profit and loss, the main challenge is finding the investment to investigate the potential opportunity and develop the business case.

Commit resource:
In larger environments, one way to ensure that a sufficient amount of CSI activity is reviewed, investigated and executed, is to establish committed resources to perform those activities. If this is a sourced service, its success can then be measured by service improvements or cost reduction achieved across all of the services. As long as the process is seen to be independent from the other Service Providers in the ecosystem and the benefits selected for further investment are actually delivered, this approach can provide significant advantages.

This approach was used in the **Case study 2 – Global energy company** in Section 1.9.2 and resulted in significant service improvements without major contractual change.

Contractual stepping mechanisms:
In longer-term contracts, contractual stepping-stones can be used to facilitate CSI:
- Cost mechanisms – contractual frameworks where the unit cost of services step-down over time thereby putting the onus to drive efficiencies on the Service Provider;
- Performance measures – building in step-ups in the service levels at intervals throughout the contract term can drive improvements in service over time.

An example of this type of contracting arrangement can be seen in **Case study 3 – European bank**, Section 1.9.3.

A study into one organization's use of shared key performance indicators (KPIs) performed by the Boston Consulting Group (Hakkenberg, 2011) concluded that the benefits included:
- Shared KPIs that are based on the company's business objectives compel Service Providers to think outside their own functional areas;
- The Service Providers themselves collectively address any problems;
- A shared focus on business outcomes drives Service Providers to find optimal solutions for the company.

Opportunity:
One of the key performance indicators of a large project leader is 'base growth' – the ability to grow the total spend or 'wallet share' with the customer through winning additional business. Recognizing this can support providers in using their opportunity budget – money not included in the service base costs, but considered as cost of sale – to support the early identification and business case creation phases of CSI. As long as there is alignment between the organizations investing in the discovery and the organizations winning this business – this can generate additional investment into CSI activities. The risk with this approach is predatory investigations into other areas that can discourage collaboration; this can be mitigated through full disclosure of the areas being investigated and a transparent process.

Seed funds:
In more mature environments, the concept of committed resources has been extended. For example in a global mobile phone provider, suppliers into the environment commit a specified amount of investment to a 'CSI seed fund'. The proposals for larger CSIs are

then presented to a Dragon's Den (or Shark Tank) style committee that is made up of leaders from each organization to compete for investment from the seed fund pot. Savings from nominated CSIs are then channeled back into the fund and profits released to the organizations involved. This type of model extends the collaboration concept significantly by offering true financial incentives. This approach can be applied initially at a Service Provider or contract level and extended to multiple Service Providers once the approach has been established and proven.

Business outcome contracts:
In the largest deals, there is a growing model of contracts where most if not all of the fees are based on the financial performance of the business being supported. In this model, improvement is owned in its entirety by the Service Provider and driven directly by the needs of the business. These types of deal have yet to be seen more broadly in a multi-sourced environment however, apart from a very few instance where joint ventures have been spun-off from the larger organization with shared ownership and independent management teams.

7.5.4   CSI inhibitors
Along with clear direction about what *is* required and expected to drive continual improvement, it must be made equally clear what will *not* be tolerated and agreement reached across the community on how such behaviors will be addressed. Any inhibitor to trust and open communication will reduce the potential benefits of CSI and should be strongly discouraged. There are a number of very specific issues that have come to the top of the list through experience of working in many multi-sourced environments:

> **Practitioner tip:**
> Any inhibitor to trust and open communication will limit the benefits of CSI.

Mismatching priorities:
During the negotiation phase of any contract there are many hours spent talking about the transition, transformation and innovation items. What will they be? How much will they cost? What benefits will they deliver? What dependencies does the Service Provider have on the customer to achieve them? Yet more often than not, once the contract is signed and the resources arrive to do the work, they find that the projects that have been agreed are not on the list of priorities for the resources in the retained organization. The unwanted distraction of the Service Provider transition/transformation resources is an annoyance and it gets in the way of meeting their own goals. As part of the negotiation process, it is critical that this is addressed; stakeholder management on the customer side needs to ensure that the items in the agreed solution transformation are clearly on the organization plan and have sufficient stakeholder and sponsor support to be successful. Otherwise, the value paid for in the contract cannot be delivered.

Lack of Transparency:

One of the biggest behaviors to affect the customer/supplier relationship is transparency and lack of solidarity by the retained organization. This is the case when the retained organization uses the "the supplier didn't perform" excuse for a service delivery failure instead of taking the blame from an end-to-end service delivery perspective towards the business and punishing any Service Provider afterwards as part of an internal service delivery discussion. This is probably the most damaging behavior to trust and collaboration between suppliers and customers and its removal needs to be a priority for any organization looking to succeed in this area. In addition to this, since the role of the retained organization in a multi-sourced model is to select and orchestrate the best partners for the business, this approach can also cause significant damage to the relationship with the business as well.

Punitive measures:

In some organizations the role of the customer (or at least its procurement arm) is to be as difficult as possible, minimizing cost and maximizing the service received. While this may have very short-term benefits, it will not encourage partnership or proactivity. As discussed in Chapter 2 of this book – see 'What type of integrator are you?' – there is a significant body of evidence, both academic and in industry, that demonstrates long-term collaborative relationships will deliver much better rewards.

'Greedy' behaviors:

Such behaviors do not recognize the interdependent nature of the multi-sourced relationship. From suppliers this can exhibit itself in blaming behavior or an unwillingness to take part in complex diagnosis or root cause analysis. It may also appear as predatory CSI activity through aggressively pursuing another supplier's scope without clear service or cost benefits. These types of behavior need to be addressed as part of relationship governance or they will damage the performance of the overall system.

These types of behavior can also be exhibited by the customer in the relationship in different ways. For example, when partners invest additional time and effort in the relationship, such as driving through CSI improvements, this needs to be recognized. Having an incumbent do all the investment to qualify a potential improvement or new service and then giving the business to another will not encourage loyalty. A common recognition of the business drivers for each party will recognize that cost needs to be just one factor of many and understand that the quality of delivery through additional opportunity sends a very strong message about the way to build a long term business relationship.

Just as Ostrom's research suggests (see Introduction reference) the 'community based-rules' by which all of the organizations agree to operate, must include both "built-in incentives for responsible use and punishments for overuse". These rules must be applied to both the retained organization, and the SIAM function if it is sourced, in an even more rigorous fashion. Just as the guardians of our society (police/legislature/judiciary) are punished more severely for abuse of their powers, so the Service Integrator must be held to a higher level of accountability and be severely and visibly sanctioned for misbehavior.

7.6   Contracting for CSI

When planning the contracting arrangements to sit around CSI, there are four primary contractual vehicles for classifying improvement activities:
- Transition– improvements that are understood in terms of both cost and benefits, and can be performed as part of transitioning services to the new provider. Transition items can be included in the financial base case for the service with committed resources and benefits;
- Transformation – transformation items are those for which the costs and benefits can be estimated, typically based on the providers' experience of implementing them in other environments. Providers need transformation outcomes to achieve the committed benefits. Commercial risk will typically be minimized by management of scope and assumptions;
- Innovation – innovation items are typically 'other' services and value-adds that the supplier would propose to bring to the relationship, but have not as yet been brought in scope for the specific contract or service. These items are a list of – 'other things to be discussed' and are kept on the radar as potential added services to the customer or additional revenue opportunities for the supplier;
- Continual service improvement (CSI) – at the point of contracting, the specific items that will make up this category are not necessarily even known. Some desired outcomes can be defined, but not the specific activities. Those that can be defined can be incorporated into agreements; those that need further definition or will operate across providers can be defined as shared KPIs.

The alignment between these different categories of improvement and the level of certainty around cost and benefit can be described using the diagram in Figure 7.5.

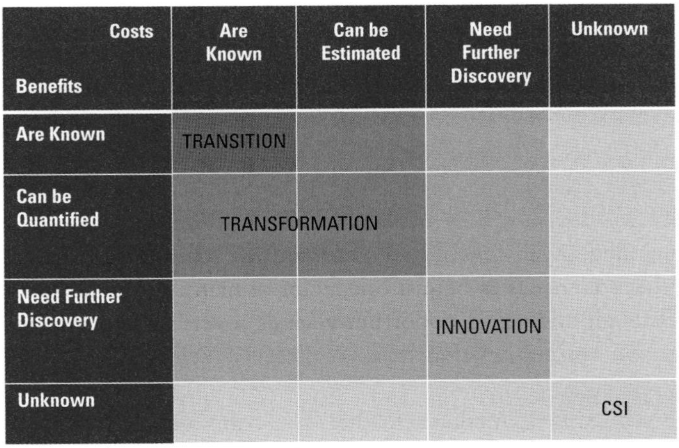

Costs / Benefits	Are Known	Can be Estimated	Need Further Discovery	Unknown
Are Known	TRANSITION			
Can be Quantified	TRANSFORMATION			
Need Further Discovery			INNOVATION	
Unknown				CSI

Figure 7.5   Contract Phases for CSI

Traditionally large services contracts have had significant expectations in terms of transformation and outsourcing contracts have been considered as vehicles of change. In industries where change is significant, this model is challenged by the fact that by the time the contracts are negotiated and signed, the business context into which the IT services will be delivered has changed. Consequently, a more dynamic approach is required in these industries.

In organizations with rapid change, there is a significant potential for a 'legitimacy gap' (S. P. Sethi, 2007) to develop over time, a gap between delivery and expectations. This gap can develop between the IT organization and its Service Providers and more critically, between IT and its customers.

Some of the contributors to this gap can be articulated using the PZB Service Quality Model (Zeithaml, 1988) which identifies five possible gaps that can exist between the expectations of service and the service actually being delivered. See Figure 7.6.

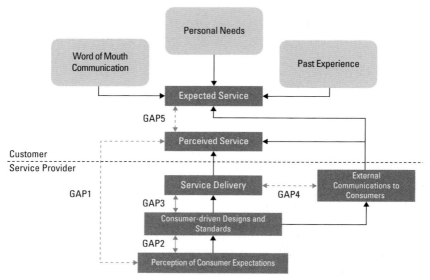

Figure 7.6   The PZB Gap Model

In the context of a Service Provider delivering service to a retained organization, these five gaps are:

- GAP1 – The Knowledge Gap: the difference between the customers' expectations and the perception of the service being delivered;
- GAP2 – The Standard Gap: the difference between the perception of customers' expectations and the specification of the service;
- GAP3 – The Behavior Gap: the difference between the service specification and the service actually being delivered;
- GAP4 – The Communications Gap: the difference between the service being delivered and the communication of the service to stakeholders;
- GAP5 – The Expectation Gap: the difference between the customers' expectations and the actual service performance.

Any one of these gaps can have a profound impact on the relationship between the Service Provider and the customer in a multi-sourced environment. Where the perception of the resulting aggregate service is impacted by all five gaps across multiple Service Providers then the net impact can be even more significant. Moreover, when typical outsourcing agreements are between three and five years, even in the perfect world where the gaps are minimized at contract signature, they will inevitably grow over time.

Practitioner tip:

In industries where change is significant, by the time the contracts are negotiated and signed the business context into which they are delivered will have changed.

In the global energy company described in the case study in Section 1.9.2, a SIAM service had been procured with a three month transition and three year transformation roadmap to implement and optimize almost all of the ITIL Service Management processes, with steps down in cost that would reflect the improvements being made across all Service Providers. As priorities changed in the business environment, including a halving in the price of a barrel of oil, the ongoing program of transformation needed to be adapted. The result was a move to a contractual construct based on quarterly tactical improvements that are measured by their outcome rather than the more traditional deliverables. Each quarter a new set of outcomes is defined which require all of the Service Providers to contribute, and the SIAM service takes the lead in delivering. Outcomes are measures of implemented improvement such as 'reducing the number of p1 incidents by X' or 'increasing customer satisfaction by Y'. All Service Providers review and commit the resources to achieve those outcomes on a quarterly basis and work through a CSI working group to achieve the desired outcomes. This approach offers a number of benefits including:

- The contractual construct enables new outcomes to be defined on a quarter-by-quarter basis making CSI a very agile process;
- All Service Providers commit the time and resource to achieve the outcomes and recognize their value to them individually as well as to the IT organization as a whole;
- Larger improvement outcomes can be split over a number of quarters while keeping the focus on short term goals.

The application of more dynamic contracting models for CSI and innovation across the Service Providers in a multi-sourced environment provides the opportunity to identify the gaps between perception and service delivery and address them on an ongoing basis.

8 Conclusion

While continuing developments in IT services and the way in which they are delivered mean that multi-sourcing is here to stay, there are still many ways to be successful and even more ways to fail. The growing case for cloud and the potential benefits of organizations being able to leverage service providers and concentrate on their core competences are well established.

Service Integration in IT was said to be in the 'Trough of Disillusionment' in 2013, having failed to deliver on earlier inflated expectations. However, there are organizations who are effectively realizing the benefits of SIAM, and three of them are case studies within this book.

Analysts agree on its importance:
- "Clients continue to struggle with the requirements for multi-sourcing, including contractual oversight and Service Integration" (Martorelli, 2011);
- "Without a MSI role CIOs often experience many boundary issues among Service Providers, with the usual "finger pointing" and siloed behavioral problems" (Longwood, 2012).

The key message to take away is that the 'technology trigger' has been pulled (and cannot be un-pulled) so this journey is going to continue and the choice is one of how and when, rather than if.

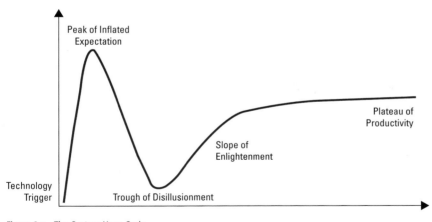

Figure 8.1   The Gartner Hype Cycle

There are a series of case studies and enablers that have been good indicators of success. Each of these has some aspect which is different in multi-sourcing than in a wholly retained IT organization (archetype A as discussed in Chapter 2: Basic Concepts and Terminology) or a sole sourced environment (Archetype B), and these have been discussed in the previous chapters. While these differences can be reduced through careful planning, appropriate service encapsulation and level of granularity, due to the dependent nature of services, they can never be eradicated.

In defining a Service Integration function to help the retained organization manage the services delivered from multiple Service Providers, the focus has been on people and process; tools and data, sourcing and governance. Figure 8.2 restates the enablers that have been used as a reference for the topics in the main chapters in this book.

Chapter	Covers...	...and is (partly) covering COBIT enabler...
2 Basic concepts and terminology	Definitions of the SIAM function and conceptual models for Service Integration	Principles, Policies and Frameworks
3 People and process	People and processes to run a SIAM function	Process Culture, Ethics and Behavior People, Skills and Competences
4 Data and tools	Tooling framework to record, gather and analyze data to share information	Information Service, Infrastructure and Applications
5 Sourcing multiple Service Providers	The sourcing process of a Service Integration ecosystem and contractual aspects	Organizational Structures
6 Governance	Governance of Service Integration	Organizational Structures Culture, Ethics and Behavior
7 Continual service improvement	Improvement over time	Process
8 Conclusions	Wrap-up and final considerations	Not applicable

Figure 8.2   The COBIT enablers revisited

Now it is time to recap the most important lessons learned and key success factors that the authors believe will get the best out of these enablers.

8.1   Basic concepts and terminology

Planning for a SIAM environment is akin to defining a long-term strategy; at face value it can seem very straightforward, while the implications of incorrect selection can be significant. Introducing contractual and organizational boundaries between the different parts of a highly effective IT organization can, if not done carefully, severely impact services to the end-user. This means that the decisions made in the design of the framework cannot be taken lightly as they will impact cost and service quality over a significant period of time.

The alignment of accountability and authority is a basic management concept. There is a tendency for organizations to outsource a role and then define *how* it is done. This is generally counter-productive in the longer term because when one party instructs another as to how to do their job, they become at least partially responsible for the outcome. This micromanagement makes holding suppliers accountable much more difficult.

The task of defining a SIAM function has been complicated by two factors over the last few years:

1. Since most of the material on this subject is produced by Service Providers, the difference between an SIAM function that needs to be delivered and the SIAM function that Service Providers can sell remains unclear. While not an intended consequence, commercial concerns have tended to confuse the message, resulting in many different definitions of what Service Integration includes and should intend to deliver.
2. The lack of clarity about the difference between an SIAM function and a retained organization. Despite 10 years having passed since the first Gartner book on multi-sourcing, the difference in scope and responsibilities between these two areas is still not clear. For the purposes of this book, the following split has been assumed:
   a. The SIAM function will be responsible for integrating sourced services and their associated providers;
   b. The retained organization as a whole remains accountable for service strategy and overall delivery of all services; retained and sourced.

A further aspect of defining the mission of the SIAM function is deciding if it will be an enabling function which is focused on integrating services and Service Providers, or an accountable function which is responsible for the delivery of business services across the sourced ecosystem.

- An enabling SIAM function is not directly accountable for the delivery of IT services to the business, its role is to ensure that sufficient rigor, standardization and control exists so that the individual Service Providers can collaborate effectively as required;
- An accountable SIAM function includes the service ownership role and is responsible for the delivery of IT services to the business that are sourced from multiple Service Providers.

The authors of this book have seen both models successfully deployed using a variety of methods and these are discussed throughout, and covered in the case studies detailed in Section 1.9.

Experience does indicate that there are some clear critical success factors however. All of the successfully planned and executed multi-sourced environments appear to have some things in common:

1. They focus on the outcome for their customers and consumers more than the output of their suppliers.
2. They build relationships with their suppliers which have clear expectations on both parties and are based a basic trust and an understanding of the goals of each party and the shared goals of the ecosystem.
3. Service enablers (process, people, tools etc.) are designed to the specific integration environment and the aggregated outcome sought. They are common to every participating service and its provider, but they are not hard rules and standards for everyone to participate by. There must be room for nuances and dialects according to the participating provider's prerequisites and capabilities. The Service Integrator is responsible for uniting different implementations of enablers into homogenous service management. This is

not a contradiction - the better and more mature the Service Integrator, the larger the differences between implementations of service enablers that can be allowed.

4. Service Integration is about integrating services, not providers or components. Service Integrators and providers that stay true to service orientation are more successful. Because of this, SIAM techniques and functions may also be very well established within a single source environment.

5. In Service Integration integrators and providers will both interact with multiple parties but cannot apply multiple behaviors. At least not if they want to stay effective and efficient. Service encapsulation is a technique for being successful in this. Having an external facing set, or setup, of enablers that can be altered according to the specific situation and an internal facing setup of the same enabler that is consistent independent of situation.

6. Today's landscape of IT-provisioning and Service Integration often forms matrixes of Service Integrators and providers (Archetype D) where behaviors and activities within one integrating environment might propagate or impact on another environment or even customer. Service Integration is not only about the provider enabling the Service Integrator to be successful, it is also about the Service Integrator making the provider successful.

7. Service Integration is recursive to any level. Hence Service Integrators are also providers and vice versa. Organizations that have the capabilities for playing both parts are more likely to be successful.

8.2   People and process

The people and process related aspects of a Service Integration function are clearly critical success factors. Organization features and the way that the processes interact are quite different in a Service Integration framework when compared to a 'monolithic' approach. The Service Integrator has to permit the actual execution of the processes by the Service Providers and focus on the outcomes of the processes and how they support the end goals of the IT organization and the business it serves. The people and processes support the management and governance principles and rely on the tools and data to perform the functions required.

The goal of the Service Integrator is to create an environment where the suppliers of the actual IT services are:
• Made aware of their accountabilities;
• Enabled to perform their accountabilities;
• Held to account for their performance.

Therefore, it becomes clear that the way people are organized around the Service Integration functionality that defines the processes is an important first step.

Good practices in this area include:
- SIAM requires different competences:
  - The move from service provider to Service Integrator requires new capabilities within the retained organization;
  - Commercial awareness, collaboration and negotiation are becoming core skills for the retained organization;
  - Skills assessments via SFIA or e-CF are useful tools but the so-called 'soft skills' are very important as well. SFIA version 6 improves approaches to soft skills but the IPMA Competence Baseline (ICB) has a very good section on behavioral competences;
- Successful leaders are succeeding through collaboration and managing relationships as much as contracts:
  - Service Provider relationships often include more than one contract and they need to be managed differently, but within the same overall relationship;
- The scope and accountabilities of the SIAM function must be clear and unambiguous;
- Defining SIAM just at a process level is not sufficient. The mandate IT has on behalf of the organization must be determined and communicated so the position of IT is clear;
- Sourcing is a critical decision for SI:
  - Sourcing SIAM services from outside the organization can bring new skills and intellectual capital, but can lead to unclear boundaries if not defined and managed carefully.

8.3   Tools and data

While one of the most commonly used phrases in IT is 'people, process and tools', there has long been a recognition that data matters. Processes are designed to react and adapt to changes in data and any interaction between two parties is dependent on them having a common understanding of the topic of their discussion. Having a 'single version of the truth' is one of the most fundamental requirements for collaboration between different parties.

Tools and data are often dealt with as after-thoughts in both the design and sourcing processes, but they are the fundamental building blocks of efficiency and can cripple successful interactions between different suppliers if either left unplanned or over-implemented.

Good practices in this area include:
- Focus on the outcome of the organization, not the output of the supplier (again):
  - Tools deployed and data sets managed for the sole purpose of checking the supplier's performance are of limited value, if supplier performance is not aligned to business service performance then there is something missing;
  - The retained IT organization should only retain the tools needed to measure and manage the experience of their end users;
- Balance the value of integration across the overall environment with the integration within a service provider:

- Since tools and data quality are the primary drivers of operational efficiency, there are many times when the benefits of efficiency within each Service Provider can outweigh the benefits of integration;
  - Integrate ITSM tools at the highest level possible to maximize supplier accountability and manage the total cost of delivery:
- Standardize and centralize only that data which is necessary to integrate the services and the providers:
  - While a theoretical approach would dictate creating a federated CMDB which knows **everything** about **everything**, the cost of implementing and maintaining this level of control is often more trouble than it is worth:
  - Define a **subset** of common data elements, and their master source, which **must** be the same for all services and allow the Service Providers to manage the rest:
  - Use the data to help improve the service capability by analyzing and providing input to the CSI role of the Service Integrator.

8.4   Sourcing from multiple Service Providers

The world of IT services is a world of sourcing. Today, many organizations choose to focus on their own core competences and IT services is one of the more obvious areas to consider for outsourcing. Dividing the scope of services between multiple parties creates complexity and has been the trigger for organizations to start thinking about integrating services. Then the question should be answered as to whether or not Service Integration is a core competence for an organization? There are several different models for Service Integration today, although the functional model itself does not differ whether the Service Integration role is retained or outsourced. The sourcing process will focus on different elements, however, depending on the chosen sourcing model.

Once the contracts with the service suppliers in the multi-sourced environment have been signed these need to be managed in a consistent way, enabling optimal collaboration between Service Providers in a competitive world.

Good practices in this area include:
- Get professional help - do not underestimate the complexity of the effort to implement a multi-supplier sourcing environment. Learn from other's experiences;
- Organize and structure demand - the requirements for IT services should be consistent with regard to service descriptions, service parameters and service levels. Therefore a service framework and a process framework using standard definitions should be developed up-front to enable aligned request for proposals across the service portfolio;
- Partner with the Service Integrator - when (partly) outsourcing a Service Integration function, develop a different kind of relationship with the Service Provider: referring to the Henderson portfolio described in Section 2.2, it's not just a transactional relationship that is required; go for a 'value add' or even a 'special' relationship.

Not 'us and them' but 'we' - define the environment and incentive for a collaborative culture amongst both internal and external Service Providers and ensure that the environment is maintained. Include incentives in the contracts, not just penalties. Jointly celebrate outstanding service delivery.

8.5   Governance

Arguably, the governance of a multi-supplier or SIAM environment is similar to any other structure. Loose governance that may be 'good enough' in simpler environments simply will not suffice for SIAM. With the use of commander's intent to manage SIAM there is an implication that the evaluate-direct-monitor cycle must very clearly and unambiguously ensure that the goals are stated so the outputs can be measured. This implies a level of rigor and formality.

To focus on lessons learned from previous implementations:
- Clean the slate to start – resolve any outstanding issues and disputes. Don't allow historical issues to cloud the way forward. This can take significant effort and goodwill if there is a large backlog;
- Where escalation is required it should be done quickly and in a positive way. Escalation is *not* a form of punishment – it is a way to raise issues to a locus of control that can resolve them;
- The need for role clarity, supported by the contracts, is crucial;
- Given the need for organizational change, the mandate for change must be provided as part of the governance of the IT organization;
- The separation of duties between the Service Integrator and Service Providers (and indeed role clarity between the providers) must be enabled by the governance regime.

Maintenance of good relationships between the parties is very important. This is supported by, rather than in conflict with, rigorous governance. As the adage goes 'Good fences make good neighbors'.

8.6   Continual service improvement (CSI)

In a multi-sourced environment, it becomes clearer than ever that the trust and leadership between the retained organization and its Service Providers is the essential ingredient. Contracts which are locked into long-term transformation programs are not flexible enough to deliver in a multi-sourced world and one answer is to drive continual service improvement. Successful leaders in this area are those who treat anything which impacts the trust between all of the teams involved in delivering IT services as a serious issue which must be communicated and addressed. Ultimately the organizations that deliver sourcing services are groups of people and the same relationship rules apply at the individual level as at the organizational level:

- The cultural perspective of continual service improvement is fundamental, it does not matter where the suggestion comes from, if it is better, it should be adopted;
- Recognize the unique aspects of driving improvement in a multi-sourced environment and lay a foundation within which CSI becomes an everyday activity;
- Improvements in the way to deliver something can often result in innovations that are as profound as the changes in the services delivered;
- Cross-supplier improvement initiatives are where most of the value is;
- Developing and delivering a true culture of continual service improvement requires trust and leadership. Many of these relationship practices are second nature to good leaders and it is vital to recognize that a sourced relationship does not remove the need to *lead* as a key element of success;
- Any inhibitor to trust and open communication will limit the benefits of CSI.

8.7   Ready to jump?

This book has illustrated the parallels between formation skydiving and SIAM that we mentioned in the Foreword. Like a SIAM-based enterprise, a sky-dive that is working well has very little tension. Every skydiver (supplier of 'body flying') has to know their position and fly solidly in that position. They accept that they will be held accountable for their performance, yet focus on sharing the success of a common goal.

They commit to not causing tension by pushing or pulling the formation, yet accept that they may have to compensate a little for what happens around them knowing that the coaches (SIAM) will manage poor performance during the debrief.

The coach for the formation must select the participants based not only on their individual skills but their commitment to the common goal – and that commitment to a common goal may be a new factor for some. The individual skydivers may also need some coaching to ensure that they have the best chance of success. This should be identified from the outset!

The coach also knows that the formation itself must be sufficiently robust for the skill of the skydivers – or the formation may not succeed. More skillful skydivers can build bigger formations with more variations of formations possible.

Thus we conclude that the metaphor remains valid. Like the SIAM the coach must ensure that skydivers:
- Are fully aware of their outcomes, expectations and accountabilities;
- Are enabled to deliver those outcomes;
- Are held clearly accountable for these outcomes.

Know your slot… Fly your slot…

We hope this book has provided a set of helpful ideas and tools to jump into the exciting world of SIAM.

Annex A Glossary of Terms

The table below contains definitions of the terms used throughout the book. The first time a term is used it will be printed in *italic*, which will notify the reader that the definition of that term can be found in this glossary.

Term	Definition
Accidental Multi-sourcing	Multi-sourcing where the outsourcing structure has happened organically, without planning.
Accountable Service Integrator	The Service Integrator that holds end-to-end accountability for the delivery of services to the SLA of the service portfolio in scope. See also Delegation and Enabling Service Integrator.
Aggregate service	A service that is assembled from multiple services, whose implementation uses, or consumes, other services as main resources to provide its agreed outcome Aggregation differs from composition in that it does not imply ownership. In composition, when the owning object is destroyed, so are the contained objects. In aggregation, this is not necessarily true.
Architecture	1. A formal description of a system, or a detailed plan of the system at component level, to guide its implementation (source: ISO/IEC 42010:2007). 2. The structure of components, their inter-relationships, and the principles and guidelines governing their design and evolution over time.
BAU	Business As Usual – the continuous delivery of IT services.
Business	The part of the organization that delivers/sells products and/or services to external actors, supported by IT products and IT services provided by the IT function. Business and IT together form the company or enterprise.
Business process	The business activities executed to deliver products or services to external customers. Business processes are supported by and consume IT services to achieve their objectives.
Business value	In management, *business value* is an informal term that includes all forms of value that determine the health and well-being of the enterprise in the long run.
Capabilities	Abilities that an organization, person, or system possesses. Capabilities are typically expressed in general and high-level terms and usually require a combination of organization, people, processes, and technology to achieve. For example, marketing, customer contact, or outbound telemarketing.
CI	Configuration Item.
Client	See Customer.
COBIT	Control Objectives for the Business of IT, *framework* for the governance and management of enterprise IT owned by www.isaca.org.
Company	A legal entity which will consist of one or more organizational units. Business and IT together form the company. An enterprise may contain one or more companies.
Competence	A demonstrated ability to apply knowledge, skills and attitudes to achieving observable results (source: e-Competence Framework).
Consumer	The individual, function or process that uses the services.

Term	Definition
Core competence	A harmonized combination of multiple resources and skills that distinguish a firm in the marketplace (Source: Prahalad, C.K. and Hamel, G. (1990) "The core competence of the corporation", Harvard Business Review (v. 68, no. 3) pp. 79–91).
CSI	Continual Service Improvement, as defined in ITIL.
CSF	Critical Success Factor – a factor that has significant impact on achieving goals or objectives. KPIs are used to help achieve CSFs.
Customer	The organization which has contracted services using *multi-sourcing* from multiple Service Providers.
Delegation	Delegation is a process whereby the authority to act is entrusted to another party. The accountability for the outcome is *shared* between the delegator and delegate. Note: when using RASCI charts, the 'A' is assigned to the lowest level of delegation. It is *assumed* that those that have delegated also remain Accountable due to the shared accountability.
Enabling Service Integrator	A Service Integrator that provides the enablement and cross Service Provider processes to allow those Service Providers to deliver in a multi provider environment. An Enabling Service Integrator does not have direct accountability for the aggregated services – the Service Providers have direct accountability.
End-to-end	The complete scope of integrated IT services. However note that this principle is contextual and always has to be accompanied by a definition of the scope: a service, a set of services, an IT process, a business process, etc.
Enterprise	The highest level (typically) of description of an organization that typically covers all missions and functions. An enterprise will often span multiple companies or organizations.
Enterprise service bus	An enterprise service bus is a software architecture model used for designing and implementing communication between mutually interacting software applications in a service-oriented architecture.
External	Outside the organizational boundaries of the enterprise.
Function (organizational)	The functional view of a set of activities that are performed; this can span multiple departments of an organization, or even across companies, depending on the sourcing of the activities.
Function (job)	A formal position in an organization. A function can perform multiple roles.
Governance	Governance ensures that stakeholder needs, conditions and options are evaluated to determine balanced, agreed-on enterprise objectives to be achieved; setting direction through prioritization and decision-making; and monitoring performance and compliance against agreed-on direction and objectives (source: ISACA, COBIT v.5).
Integrated	Role of the function whose delivered service(s) is integrated into an aggregated service.
Integrator	Role of the function that integrates other services to deliver an aggregated service.
Internal	Within the organizational boundaries of the enterprise.
ITIL	A set of best practice publications for IT Service Management. ITIL® is a Registered Trade Mark of AXELOS Limited.
IT function	The functional view of the activities that are performed to develop, run and continually improve IT services for the business.

Term	Definition
IT service	A service provided to one or more customers, by an IT Service Provider. An IT service is based on the use of Information Technology and supports the customer's business process. An IT service is made up from a combination of people, processes and technology and should be defined in a Service Level Agreement (SLA) (source: AXELOS, ITIL).
ITSM	IT Service Management (ITSM) refers to the entirety of activities – directed by <u>policies</u>, organized and structured in <u>processes</u> and supporting <u>procedures</u> – that are performed by an organization or part of an organization to plan, deliver, operate and control IT services offered to customers (source: AXELOS, ITIL).
KPI	A key performance indicator (KPI) is a type of <u>performance</u> <u>measurement</u>. KPIs evaluate the success of an organization or of a particular activity in which it engages. KPIs are used to help achieve Critical Success Factors (CSFs) and are used to define one or more metrics
Management	Management plans, builds, runs and monitors activities in alignment with the direction set by the governance body to achieve the enterprise objectives (source: ISACA, COBIT v.5).
Metric	A measurement used to support the monitoring of a key performance indicator (KPI). A metric can have targets and then can be used as a service level.
MSI	Multi-Supplier Integration or Integrator, refer to Service Integrator.
Multi-sourcing	The practice of contracting with multiple Service Providers to deliver a portfolio of services.
OLA	Operational Level Agreement defines the interdependent relationship between Service Providers in order to support a service level agreement (SLA).
Process orchestration	The coordination of events and activities between multiple processes amongst multiple Service Providers, to help achieve objectives laid down by the business.
RACI	See RASCI.
RASCI	Acronym for Responsible, Accountable, Supporting, Consulted, Informed. A mechanism used to document roles performed by parties in a collaborative process or activity.
Retained organization	The functions within an IT organization which have not been outsourced to external Service Providers. This book regards internal Service Providers as part of the retained organization.
Role	A set of responsibilities, activities, and authorities granted to a person or team. A Role is defined in a Process. One person or team may have multiple Roles, for example the Roles of Configuration Manager and Change Manager may be carried out by a single person (source: AXELOS, ITIL),
Service bundle	A group of interrelated services, which are combined in a single statement of work.
Service Integration	The set of principles and practices which facilitates the collaborative working required to maximize the benefit of delivering services using multiple Service Providers. Service Integration links services, the technology of which they are comprised and the delivery organizations and processes used to operate them, into a single ecosystem, which is capable of meeting the needs of the business it supports.
Service Integration and Management	Also known as SIAM, alternative term for Service Integration.

Term	Definition
Service Integration function	The function that includes the activities that are performed in the definition and execution of Service Integration; this function can be established within a specialized unit, span multiple departments of an organization, or even across companies, depending on the specific situation and sourcing strategies of Service Integration.
Service Integrator	The service provider primarily responsible for performing Service Integration activities. The Service Integrator can be *accountable* or *enabling*.
Service Integrator role	The sum of activities and responsibilities as defined in a statement of work as part of the sourcing process for a multi-service provider ecosystem or being executed in an implemented ecosystem.
Service level	A metric for which a target is defined as part of a service level agreement (SLA).
Service Level Agreement	An agreement between Service Provider and customer with regard to the scope, structure and quality of the services.
Service orchestration	A term used in service oriented architecture (SOA) to describe the automated combination of services into an aggregated service.
Service Provider	The organizational unit primarily responsible for delivering a service. A Service Provider can be *internal* or *external*.
Services	In the context of this book services primarily refer to IT services.
SIAM	See Service Integration and Management.
SLA	Service Level Agreement, Note that the term SLA is also used to refer to individual service levels.
SMA	An SMA (Service Management Architecture) is the service provider's overall capability to deliver its services effectively and efficiently, covering process, products, people, organization etc.
SPOC	Single Point Of Contact - the unit or function where all day-to-day communications are channeled through. Typically for IT Services, this will be the s service desk. This ensures that Users are able to contact trained staff and all contacts can be recorded consistently.
SPOS	Single Point of Service – the organizational unit where all communication regarding the delivery, management and altering of any participating service is channeled in a multi-service environment. Typically this will be the Service Integrator. This ensures that Customers and Consumers are able to govern, impact, elaborate and enhance the aggregated outcome of multiple services.
Supplier	The organization contractually responsible to deliver hardware and/or software assets to a customer.
Third party	See external.
UC	Underpinning Contract between two organizations (companies) where one organization provides assets and/or services to the other organization. The assets and/or services are components of the service that the receiving organization will deliver as a Service Provider.
User	Any individual who uses the IT service.
Value	See business value.
Value chain	A *value chain* is a set of activities that a firm operating in a specific industry performs in order to deliver a valuable product or service for the market.

Table of Figures

Bibliography

Axelrod, R., & Hamilton, W. D. (1981). The Evolution of Cooperation. *Science*, 1390-96.

Balmelli, L., Brown, D., Cantor, M. & Mott, M., Model Driven System Development. *IBM Systems Journal*, 45 (3), 569-585.

Bell, S.B. & Orzen, M.A. (2010). *Lean IT, Enabling and Sustaining Your Lean Transformation*. Productivity Press.

Bree, T. L. (2014, October 30th). Retrieved from The Guardian: http://www.theguardian.com/media-network/2014/oct/30/retailers-tech-high-street-stores

Davis, V. D. (2014). *Impact of Multi-Sourcing on the IT4IT Reference Architecture*. IT4IT Consortium.

Doran, G. (1981). There's a S.M.A.R.T. way to write management's goals and objectives. *Management Review (AMA FORUM) 70 (11)*, 35–36.

Ferris, K., & itSMF (2011). *Balanced Diversity - A Portfolio Approach to Organisational Change*. Van Haren Publishing.

Fischbacher, E. F. (2003). The Nature of Human Altruism. *Nature*, 785-791.

Gartner (2015, August 1). *Gartner IT Glossary*. Retrieved August 1, 2015, from http://www.gartnercom: http://www.gartner.com/it-glossary/cloud-services-brokerage-csb

Gartner (2013). *Gartner Outsourcing Trends*. Stamford, CT - USA: Gartner.

Hakkenberg, H. K. (2011). *Shared KPIs in Multivendor Outsourcing*. BCG.

Henderson, J. C. (1990). Plugging into Strategic Partnerships: The Critical IS Connection. *MITSloan Management Review*.

Holland, K. (2015, May). Retrieved from Axelos.com: https://www.axelos.com/case-studies-and-white-papers/an-example-itil-based-model-for-effective-siam

Holland, K. (2015, January). Retrieved from Axelos.com: https://www.axelos.com/case-studies-and-white-papers/introduction-to-service-integration-management

ISACA (2012). *Cobit 5*. Rolling Meadows, IL - USA: ISACA.

IT4IT Forum (n.d.). *IT4IT Forum*. Retrieved from The Open Group: http://www.opengroup.org/getinvolved/forums/IT4IT-forum

Kotter, J. P., & Rathgeber, H. (2005). *Our Iceberg Is Melting*. St Martin's Press.

Lencioni, P. (2002) *The five Dysfunctions of a team*.Jossey-Bass.

Longwood, J. (2012). "*Outsourcing Trends, 2011-2012: Exploit the Multisourcing Service Integrator Market*. Gartner Inc.

Martorelli, B. (2011). *Should ITO Customers Also Outsource Service Integration*. Forrester Research Inc.

McKenzie, G. (2015, March). *Art of IP War*. Retrieved August 15, 2015, from Art of IP War: http://www.filament.com.au/upload/Gregory-McKenzie-Art-of-IP-War.pdf

McKenzie, P., & Murphy, P. (2013). Model Driven Operational Architecture and Multi-Supplier Outsourcing. *The Open Group Conference*. Sydney.

McNicholl, D. (2005). *http://www.conexl.com/docs/101/Dan%20McNicholl%20Master%20of%20Outsource%20Game%20Interview.pdf*. Retrieved 2015, from http://www.conexl.com/docs/101/

Ostrom, E. (2009). *Tragedy of the commons*. Retrieved from Wikipedia: http://
    en.wikipedia.org/wiki/Tragedy_of_the_commons

Patrick M. Kerin, S. J. (2013). *Why Partnering Strategies Matter*. Armonk: IBM Center for
    Applied Insights.

Rasiel, E. M. (1999). *The McKinsey Way*. McGraw Hill.

Sethi, S.P. (2007). *Advocacy Advertising and Large Corporations*. Lexington, MA: Lexington
    Books.

Solli-Saether, P. G. (2006). Maturity model for IT outsourcing relationships. *Industrial
    Management and Data Systems*, Vol 106.

Stevens, W., Myers, G., & Constantine, L. (1975). Structured Design. *IBM Systems
    Journal*, 115-139.

Taylor, F. W. (1911). *The Principles of Scientific Management*. Harper and Brothers.

The Open Group. (2015, May). Retrieved from IT4IT: http://www.opengroup.org/IT4IT

Weldon, L. (2012). Scoping the Office of the CIO. Gartner.

Wiggers, P., Kok, H., & De Boer - de Wit, M. (2004). *IT Performance Management*.
    Oxford, UK: Elsevier (Butterworth Heinemann).

Wikipedia. (2015, July 30th). Retrieved from Lean Manufacturing: https://en.wikipedia.
    org/wiki/Lean_manufacturing

Wikipedia. (2015, July 30). Retrieved from Six Sigma: https://en.wikipedia.org/wiki/
    Six_Sigma

Wikipedia. (n.d.). *Auftragstaktik*. Retrieved from Wikipedia.com: https://en.wikipedia.org/
    wiki/Mission-type_tactics

Zee, H. van der, Blijleven, V. & Gong, Y. (2015). *Lean IT Partnering*. Van Haren
    Publishing.

Zeithaml, V. B. (1988). *Communication and Control Processes in the Delivery of Service*.
    Journal of Marketing, April 1988, Vol. 52, Issue 2

Author Biographies

Dave Armes has spent more than 20 years working in the area of IT Service Management and is currently leading transformation for a global energy company. During his 19 year career with IBM, Dave has demonstrated a proven track record of innovation with clients to deliver business value. Since 2002 Dave has been working with enterprise clients focused on solution and strategy development to assist in the architecture, implementation and operation of IT solutions as part of major outsourcing contracts in multi-sourced environments. Dave has worked in almost all of the core professions; technical specialist, management, consulting and architecture and with all aspects of IT; hosted infrastructure, end-user services and business applications.

Niklas Engelhart has more than 30 years of experience working every corner of ITSM. For the last 10 years he has been establishing ITSM processes and governing models within the banking industry and the public sector in Sweden. Primarily working within application lifecycle management environments he has experience of both vertical and horizontal integration of services. In his latest assignments Niklas has been designing and establishing integration services for Stockholm county e-health services, including their integration to national services. These services make it possible for hundreds of healthcare providers to share locally stored information, thereby improving healthcare efficiency and patient safety. Niklas is also a member of the tactical national governance board of the National Patient Overview e-health service in Sweden.

Peter McKenzie has 30 years in the IT industry with more than 20 years managing aspects of outsourcing and service delivery from both the consumer and suppler perspectives. Much of this time has been spent in ITSM management, sourcing transition and service improvement projects across multiple industries.

In 2004, Peter was a strategist providing sourcing advice supporting a successful bid for the General Motors Infrastructure Integration Management/Operations Management (IIO/OM) tender, an early SIAM implementation. Peter assisted with the global transition of those service contracts in 2006 and the subsequent transformation through 2007.

Currently, Peter is the Principal Consultant for his own consulting company (Sintegral) working with multiple clients ranging from medium sized enterprise to federal government, across multiple industries. He continues to be active member of the Service Management community.

Peter Wiggers has 30 years in the IT industry of which 20 years as a consultant on many aspects of IT strategy, including cost and value of IT, sourcing, enterprise governance and service management. He is lead author of the book IT Performance Management (2003) which focuses on multiple aspects of IT strategy and the service management lifecycle. Since 2008 he has worked as a subject matter expert on outsourcing governance, partnerships and service integration to support the outsourcing division of IBM across Europe. He holds a master degree in Business Information Management and is certified in the Governance of Enterprise IT from ISACA (CGEIT).

Index